The
Right
to
Die

The Right to Die

Policy Innovation and Its Consequences

Henry R. Glick

Columbia University Press

New York

Columbia University Press
New York   Oxford
Copyright © 1992 Columbia University Press
All rights reserved

Library of Congress Cataloging-in-Publication Data

Glick, Henry Robert
    The right to die : policy innovation and its consequences /
Henry R. Glick.
       p.   cm.
    Includes bibliographical references and index.
    ISBN 0–231–07638–X
    1. Right to die—Law and legislation—United States—
States.   2. Right to die—Government policy—United
States—States.   I. Title.
KF3827.E87Z954   1992
344.73′04197—dc20
[347.3044197]   92–12693
                                                       CIP

⊗

Casebound editions of Columbia University Press books are
Smyth-sewn and printed on permanent and durable acid-free
paper.

Printed in the United States of America

c 10 9 8 7 6 5 4 3 2 1

To
Lee Glick,
a model for living life fully

Contents

Preface

This is the political story of the right to die—how it developed from a limited and peripheral issue in the 1940s to a highly visible and controversial public policy in the 1980s and 1990s. I examine when and why the issue began to receive increased media and public opinion attention, obtained a hold on the political agendas of state courts and legislatures, and reached the U.S. Supreme Court and Congress.

The distinguishing feature of my approach is that I emphasize the growth of the right to die as a social and political issue, its movement onto the social and governmental agendas, and its transformation into concrete policy innovations. Most other studies of the right to die examine the ethics and pros and cons of treatment decisions, euthanasia, and other proposals. While these are important in the politics of the right to die, my main concern is the social and political process, not a reexaminaton of right to die issues or the merits of various perspectives.

The politics of the right to die has not peaked, and there are many indications that the issue is shifting from the withdrawal of treatment for the hopelessly ill, which is widely accepted, to more controversial issues of voluntary active euthanasia and assisted suicide. The right to die will be on the political agenda into the next century.

My research on the right to die began as an exploration into the innovative policy-making role of state supreme courts. Right to die litigation clearly showed that state courts were moving into new territory. Their decisions potentially were important to millions of people, but they also were exceptionally controversial. I quickly learned, however, that the right to die involved much more than merely courts responding to individual demands for freedom from unwanted medical treatment. The issue also involved state legislatures through living will and other legislation; powerful, active state and national interest groups; and state legislators and other individuals who felt strongly, both in favor and against, about transforming this emerging social issue into public policy. Consequently, my research soon enlarged into a full examination of the right to die as a social and political issue in state and national politics.

The realization that the right to die involved many parts of the political process also convinced me that policy analysis too often is compartmentalized and limited by separate studies of legislatures, courts, and administrative and executive agencies, and that understanding policy-making and the content of individual policies requires bridging research into several governmental institutions and various participants at the same time. Had I limited myself to a study of state courts, for example, I would not have fully appreciated the power and contribution of interest groups and legislatures, or how courts and legislatures have shaped each other's political agendas, options, and policies.

Although the right to die is an important, timely, and striking political issue, I was interested in doing more than telling the story of the controversy and emergent policy. Political analysis has the potential of contributing generally to understanding the policy-making process if policies are analyzed within the context of empirical political theory. The theories that contributed most to my research were a combination of political agenda setting and the diffusion of policy innovations. I have employed and expanded on these theories to enlarge our understanding and appreciation of the nuances of policy-making. The result, I hope, is the story of the right to die as well as a broader contribution to the study of state politics and policy-making.

I would like to acknowledge the support of many people who helped make this research possible. Dr. Charles F. Cnudde, dean of the College of Social Sciences, and Dr. Marie E. Cowart, director of the Institute on Aging at Florida State University, provided facilities and institutional support that gave me the time and resources for conducting this research. Dr. Burton M. Atkins, chair of the Department of Political Science, also contributed department resources. My colleagues in the Institute on Aging—particularly Dr. Melissa Hardy and Dr. Jill Quadagno—and Dr. Paul Allen Beck of

Ohio State University also contributed to this project through their valuable suggestions and comments on various manuscripts. I especially appreciate the careful and unflagging research assistance of Dr. Scott P. Hays, now assistant professor of political science at Southern Illinois University. Some of the data gathered for this project are included in an article that Professor Hays and I coauthored for the *Journal of Politics*. I also appreciate the willingness of legislators, interest group representatives and lobbyists, legislative aides and staff, and state administrators who agreed to be interviewed for this project, many of whom also provided their private files for my search for the details and hues of state policy-making. Finally, but certainly not least, my wife, Joy, contributed her moral support, a willing ear, and helpful responses to my stories and discoveries about the right to die.

I dedicate this book with love to my mother, Lee Glick—over eighty and a model for living life fully.

1 Death, Technology, and Politics

Nancy Cruzan, an attractive and vivacious twenty-five-year-old, probably fell asleep while driving home from work at the cheese factory near her home in Carterville, Missouri. She lost control of her 1963 Nash Rambler on lonely Elm Road and was thrown out of the car as it crashed. Nancy lay face down in a roadside ditch for about fifteen minutes without breathing or having a heartbeat before a state highway patrolman and paramedics discovered her and began resuscitation. Her lungs and heart began to work again, but since permanent brain damage begins after about six minutes without oxygen, Nancy was in a coma and soon descended into a permanent unconscious vegetative state. Not brain dead, her body performed respiration, circulation, and digestion without medical devices, but she would never regain consciousness or become aware of her surroundings.

Shortly after the crash, which occurred in January 1983, her then husband, hoping that she might awaken and recover, agreed to have a feeding tube implanted in Nancy's stomach. Later her parents, Lester "Joe" and Joyce Cruzan, brought her home from the Missouri Rehabilitation Center forty miles east at Mt. Vernon, hoping that familiar surroundings would stimulate her, but nothing worked. Years passed, and Nancy lay in a tightly contracted fetal position with her muscles and tendons irreversibly damaged, spinal fluid gradually replacing destroyed brain tissue. There was no hope whatever that Nancy Cruzan would change for the better, although

1

with food and water administered artificially through the stomach feeding tube, she could have lived for several decades. Her care cost $130,000 per year, paid by the state of Missouri. Social Security contributions for medical care had long been exhausted.

Four years after her accident and with no change in her condition, Nancy's parents tried to reverse the early approval of the artificial feeding tube so that Nancy could be, in her father's words, "turned loose" and allowed to die. Medical personnel refused, however, and the Cruzans asked the Missouri chapter of the American Civil Liberties Union for help. In turn, the ACLU obtained the free services of a young and vigorous attorney from a large, prestigious Kansas City law firm. Again, the rehabilitation center refused, and the only remaining path was a lawsuit to persuade a local judge to order the feeding tube removed.

A trial began in March 1988 with the Cruzan's lawyer presenting medical testimony from several neurologists, who confirmed that Nancy was in a persistent vegetative state, and from her family and friends, who testified that Nancy had clearly told them that she would not want to be kept alive in her condition. The state rehabilitation center, represented by an assistant state attorney general, countered with doctors and nurses who said Nancy sometimes exhibited awakelike reactions, such as crying, grimaces, and eye movements, that seemed to indicate awareness. Nurses also testified that they did not want to see Nancy's treatment stopped. But the doctors admitted that Nancy's reactions, including tearing, were common in a vegetative state and did not indicate that Nancy was interacting with her environment. A few months after the trial began, Judge Charles Teel, Jr., ruled that a patient has a state and federal constitutional right to refuse medical treatment and that Joe and Joyce Cruzan, acting as Nancy's guardians, had the right to act in her best interests and to order the withdrawal of treatment, including the artificial feeding and hydration.

But the dispute did not end. The state appealed to the Missouri Supreme Court, and Nancy Cruzan's plight quickly changed from a personal tragedy to a state and national issue. Seven medical, right to die, and right to life organizations and advocates for the retarded and disabled filed friend of the court (amicus curiae) briefs on both sides of the issue.

In November 1988, in a 4–3 split decision, the court reversed the trial judge (*Cruzan v. Harmon*). It concluded that there is no right to privacy that allows a person to refuse medical treatment in all circumstances and that removal of the feeding tube would result in death by starvation; it found that Nancy's wishes expressed to a friend were unreliable and denied that Nancy's parents had the power to act on her behalf. The court also ruled that, although Nancy had not executed a living will and was not terminally ill, Missouri's living will statute indicated the legislature's intended policy in such cases; the statute has a prolife preamble, and the law prohibits the withdrawal of food and hydration from terminally ill patients. Also, to the court majority, Nancy was alive and the treatment was not a burden to her. Therefore, the state had a legitimate interest in preserving her life.

The Cruzans' lawyers quickly filed a petition for certiorari with the U.S. Supreme Court. In the past the Court had declined to hear right to die cases, but this time it granted the request. The Bush administration filed an amicus brief in support of Missouri's appeal. On June 25, 1990, the U.S. Supreme Court upheld Missouri in a 5–4 decision (*Cruzan v. Director, Missouri Department of Health*). Writing for the majority, Chief Justice William Rehnquist agreed that Missouri had the right to require clear and convincing evidence of Nancy's wishes not to be kept alive if she were in a vegetative state, and that the state may guard against potential abuses by a patient's surrogate or guardian.

The majority also indicated that oral agreements and instructions were generally suspect in legal transactions but that written instructions concerning medical treatment left by a competent patient would be binding. But, unlike Missouri, the Court did not distinguish between food and hydration and other medical treatment, indicating that both could be withdrawn if a patient had requested. In a concurring opinion, Justice Sandra Day O'Connor urged adults to use living wills or the durable power of attorney to convey in writing their advance wishes concerning final medical care. The dissenters argued that the Cruzans should be permitted to order the withdrawal of Nancy's artificial feeding.[1]

Nancy Cruzan's case continued. Her court-appointed guardian and her lawyer returned in November to the Missouri trial court

3

where the case had begun with three newly discovered former friends who testified that Nancy Cruzan had told them she would not wish to be kept alive if she were in a vegetative state. This time the state of Missouri did not contest the renewed request to disconnect the feeding tube, and within a few weeks Judge Teel ordered its removal so that Nancy could die.

The Society for the Right to Die praised the Cruzans and the decision while right to life protesters denounced what they termed the frenzy to kill Nancy Cruzan. Right to life organizations filed several unsuccessful petitions in state and federal courts to overturn Judge Teel's ruling, and twenty-five protesters were blocked and arrested as they tried to get to Nancy Cruzan's hospital room to force the reconnection of the feeding tube. The day after Christmas 1990—twelve days after the feeding tube had been withdrawn, nearly seven years after her automobile accident, and almost three years after the first court hearing—Nancy Cruzan died.

In January the Missouri legislature considered a bill allowing individuals to designate another person to make health care decisions in the case of incapacitation. However, since the governor has vowed to veto any right to die legislation, bill sponsors have planned to place the issue on the November 1992 ballot (*New York Times,* 23 January 1991:A12).

Introduction

The Cruzan case is only a recent part of the right to die story. The campaign for a government-sanctioned right to die did not begin with Nancy Cruzan in 1988 but started much earlier in other states. However, identifying particular earlier events also oversimplifies the origin of the issue, and it is impossible to find a single starting point.

The issue became most visible in the United States in 1976 with the first appellate court case involving Karen Quinlan, another young woman in a vegetative state whose parents sued to have life support systems removed. It also began independently in California that same year with the first living will law in which competent adults were empowered to indicate their wishes in writing concerning final medical treatment. But it began earlier than 1976 as well, since right to die proposals had been placed before the Florida and California legislatures in earlier sessions, and the issue gradually had been penetrating the consciousness of Americans at lease since the 1950s. New awareness reflects major changes in modern medical technology and social beliefs concerning appropriate medical treatment and the quality and sanctity of life.

Just as the right to die has no single starting point, it has not ended with the Supreme Court's decision in the Nancy Cruzan case. First, the impact of the Supreme Court's decision is mixed and uncertain. The Supreme Court ruled that conscious, competent adults have the right to refuse unwanted medical treatment, including the artificial administration of food and hydration. However, a person's desires need to be clearly expressed while competent and conscious. Ideally, they need to be written down so that an unconscious or incompetent patient's wishes can be honored later.

But the Court also accepted widely quoted evidence that only 15 percent of Americans have living wills directing their final medical treatment, and that perhaps ten thousand people currently are being maintained on life support equipment. Therefore, from one perspective the Court's decision is a victory for those who argue for a right to die and who stress the importance of living wills and other written instructions, but the decision leaves the Nancy Cruzans in medical limbo—forever unable to express their wishes concerning medical treatment but sustained indefinitely by medical technology. It also leaves vulnerable the vast majority of Americans who have no living wills or other written medical instructions.

Equally important the Supreme Court has imposed no particular policy requirements on the states: in the absence of a written living will, the states may require various standards of evidence concerning a patient's prior wishes. The states also may develop their own rules regarding the form and implementation of living wills and other advance medical directives. Policy-making on the right to die will continue.

Politics and the Right to Die

Much has already been written about the right to die in mass circulation magazines and newspapers, in religious, legal, and medical journals, and in book-length treatments. In most of this literature, clergy, journalists, ethicists, lawyers, and doctors grapple with the moral issues involved in the right to die, the conditions when life-saving equipment should be withdrawn, and who should decide for patients who are unable to indicate their own wishes. Examining particular court cases, legal writers explain the logic of judges, describe differences among closely related decisions, and provide guidance for doctors, nurses, and others making treatment decisions. Still others examine differences in the details of state statutes. Much of the writing is prescriptive and is designed to influence policymakers and practitioners.[2]

There is little political analysis of the right to die, and most of that examines public opinion about new health policies. Surveys typically measure support for limiting the use of technology to preserve life in hopeless situations, and numerous social characteristics, such as age, religion, and region, have been related to differences in opinion.

My examination of the right to die takes a different approach. It is not designed primarily to add to the debate over the pros and cons of the right to die but to analyze how policy originated and evolved in state politics and how state governments responded to it. It is principally a book about the right to die rather than a prescription for making policy or decisions in individual cases. The theme is that the right to die became an issue on state social and political agendas long before state courts and legislatures confronted the problem. Later, over a fifteen-year period, the states produced different innovative policies for dealing with it.

Although there are many similarities among state laws and court cases, they are not identical, and there is no single right to die policy accepted throughout the nation. Instead, the states have produced distinctive policies with important consequences for its citizens. Additionally, innovation in right to die policies has not been the preserve of one branch of government but has involved important and sometimes intense political conflict between courts, legislatures, and the executive branch. To understand the content of right to die policy and, equally important, how it came to be, it is necessary to consider the political roles of all three institutions. Finally, a complex web of political influences accounts for state right to die policies. National political and social trends combined with state political environments, the power of state interest groups, and the power of individual politicians tells us much about how the right to die emerged and the forms it takes in the various states.

Besides analyzing the politics of the right to die, this book is intended to contribute to new ways of studying state policy-making. Drawing on previous research on agenda setting and policy innovation, I wish to expand the way that social scientists approach the policy-making process and the content of state policy. A central theme is that agenda setting and innovation are closely related political activities that need to be considered in tandem in order to develop a much more comprehensive view of how innovation occurs.

Furthermore, we need to devote much more attention to the content of state policy. Most research on policy innovation concentrates on either state legislatures or courts and frequently treats all policies in a particular subject area as if they were the same; the only important difference is *when* states adopt a particular policy, not the content of different state's policies. This research will show that the content of policies differs from state to state and over time, and that these substantive differences are important and worthy of more thorough analysis.

Finally, much state policy analysis focuses on comparing the states according to the amounts of money they spend on particular programs, such as education, welfare, and highway construction, or how much money is raised through various forms of taxation. Many other policies, however, give citizens rights to engage in particular conduct. These policies govern the right to die, divorce and child support, abortion, landlord-tenant relations, and many others. These policies cost the states little or nothing, but they have enormously important consequences for individuals and, since the content of the policies varies widely, individuals are affected differently depending upon where they live. Additional attention needs to be given to these different kinds of issues.

The data for this project are derived from numerous sources. I have obtained all original living will laws and amendments and coded them for date of adoption and for differences in policy content. In addition, I have examined all available bill files for states that have considered the right to die. For judicial policy, I have coded the date and content of right to die decisions of state supreme courts and intermediate courts of appeals in states where the highest court has not heard a right to die case. I also have gathered extensive social and political data for all the states and the frequency of publication of popular and professional articles about the right to die, which may help to account for variations in the adoption of policy. I have also obtained all available surveys on this issue. Finally, in addition to the fifty-state data, I have done intensive case studies of the right to die in three states, which involved interviews with bill sponsors, lobbyists, and legislative aides, and archival research, both in legislative files and the private files of various organizations.

Definitions

Before beginning the story of the right to die, it is important to discuss what the right to die means, the controversies that constantly swirl around it, and its origins.[3] There is no complete agreement on the meaning of the right to die. Terms such as *the right to die with dignity, death with dignity, a natural death, passive euthanasia,* and *abating treatment* are all used to convey a similar but often unclear notion of an ideal environment for and form of final treatment.

Figure 1.1 portrays right to die policies and proposals as a continuum from the least to the most active measures, according to the current levels of public support for each one (chapter 3). It is provided as a guide to the definitions and discussion that follow. Most contemporary policy proposals and law in support of the right to die concentrate on the withdrawal or withholding (abating) of treatment. They generally do not include more active ways of ending life, such as assisted suicide or active euthanasia. However, assisted suicide in particular is fast becoming a new item on the social agenda.

Withdrawing and Withholding Treatment

Withdrawing and withholding treatment is the least active and most widely accepted policy. It is legal and is practiced widely as part of

FIGURE 1.1 *Continuum of Right to Die Policies and Proposals*

Least Active/Most Accepted ⟵⟶ Most Active/Least Accepted

Withdrawal/withholding treatment (also passive euthanasia, abating treatment, natural death; most common meaning of right to die)	Voluntary active euthanasia	Assisted suicide	Involuntary active euthanasia

ordinary medical procedure where doctors use their professional judgment in making appropriate treatment decisions. In hopeless cases, many doctors routinely stop treatment and withdraw life-sustaining measures. However, the large number of court cases involving disputes over the withdrawal and withholding of treatment also makes it clear that some doctors and health care institutions are uncertain and unwilling to end treatment without explicit legal protection.

State living will laws and court cases generally include two related processes in defining and implementing this definition of the right to die. First, a patient's wishes concerning final medical care in the case of terminal illness and, in a few states, permanent vegetative state, are to be honored by attending physicians, other medical personnel and medical institutions. Second, presuming the patient does not wish to have his or her life extended through aggressive medical treatment, the right to die requires the withdrawal and withholding of treatment that only postpones the process of dying. However, as discussed below, getting agreement on the definition of a terminal illness and exactly what constitutes life-sustaining treatment and when it should be withdrawn or withheld is elusive and at the center of political conflict over the right to die.

For patients who have become permanently unconscious, their recorded prior wishes are to be honored, but if their wishes are unknown, their situation is uncertain. In a dozen states, appellate courts have allowed designated surrogates or court-appointed guardians to make medical treatment decisions on their behalf and in the best interests of the patient. Some state living will laws have similar provisions. But a few courts, such as in Missouri, have required absolutely clear, written proof of a patient's prior intent before treatment may be ended. In addition, most states have recently enacted durable power of attorney or health care proxy statutes that permit individuals to designate another person to make medical treatment decisions on their behalf, but several of these do not cover life-sustaining treatment or do not address the withdrawal of treatment.

As applied to ending treatment, the right to die is synonymous with passive euthanasia; however, that term generally is not used by supporters of the right to die because euthanasia is an emotionally and politically charged word that often is confused with active euthanasia, or is presented by opponents as just one step down the "slippery slope" to active euthanasia. Organizations, such as the early Euthanasia Society of America, have changed their names to more innocuous ones, such as Concern for Dying and Society for the Right to Die (recently recombined as Choice in Dying), to avoid the charged connotations associated with the word *euthanasia*.

Active Euthanasia

Active euthanasia occurs when doctors or others act directly to end a patient's suffering before a natural end to life. Active euthanasia is divided into two categories: voluntary active euthanasia and involuntary active euthanasia. In the former, a patient and/or the family asks another person, most likely a doctor, to terminate the patient's life. In the latter, others take it upon themselves to kill the suffering patient. Active euthanasia differs from the withdrawal or withholding of treatment in which the disease or injury is allowed to take its course, with only "comfort care" provided by hospital or hospice staff. Both forms of active euthanasia are mercy killing and criminal, possibly murder, although convictions for manslaughter with suspended sentences or probation are typical (Humphry and Wickett 1986).

While active euthanasia refers to ending the suffering of the dying, it sometimes is seen as the modern forerunner or even synonymous with Nazi-like "euthanasia" programs in which millions of the medically and mentally handicapped, homosexuals, Jews,

10

Gypsies, and other "undesirables" were murdered through explicit and planned government policy.

Although active euthanasia is criminal because it hastens death, many doctors and a growing majority of Americans believe that voluntary active euthanasia should be legal. Support for passive euthanasia has been high and increasing since the 1950s (Adams, Bueche, and Schvaneveldt 1978; Crane 1978; Huag 1978; Singh 1979; Duff and Campbell 1980; Ward 1980; Perlin 1989; *Washington Post National Weekly Edition,* 1 April 1985:n.p.).

Assisted Suicide

The usual meaning of the right to die has not included assisted suicide, in which others, probably doctors, are enlisted by patients to help end their lives. It usually entails providing the means of death, such as a prescription for sleeping pills or other device. Assisting a suicide is illegal in many but not all states.

Assisted suicide is a quiet but accepted practice in the Netherlands, and it is receiving more attention in the United States (*New York Times,* 31 October 1986:6). The Oregon based Hemlock Society (formerly located in California) has sought, unsuccessfully so far, to place a citizen's initiative on the California ballot legalizing assisted suicide. However, a similar effort was successful in Washington state, although the measure was defeated (*New York Times,* 6 July 1990:A7, 7 November 1991:A10).

Increased professional and public interest in assisted suicide is also underscored by the recent cases involving Dr. Jack Kevorkian's "suicide machines" of lethal drugs and carbon monoxide, which were used in the planned death of Alzheimer's sufferer Janet Adkins in Michigan and later in the deaths of two other women, and Dr. Timothy E. Quill in Rochester, who described in the *New England Journal of Medicine* his decision to provide a prescription of barbiturates knowing that a leukemia patient he had been treating would use them to kill herself. Dr. Quill wrote the article because he believed it important for doctors to begin to explicitly discuss their duties and obligations to terminally ill and suffering patients (*New York Times,* 6 and 7 June, 1990:1; Altman, *New York Times,* 12 March 1991:B6; *New York Times,* 3 July 1991:1, 25 October 1991:1).

11

Locating voluntary active euthanasia as less "active" than assisted suicide in figure 1.1 may seem incorrect or arbitrary, and individuals might change the order to fit their own views of proper policy. However, the public supports voluntary active euthanasia more than assisted suicide, possibly because voluntary active euthanasia has been a social issue for many decades.

There also is disagreement in society concerning how "active" each of these measures is. Some individuals and organizations consider all measures, possibly other than the withdrawal or withholding of treatment, to be extreme and unacceptable ones. But others argue that helping a patient to commit suicide requires less action by others than either form of active euthanasia, and that assisted suicide places more responsibility on the patient who wishes to die than on a doctor or others who might help. Still others view voluntary active euthanasia as a logical extension of medical care. If doctors are able to sustain life through modern medical technology, they ought to be able to painlessly end life in hopeless situations as well, so long as patients and/or their families request it.

Finally, both assisted suicide and voluntary active euthanasia are often discussed together in the news media as equally controversial policy proposals. However, practically no support exists for involuntary active euthanasia, which is mercy death administered by doctors or others without patient consent or request. Most would agree that it is the most extreme and least acceptable measure.

Origins and Impact

The right to die has been a social concern for eons. The term *euthanasia* is derived from the Greek meaning good or easy death, a process that the Greeks and Romans wrote about and practiced. In the sixteenth century Catholic theologians distinguished between a patient's obligation to undergo "ordinary" medical treatment to sustain life and the right to forego "extraordinary" procedures (Weir 1989:216–17). Euthanasia also was an issue in Great Britain and the United States in the early 1900s, but the concept of euthanasia was blackened as a result of Nazi policy, and the word is still not used often or openly in Germany (*New York Times,* 6 December 1986:6). However, euthanasia has received increasing attention since the 1950s with the fading of World War II, and in 1957 Pope Pius XII formally addressed the differences between ordinary and extraordinary care.

Modern Medicine

Before the 1950s, the right to die was not of great concern because medical science was unable to appreciably extend the lives of terminal patients. Those in a permanent unconscious state died quickly from additional illnesses and complications or because they were unable to eat and drink. Before the widespread use of antibiotics and the control of communicable diseases, people also died quickly when they contracted pneumonia, tuberculosis, and influenza—the common illnesses of the early 1900s. Those with cancer and heart disease or victims of debilitating accidents frequently contracted pneumonia and died before their otherwise terminal illness took its toll. Until midcentury most people also died at home without extraordinary medical equipment or treatment. Today, however, probably less than 20 percent of the population die outside hospitals or nursing homes.

With victory over most common communicable diseases now possible and lengthening life spans, the nature of illness has changed, and modern medicine is able to treat today's common degenerative diseases such as cancer and heart disease. In the 1950s surgical techniques improved, and cancer patients, for example, could undergo surgery that might not cure but could postpone the ravages of illness. Developments during this period included intravenous feeding, new drugs to fight infection, and cardiopulmonary bypass machines and coronary angiography for open heart surgery and for studying coronary circulation. In the 1960s ventilators, cardiac resuscitation, kidney dialysis, organ transplants, artificial heart valves, and more antibiotics were added to the medical arsenal. Computer axial tomography (CAT scanners) and nuclear magnetic resonance imaging, which were superior to x-rays, appeared in the 1970s and 1980s. New drugs for fighting the progression of AIDS and other diseases are on the way, and organ transplant and artificial skin technology is improving. There is no end to medical innovation and the power of doctors and new machines to prolong life.

Advances in technology and knowledge and the cost of new medical treatment also have led to increasing medical specialization and large, centralized, and impersonal medical centers and hospitals. Increasing urbanization and population mobility inevitably produce growing impersonality in many business and professional relationships, and traditionally close doctor-patient bonds that last a lifetime have given way to constantly changing faces and institutions. With any condition out of the ordinary, family practice physicians quickly refer patients to one of perhaps several specialists who have not had any prior relationship with the patient and cannot know the patient's concerns and desires. Inevitably, busy doctors in impersonal settings focus on treating particular physical problems rather than learning about a patient's outlook on illness, treatment, and the quality of life.

Changes in the technology and practice of medicine, coupled with traditional medical training and ethics that champion conquering disease and preserving life, and doctors' fears of liability for discontinuing treatment have all created a specter of a lingering death for many terminally ill or comatose patients and the growing elderly population. Modern medical tools are valued lifesavers for accident victims and those suffering from reversible serious illness or undergoing surgery, but the new technology can also be a threat to the elderly and the hopelessly ill who inevitably will die, but not quickly or easily because the same machines that preserve life can exacerbate inevitable death.

Individuals have had the legal right to refuse unwanted medical treatment for many decades, but this was before the advent of powerful and modern medical technology. Now, there is heightened social and political concern with the right to control the use of medical technology and to establish the rights of individuals to determine the course of their own treatment.

Karen Quinlan and Beyond

Social concern with the right to die is evidenced by articles in newspapers and popular magazines and legal and medical journals which appeared sporadically since the 1950s, but the galvanizing event which stimulated a rapidly rising chorus of concern is the 1976 Karen Quinlan case (*In the Matter of Karen Quinlan*). Then, a young woman in a coma, but not brain dead, was placed on a respirator in "an altered state of consciousness" with no hope of recovery. Her parents pressed attending physicians to remove the respirator so that she could die, but were refused. The New Jersey Supreme Court, relying on an expansive interpretation of the constitutional right to privacy and the right of parents to act as guardians, finally ordered the respirator removed. Although the respirator was withdrawn, Karen Quinlan was fed artificially and lived for another ten years. The case inaugurated new policy for allowing patients and/or their families to make decisions concerning the use of life prolonging medical treatment.

When this case first entered the New Jersey trial courts in 1975, and continuing through 1976, newspaper, magazine, and journal coverage of the right to die zoomed. The total number of articles published in 1975 and 1976 equaled or exceeded all articles published in the previous decade.[4] From 1976 until the end of 1990, dozens of appellate court cases were decided in 17 states affecting the use of life-support systems and other treatment for the terminally ill and those in a permanent vegetative state. Generally, the states have endorsed the policy produced in the Quinlan decision, but other courts have produced distinctive policies. In 1976, California enacted the nation's first living will law, followed in 1977 by similar laws in seven additional states. Nearly all states had living will bills before the state legislature in 1977 (Society for the Right to Die 1988). By the end of 1990, forty-one states and the District of Columbia had enacted living will legislation.

As indicated earlier, living will laws allow individuals to specify their wishes in advance of a terminal illness concerning the administration of life-saving treatment. In contrast, the court cases generally deal with terminally ill or permanently comatose patients who have not executed living wills and where there is doubt concerning a patient's wishes or doctors require a court order to disconnect equipment. However, certain court cases have interpreted legislation and on occasion have sanctioned the validity of living wills in the absence of legislation.

Dilemmas and Ambiguities

Despite the quantity of state law produced in the past fifteen years, the right to die is not a settled issue. There are numerous dilemmas and ambiguities and associated political conflicts that continually crop up and keep the right to die a frequent if not permanent issue on state political agendas. Disagreement over the meaning and availability of the right to die is reflected in wide variation in state law. Some states have generally permissive or facilitative laws while others have imposed serious limitations on patient control. Most state courts permit the withdrawal of treatment in most hopeless cases and generously interpret the meaning of terminal illness, but others require absolutely clear evidence of patients' wishes, have narrowly interpreted the meaning of terminal illness, and have restricted the types of treatment that may be withdrawn.

As indicated earlier, a complete examination of the legal, medical, and ethical issues involved in the right to die is beyond the scope of this study. But as background to the politics of the right to die, it is important to recognize that many of the concepts and practices involved in treating terminally ill or comatose patients are unclear and unsettled. Some have been the focus of many political battles in the states while others have been addressed by courts but not by legislatures.

The Continuum of Care

Aggressive medical care and passive and active euthanasia are three elusive points on a treatment dimension that is even broader than the right to die proposals depicted in figure 1.1. At one extreme end of the continuum, a minority of doctors object to any withdrawal or withholding of treatment and would continue to sustain any patient who is not brain dead. At the other end, a few doctors publicly—and probably more, privately—condone ending the life of a patient who is suffering and cannot be restored to any reasonable level of health. Most others are in the middle. They would refuse to kill a patient out of mercy, termed an act of commission, knowing that such action clearly is illegal. Most also resist enlarging the role of medicine to include assisted suicide since doctors are pictured as

healers, not killers or abettors of death. Involving doctors in mercy killing or suicide confuses the traditional medical role and suggests to some that medicine could become an agent of state policy permitting or encouraging active euthanasia.

But most physicians also recognize that there is a time for ending futile treatment which can only postpone the inevitability of death. However, doctors and medical institutions sometimes fear medical malpractice suits or even criminal liability for withdrawing treatment, which occurs through omission, i.e., not doing everything possible to sustain life.

Medical fears of liability for not doing everything possible to preserve life are the basis of most lawsuits concerning requests by patients and families to withdraw medical treatment. However, occasionally disputes arise when family members disagree over whether treatment should be stopped and doctors refuse to end treatment without the legal protection of a court order. Living wills are designed to prevent such conflicts, but even with living wills, doctors sometimes are satisfied only with an explicit court order which absolves them of criminal or civil liability for ending treatment.

There apparently have been only two disputes with the roles reversed—in which the families of patients on artificial life support objected to its removal, and doctors and the hospital have gone to court to get permission to end what, in their view, was futile and inhumane treatment. In a case in Minneapolis, the patient's husband stood by strong religious beliefs which require preserving life, whatever its condition. In Atlanta, the parents of a thirteen-year-old girl disagreed about her treatment, and the father insisted he was waiting for a miracle. Trial judges in both cases ruled that families were in the best position to decide for the patient. The hospital in the Minneapolis case said it would not appeal, and the patient died a few days later (*New York Times*, 10 January 1991:1; 2 July 1991:A3; 6 July 1991:8).

Ending life-sustaining medical treatment also may seem easy to specify, but there is disagreement and confusion concerning the particular treatments that patients should and should not receive and what constitutes ordinary and extraordinary care. Artificial respiration and heart resuscitation are the "extraordinary" life-sustaining treatments that are withdrawn most frequently, but other routine or

17

ordinary medical procedures, such as the use of antibiotics to fight pneumonia and other infections, also postpone inevitable death from the underlying terminal illness or injury. Should they be used because they can fight a treatable illness or employed as "comfort care" because they keep a patient comfortable while they die? In contrast, pain killers used as comfort care procedures also can hasten death by depressing breathing and circulation, and further blur the distinction between passive and active euthanasia. These details of treatment generally are not addressed by legislatures, and ambiguity surrounding day-to-day medical decision making increasingly are seen as shortcomings and problems in living will laws.

Withholding and Withdrawing Treatment

Disagreements also flare over the ethical difference between withholding and withdrawing life-sustaining procedures. Some doctors feel more comfortable not beginning a life-prolonging treatment than withdrawing it, which fits within broader concerns over the difference between acts of commission and omission. To omit a treatment is justified as passive euthanasia since a doctor stands aside while illness takes its toll, but removing a device or stopping a treatment requires action and possibly seems closer to the commission of active euthanasia. Clearly, the result to the patient is the same and many commentators and ethicists no longer see a difference between withholding and withdrawing or between a decision not to act (i.e., not starting treatment) and a decision to act (i.e., withdrawing treatment). The courts also generally have taken this view, but the conflict still plagues daily clinical decision making.

Food and Hydration

Political battles have raged most recently in state legislatures and courts over the artificial administration of food and hydration. Patients who are unable to take food and liquids by mouth often are routinely given them through intravenous, nasogastric, or implanted stomach tubes. Artificial feeding frequently is considered part of regular patient maintenance and comfort care that all patients—regardless of their condition—should receive. Many patients, such as Nancy Cruzan and other young people in a permanent vegetative state, could be kept alive for years or decades through such procedures.

Since the mid–1980s many states (but by no means all) and the U.S. Supreme Court have concluded that there is no meaningful distinction between ordinary and extraordinary care, and that the artificial administration of food and hydration is a medical procedure that can be withdrawn or withheld like any other. But to opponents, the withdrawal of sustenance, however administered, is enforced starvation and active euthanasia. Political battles between state courts and legislatures and interest groups continue to be fought on allowing or curtailing the right to end artificially administered food and hydration.

Diagnosis

A related political issue concerns the diagnosis of terminal illness. Most state living will laws specify that in order for medical treatment to be withheld and a patient allowed to die, he or she must be diagnosed by two or more physicians as terminally ill and judged that death is imminent. However, the term *terminal illness* is not very precise, and since doctors are trained and medically socialized to treat illness, not to give in to death, they sometimes are unwilling to diagnose a patient as terminally ill until death is very close and the patient already has undergone various life-sustaining procedures.

In turn, and paradoxically, treatment that preserves various organ functions may make the patient technically not terminal. Consequently, dilemmas concerning the timing of a diagnosis of terminal illness and the willingness to end life-sustaining treatment is even more basic than differences over passive and active euthanasia and the medical procedures which may be withdrawn. If doctors are reluctant to term the patient terminal or in a permanent unconscious state, various life-sustaining treatments will be administered, at least for a time, regardless of a patient's wishes.

Moral Conflicts

Finally, but certainly not least, there are fundamental religious and moral conflicts over the right to die, which have been channeled into state politics. While not condoning incessant suffering, opponents of living will laws and court decisions which permit the withdrawal or withholding of treatment see the right to die as an infringement on the power of God to control life. It also involves government in matters that ought to be managed privately by patients and their families and doctors. In this view, although man has increased the power to extend life, he should not take steps which actively seek its end. Government sanctioned passive euthanasia also is seen by opponents as a step toward mercy killing, assisted suicide, and probably involuntary Nazi-like euthanasia. In this view, the frail and poor elderly and the medically and mentally handicapped are most vulnerable, although unnamed others could be threatened in the future.

Political Combatants
Supporters

Until very recently there has been little organized political support at the state level for the right to die. National groups, especially Concern for Dying and the Society for the Right to Die, provide information and support to sponsors of legislation and aid individuals and families involved in litigation, but few in-state interest groups have actively campaigned for the right to die or supported legislators who put the issue on legislative agendas. In most states, the issue has been too controversial and divisive for organizations to take a stand. In addition, the right to die does not affect a particular group of citizens more than another, which leads no group to champion it as a legislative issue. Even the elderly, a group that is disproportionately affected by the right to die, have been divided and largely silent on this issue. Other groups that often are sympathetic to the right to die, such as state nurses' associations, have many other items on their agendas more central to their interests, so they do not devote time or resources to lobbying directly on this issue.

In the early 1970s, except for the occasional legislative testimony of individual doctors and nurses—often associated with universities—and citizens with personal tragedies to tell about the protracted death of a loved one, legislators sponsoring living will bills frequently found themselves working alone for legislation. Today, as the issue has permeated the social and political agendas, supporters include the American Medical Association and various state medical societies, bar associations, hospital associations, various Protestant and Jewish denominations, the American Association of Retired Persons and their state affiliates, other groups of the elderly, and many others. However, while these groups are supporters, they rarely lobby hard for living will laws and other legislation.

Opponents

In sharp contrast to the sporadic support among those who are sympathetic, the right to die always has had very powerful and active opponents. The most well-organized and influential opposition comes from the Catholic church through state Catholic conferences, which are the lobbying arms of the Catholic dioceses. However, the Catholic church recently has modified its position in recognition of increased public support of the right to die. It has not endorsed living will laws, but actively tries to influence their content in order to insure that Church interests are included. Additionally, various state and local right to life organizations also oppose living will laws and permissive court decisions, and they take the most extreme positions against the right to die, linking it to Nazi euthanasia and other totalitarian measures. These groups also generally refuse to compromise on living will legislation. Finally, state and national organizations representing the disabled and retarded also have opposed living will laws and permissive judicial policies, seeing them as a likely first step to ridding society of the dependent and unwanted.

Representatives of state Catholic conferences frequently claim they have no bonds with right to life groups and that they do not coordinate political activities with them, but the two have been closely linked in the past. The National Right to Life Committee and its state and local affiliates were created as separate organizations by the U.S. Catholic Conference in order to avoid jeopardizing the Church's tax-exempt status as a result of its active political promotion of prolife causes. But the right to life committees were and continue to be heavily dominated by Catholic lay persons, and various researchers and journalists maintain that the Catholic church continues to channel funds to these groups (Tribe 1990; Paige 1983; Tatalovich and Daynes 1981; Steinhoff and Diamond 1977).

The rise of conservative Protestant evangelical groups in the Republican Party in the 1980s has attached conservative Protestants to this formerly mostly Catholic movement. State Catholic conferences and state right to life committees separately manage their own political activities, but on abortion and the right to die, they have parallel political goals, and often there is a tacit but sometimes uneasy alliance between them. The Catholic church and right to life groups are not always in harmony for two main reasons. Right to life organizations often take conservative positions on a wide range of social issues on which the Catholic church is more liberal, and the right to life groups often use extreme tactics, such as sit-ins, demonstrations, searing language, and graphic advertising and other visual displays against supporters of the right to die. State Catholic conferences often officially distance themselves from these strategies while pursuing the same political objectives.

In each of the states, Catholic conferences have been much more prominent than right to life organizations or evangelical Protestants in opposing the right to die and they lobby in much more conventional ways, which gives them greater access to state legislators. However, in the past few years, The National Right to Life Committee, its state affiliates, and new right to life groups, such as the International Anti-Euthanasia Task Force, have linked the right to die to abortion in an effort to mobilize broader political opposition to the withdrawal of treatment, particularly artificially administered food and hydration (*New York Times,* 31 July 1990:1).

Converging Policies

The right to die is one element of a much larger set of medical, health care, and social issues that appeared at a similar time and evolved in response to the transformation of modern medicine. While it is not possible to thoroughly explore these other issues here, it is important to emphasize that the right to die has not emerged separate and apart from other problems and developments. The appearance of other related issues also underscores that policy innovation is much more complex than the emergence and evolution of a single policy.

Brain Death

Not only have advances in medical technology made it possible to extend life, they have made it much more difficult to pronounce death. Before the availability of brain scan technology and medical devices which can prolong breathing and circulation, death was defined as the cessation of voluntary breathing and heartbeat. However, with increased use of respirators and resuscitators, doctors have begun to rely on newer definitions which include brain death as an additional basis for the pronouncement of death.

Like withdrawing medical treatment, determining brain death may seem simple at first, but there are at least seven different definitions of death, which include a brain death component, that have been developed since 1968 (Blumberg and Wharton-Hagan 1988). All state laws require that the entire brain—the cerebellum and the brain stem—cease functioning in order for a person to be declared brain dead. Persons in a permanent vegetative state have suffered complete loss of cerebral function, but the brain stem continues to operate and these people are not considered brain dead.

Recently, critics have argued that definitions of brain death should be changed to include only the cerebellum and higher brain functions so that those in a vegetative state could be declared brain dead, which would permit the withdrawal of treatment (Meisel 1989:134–35). The Catholic church and other opponents maintain that so long as part of the brain continues to function, life exists. Brain death policies also are crucial for organ transplant policies since minimal lifelike functions can be preserved through artificial respiration and circulation which permits organ transplants from those who are brain dead.

Of the states that have adopted living will laws, nearly 70 percent previously had enacted one or another brain death statute, indicating that most of the states previously had dealt with an issue closely related to the right to die. Although brain death and the right to die are not the same thing, the adoption of one creates psychological and political linkage to the other. Previous adoption of a brain death statute "softens up" the political environment and probably makes a living will law more acceptable.

Medical Costs

Doctors and medical researchers are not the only ones in our society who have come to expect continued advances in treatment and aggressive battles against disease. Nearly everyone strives for better health and longer life and expects medical salvation for every illness. Medicine is expected to conquer the next health challenge and extend its frontiers; there is no end to our preoccupation with medical miracles. But all of the medical innovations cost enormous amounts of money and critics are beginning to argue that it is impossible to provide expensive and innovative treatments and procedures to everyone for every illness. Many people no longer can afford health insurance and those covered on the job face rising premiums and reductions in benefits. Government programs to aid the poor and the elderly cost more every year. Some limits or rationing—done either by government or through market forces—must occur, it is argued, or there will be continuing economic and social crises in providing health care.

Daniel Callahan has argued for a revolution in the way we think about health care (1987; 1990). We need to set limits of all sorts, guaranteeing a certain level of health care for everyone, but eliminating the exotic cures that save or extend few lives at great cost and which spur even more innovation and social expectations about the next generation of medical miracles. Although such a revolution in medicine has not and probably will not take place soon, discussion and debate about a national health care crisis is occurring at the same time the states have adopted right to die policies. Indeed, a few politicians and political commentators make a clear and direct link between the two, although these arguments rarely have been raised in state legislatures.

A drive to extend life through sophisticated diagnostic procedures, treatments, and life-sustaining measures means that those on the verge of death, or in a permanent vegetative state, and the infirm elderly increasingly receive huge amounts of health care resources. If society reexamines the meaning of life and death and the role of health care, our conception of appropriate treatment must come under greater scrutiny.

There is no evidence that medical costs and treatment have been reduced by living will laws or court decisions. On the contrary, some recent research and events suggest that profit motives are related to decisions to use life-prolonging technology. In 1989, a New York intermediate appellate court ruled that the family of a nursing home resident, who was in a permanent vegetative state, would not be required to pay $100,000 in nursing home fees for treatment which the family repeatedly insisted the resident did not want. The nursing home continually pressed for payment but had repeatedly refused to honor requests for the removal of a stomach feeding tube and the end to antibiotic treatment as contrary to the policies and philosophy of the nursing home (*Elbaum v. Grace Plaza of Great Neck*).

A recent survey of the use of artificial nutrition and hydration in nursing homes found that state living laws had no effect on nursing home policy regarding the use of artificial feeding. However, artificial feeding was more likely to be used in private nursing homes owned by large corporate chains. A large proportion of residents supported by private and public assistance also leads to greater use of feeding tubes. Other research has shown that highly debilitated nursing home residents are less costly to maintain than mobile and active clients, which reinforces the possibility that nursing homes may be motivated by profit to keep the very elderly and disabled alive through life-prolonging technology (Almgren 1990; Danis 1991). The Associated Press also reported recently that some privately owned hospitals in various cities lure doctors with cash payments, low cost loans, gifts of equipment and guaranteed supplemental incomes to admit more patients to fill empty hospital beds (*Tallahassee Democrat*, 17 October 1990:1). Once the patient is there, perhaps private hospitals are reluctant to cease unwanted or perhaps unnecessary treatments.

The Increasing Elderly

Occurring with changes in medical technology is a huge demographic shift in the age of the American population, with enormous implications for all types of public and private policies from advertising and marketing to health care, housing, and transportation. The proportion of the elderly is fast increasing, and the biggest jumps are yet to come. In 1900 those over age sixty were little more than 6 percent of the total population. This doubled by 1950 and increased to nearly 17 percent in 1990. The level is likely to remain fairly constant to the end of the century, but will increase again to 25 percent between 2000 and 2025 and 30 percent by 2080. While the total U.S. population tripled between 1900 and 1980, from 76 million to 227 million, those over age sixty increased sevenfold, from 5 million to 36 million. The oldest old is the fastest-growing group. The percentage of all elderly under the age of seventy is declining while the percentage of those over age seventy and especially over age eighty-five is increasing. In 1900, those age eighty-five and older were 1 percent of the total population; in 1980 they had increased to 6 percent. The meaning of "old age" is changing with the statistics.

The implications for health care are clear. Between 1965 and 1981 the nation's health care expenditures for the elderly increased from 23 to 33 percent of the total. In 1973 the number of nursing home residents age sixty-five and older was 961,500. By 1980 the number had increased 37 percent to 1,315,800. Those age eighty and above constituted nearly 65 percent of all residents. Nearly half of all nursing home care is paid by Medicaid and other government funds (Serow, Sly, and Wrigley 1990; *New York Times,* 27 March 1990:A10). In any particular year, Medicare spends six times the amount for health care for elderly who die as opposed to those who do not die. The largest increases (over 45 percent) occur within the last sixty days of life (Weir 1989:21–22).

Political debate about health care costs and the allocation of medical resources and the concerns of medical institutions are bound to focus heavily on treatment for the elderly, and the concerns will heighten as the size of the elderly population—especially the oldest old—increases. The elderly are also disproportionately involved in and affected by right to die policies. Half of all deaths in the United

States each year occur among the elderly, although those over age sixty-five constitute only 11 percent of the population. Half of all the right to die appellate cases in the states also have concerned persons over age sixty-five. Again, the right to die is not the same issue as the cost and allocation of health care, but connections between the two are being made and are bound to become more compelling in the future. Policies in one area implicate policies in others.

Legislators and judges rarely link these converging policies or produce solutions to new problems according to a large, encompassing plan. But the right to die is part of a larger process of agenda setting and innovation, and related policies have implications for each other. The simplest connections occur when the adoption of a certain policy at an earlier point in time eases the way for the adoption of related policies in the future. But some policies emerge more or less simultaneously and motivate divergent groups to support them as solutions to different problems that they have identified as important to their own constituency.

Conclusion

Although the right to die is connected to a much larger set of social and technological issues, this book focuses on the emergence and development of the right to die as public policy. As I indicated earlier, my approach differs from most other writing about the right to die as I am concerned mainly with the politics of the issue and the responses of state government to it. The adoption of right to die policies is part of the state policy-making process and it can be examined and understood through established methods of political analysis. Therefore, in addition to telling the political story of the right to die, I place it within the context of previous political research.

In the following chapter, I explore how research on social and political agenda setting and innovation provides a way for understanding how the right to die has developed as a social concern and became a subject for government action. This chapter is followed by a political history of the right to die and the emergence and political take-off of the issue in the United States. This chapter also

illustrates that the right to die has ancient political roots and various
current forms, and that it is impossible to trace a particular policy
to a single source or idea. The third chapter examines the right to
die in more detail on the political agendas of three diverse states. I
closely examine the roles of bill sponsors, litigants, interest groups,
and the interactions between courts and legislatures as a way of telling the right to die story in three different settings. This chapter
provides information about the particular political processes, individuals, and organizations that have been important in the adoption
of right to die policies, but it does so within the context of agenda
setting and innovation.

The next two chapters examine the diffusion of policy innovations throughout the fifty states. Important in both of these chapters is the theme that while the adoption of right to die policies has
spread among the states, the content of these policies varies enormously and has substantially different impacts on citizens. The first
of these chapters examines the rise of litigation and the content of
state appellate court decisions. State appellate courts contributed
enormously to establishing a common law and/or constitutional
right to die, and their decisions stimulated additional political conflict and policy-making. The next chapter explores innovation in
state legislatures, with the primary emphasis on the diffusion and
content of living will laws. In addition, I examine the interplay between courts and legislatures, the role of interest groups, and recent
state innovations. The final chapter explores the existence of a national right to die and future policy issues that are likely to occur.

2 Agenda Setting and Innovation in State Politics

Models of agenda setting and innovation link the sources and production of policy. Agenda setting focuses on how problems transform from general social concern into items for official governmental action, and innovation deals with government adoption of new programs and policies. Theories and models of agenda setting and innovation cover virtually the entire political process, which makes it difficult to develop an integrated set of specific and testable propositions about how issues arise and what government does about them. Of the two, innovation is the most fully developed, but there are many approaches to innovation, and research covers a wide range of issues, levels of government, and theoretic concerns.

In political science, the main focus of innovation research is on the relationships between political and social characteristics of the states or local governments and the date when governments have adopted various new policies. Another approach explores the extent to which particular innovations are employed by state or local governments. In contrast, theories of agenda setting lean toward description and comparison of the stages of the political process and political strategies for getting items on official governmental agendas. There has been little cross-national or other comparative research that can be used to test the impact of political contexts and behaviors on agenda setting (Cobb, Ross and Ross 1976), and few efforts to link agenda setting with innovation. However, comparative research on state agenda setting would help uncover the political processes and conditions necessary for getting new issues on governmental agendas as well as the political strategies that lead to successful innovation or delay in policy adoption.

Agenda Setting and State Politics

The large gap between research on agenda setting and innovation in state politics is due partly to the relative difficulty in obtaining necessary data. It is much easier to identify and date new laws or court decisions and the social and political conditions related to their adoption than it is to uncover the informal political processes that produce ideas and demands for new policies. It also often is unclear exactly what data is needed for identifying and measuring the processes by which an issue emerges from the social context, attains a position on the official governmental agenda, and becomes official policy (Burstein 1985). No matter how complete a search may be for participants, events, ideas, political influence, and changing social trends, there always is information left uncovered about the nuances and details of politics. Moreover, despite the emphasis in political science on fifty-state comparative research, it probably is impractical to do in-depth comparative research on agenda building since indicators of agenda setting are not readily available and the necessary information for mapping the progress of an issue is varied and voluminous (Nelson 1984:21).

The leading work on agenda setting focuses on the United States Congress or formulates propositions derived from a variety of research primarily on national politics (Kingdon 1973; Kingdon 1984; Cobb and Elder 1972; Polsby 1984). Even the work on individual state issues focuses heavily on national political trends that sweep the states along to similar legislation in a short period of time (Nelson 1984; Jacob 1988). But not all innovations spread like wildfire, and some states never get on the bandwagon, leaving much to explain about the impact of state level politics on the reception that new policies receive. Nevertheless, researchers have put very little emphasis on the varied effects of individual state social and political contexts and political strategies used to get issues onto government agendas.

Theories of Agenda Setting
Social and Historical Context

Long before an issue becomes a concern for government, it exists in a preagenda stage and has predecessors in the broad social and historical context. In a modern, complex society, bright ideas and issues may come from anywhere, and similar ones might arise almost simultaneously from different quarters. It also usually is fruitless to attempt to trace ideas for innovations to their origins or to isolate the sources of new thoughts, since every social condition grows out of something previous (Kingdon 1984:76). As mentioned in the previous chapter, the right to die can be traced to the early Greeks, but looking to the past will not help to explain contemporary policy and variations among the states. While it is perhaps fruitless to search for roots, studies that focus on the development of specific issues and policies require contextual information and background to orient the research and to place current policy within its larger social context. In contrast, the search for roots generally is unimportant if the focus is on the perceptions of legislators and others concerning the general processes by which a wide range of issues gets on the agenda (Kingdon 1973; 1984).

Agenda-setting theory distinguishes between social conditions and social problems. Many conditions, such as poverty, poor health, inadequate transportation, oil spills, etc., do not become agenda items until segments of the public and/or government officials perceive them as problems requiring a governmental solution. Until items get on the public agenda, they simply are facts of life that people might take for granted or tolerate as part of their existence. Once a condition is perceived as a problem, however, it may become part of the public and/or governmental agendas.

Public and Governmental Agendas

The public agenda includes all of the items that groups and individuals within the public perceive as problems. The public agenda is divided into two components: the *professional agenda,* which includes the views of various elites, opinion leaders, and the leaders of interest groups; and the *mass agenda,* which covers the broader polity (Nelson 1984). The *governmental agenda* is composed of fewer items, which are being considered for possible action, and the *decisional agenda* is the still smaller set of problems on which immediate government action is likely. The public, governmental, and decisional agendas operate as a narrowing funnel as the many issues circulating among the public are reduced to fewer issues of concern to government and still fewer issues on which government takes action. Not all issues of concern to the mass public or to professional groups get on the governmental agendas or stay there long enough to get serious attention. Many issues come and go and an issue's staying power is a crucial element in moving from agenda setting to innovation.

Barbara Nelson (1984) argues that the distinction between the professional and mass agendas is very important since issues often reach the professional agenda first by appearing frequently in professional literature. Later leading articles and books are noticed by journalists and publicized in the mass media. In turn newspaper and magazine articles lead the broader mass public to pay attention to a newly discovered problem. Both professionals and the mass public may demand government action to solve a problem, but that depends heavily on the persistence of the problem and the political strategies of individuals calling for innovation.

Outside and Inside Forces

There are two models for understanding how new items get on government agendas. The first is through *outside political forces,* which reflects the classic pluralist model of American politics. In this scenario political demands, composed of elite leadership, mass public opinion, interest group lobbying, and perhaps political party mobilization, are channeled into the legislative and/or judicial processes, which respond by converting demands into policy. Outside forces are at work when small specialized groups of concerned individuals—such as doctors, lawyers, or particular business people—have special expert knowledge about a problem that they believe requires official action. The professionals attempt to develop broad support for change by expanding public awareness of the issue through news coverage in the mass media. In time, public officials react to rising public concern (Burstein 1985; Cobb, Ross, and

Ross 1976). However, broadening public awareness invites opposition from groups that benefit materially or psychologically from the status quo. In keeping with classic interest group theories of politics, the unresolved conflict between opposing groups places the problem on the official governmental agenda for resolution (Cobb and Elder 1972:19).

But agenda-setting theory is contradictory on this final point. Opposition from powerful groups also frequently keeps issues from getting on or remaining on government agendas (Cobb, Ross, and Ross 1976; Bachrach and Baratz 1962; Bachrach and Baratz 1963). Lobbyists are known to watch carefully for bills that threaten their group's interests and to try to keep them from getting out of legislative committees and being voted on by the full houses of a legislature. City councils may refuse to take up controversial or fundamental issues, preferring to silently endorse the status quo and deal instead with managerial problems. Equally important, most policy-making does not involve interest group conflict, and it is largely unnoticed by the media and the public. Many problems are cast as extremely narrow, technical, and irrelevant for the general public, such as business and professional regulation, education policies, health regulations, etc. (Jacob 1988). Also, state legislation has a much greater chance of passing when there is no group conflict—a perspective on the decisional agenda that is contrary to the outside forces model (Wiggins and Browne 1982).

An alternative to the conflict-ridden, pluralist, and outsider model of agenda setting and innovation is a consensus or *inside political forces* model in which elites dominate the policy-making process. An inside forces strategy is one in which experts and sympathetic legislators or government staff try to put items on the government agenda without first placing the issue on the mass agenda. By avoiding mass participation and political conflict they hope to retain control of the definition and content of the issues and obtain more rapid innovation. Instead of attracting and using the mass media, they limit the dissemination of information and narrow the definition of policy to make it appear a routine, noncontroversial modification of law or the natural evolution of an existing policy.

An illustration is the emergence of child abuse as a social problem in the 1960s and 1970s, which came mainly from medical elites and the visibility of their published research. Although the general public and government officials could become aware of the issue via the news, medical elites presented child abuse as a special medical problem separate from poverty and neglect in order not to arouse potential conservative opponents who might see legislation as an intrusion into the sanctity of the family (Nelson 1984:14–15). Similarly, Herbert Jacob found that by making no-fault divorce reform a routine modification of existing family law, legal reformers achieved official agenda status and remarkable and rapid innovation without substantial involvement from other groups (Jacob 1988:11–15).

Characterizing a proposed change in policy as routine and undisputed or new and controversial is crucial for determining the kind of strategy that can be used. As suggested in the previous chapter, the right to die never has been a routine or undisputed issue. Sponsors of living will laws initially tried using an inside strategy because it offers the possibility of quick and painless success with much less political effort. But inside strategies have not worked. Outside strategies have always been necessary but have not always been successful either, leaving some states without living will laws and many others with delayed innovation.

Getting Official Attention

Regardless of strategy, an issue finally must attract the attention of government officials to get on the government agenda. There are many ways that an issue may receive official recognition. Frequently a cataclysmic disaster, such as a flood, mine cave-in, oil spill, etc., galvanizes officials, or issues gain attention as a result of accumulating research, recurring statistical reports, or court cases. However, disasters or prominent research alone rarely tip policymakers into action. Big events usually have been preceded by long-term conditions or minidisasters. But big events frequently open windows of opportunity for a policy entrepreneur who has been working for a long time to find a way to get an issue on the government and decisional agendas. The big catastrophe or court case can finally lead others to pay attention (Kingdon 1984:183–93).

The general public frequently is unaware of an issue until a big event motivates official policymakers to act, and many people may be surprised to see an issue surface. But issues frequently circulate previously on one or another professional agenda and usually have received some attention by the mass media. Preexisting conditions and concerns among professionals make it important to search the social agenda for emerging issues in order to understand their subsequent movement to government agendas and innovation.

Finally, to move from official consideration to the decisional agenda, policy sponsors must formulate specific solutions, possible alternatives, and potential compromises that translate a problem into a policy (Kingdon 1984:149–50). If government acts or fails to act on a proposal, items often drift off the agenda either because government appears to have dealt with the problem, or sponsors and supporters give up and go on to other issues. The ability of policy sponsors to keep an issue before the public and on the governmental agenda is crucial for getting favorable governmental policy since many controversial proposals are not enacted immediately.

For example, in eleven states in which it has been possible to trace living will legislation from the first bill to passage of a law, the date of enactment has come an average of seven years after the first bill was introduced. The longest periods were in Florida and Nebraska with twelve years and the shortest were in California and New Hampshire with two years. However, living will bills have repeatedly been before the Massachusetts legislature since 1976, but no law has passed. Only in 1990 did Massachusetts enact a different right to die law. Had bill sponsors given up after their first defeat, or been unable to resurrect earlier bills, it is unlikely that any of the states would have living will laws or other right to die policies.

Agents of change. Most agenda-setting research emphasizes the importance of chief executives, legislators, and government staff who notice a problem and decide to try to put it on the government agenda. They may bring certain issues with them when they take office or discover them later as a result of changing family circumstances or the experiences of friends and constituents. This is especially important for health issues, such as the right to die, which do not affect large numbers of people through a single big event but have their impact on thousands—one at a time. For health conditions to be cast as problems, officials and other elites must demonstrate that they are not isolated and individual or unusual events, but an aggregate of conditions that invisibly permeate society (Kingdon 1984:100–102).

Agenda-setting research generally overlooks or compartmentalizes the role of courts in elevating issues from the social to the governmental level. But it is widely recognized that courts no longer are—if they ever were—"the least dangerous branch," meaning that they produce few decisions of great consequence to society. Getting issues before the courts is an alternative to lobbying the legislature and it frequently results in extremely important policy. Equally important, judicial decisions sometimes drive issues onto legislative agendas (Melnick 1983; Bosso 1987; Dister 1988).

For example, abortion probably is the most controversial long-term domestic issue in American politics, and federal and state courts have made crucial decisions in this field, frequently overturning state laws limiting access to abortion. However, the Supreme Court's decision in *Webster v. Reproductive Health Services* (1989) permits state regulation of abortion and invites the state legislatures to enact new abortion laws, some of which already have come under new judicial scrutiny.

Similarly, the Supreme Court's Cruzan decision recognized Missouri's right to regulate the withdrawal of medical treatment, but it did not require other states to follow Missouri's policy, further inviting state legislatures to produce distinctive living will and related right to die laws. The state courts also are free to produce their own standards of evidence concerning patients' wishes and related right to die policies. As discussed in later chapters, state appellate courts have been extremely important in stimulating movement toward the adoption of state living will laws and they have influenced the content of legislation.

Interest groups seem to have a much more peripheral role in agenda setting than political office holders and institutions. Liberal interest groups, which are more likely than conservative ones to seek change, place some items on the agenda but interest groups generally are more concerned with shaping the alternatives to policy and assuring that their concerns are included once an item gets on the agenda. Consequently interest groups appear to be more important at the innovation stage than in developing new ideas and proposals.

Diverse groups also sometimes support a proposed policy as a solution for completely separate and distinctive problems. Instead of formulating and proposing new policies designed to solve a problem they have identified, organizations sometimes discover and embrace policies proposed for other situations, but which can be applied to their own problems. For example, the sponsors of living will laws see them as providing individuals greater control over terminal medical care, but living will laws also are attractive to certain medical elites as a possible way of decreasing medical malpractice suits and saving scarce resources spent on expensive but fruitless treatment. Lawyers like them because they are another item to include in estate planning. When there are "solutions in search of a problem" (Cohen, March, and Olsen 1972), and a single solution solves the problems of several different groups, coalitions can be built toward innovation. In both of these situations interest groups use or modify solutions that have been proposed by others for their own purposes. They are not responsible for posing new solutions to existing problems and working to get them onto governmental agendas.

Finally, the mass media reports on what is happening, which may help to build the mass agenda, but political elites generally do not perceive the media as determining the content of the official agenda (Kingdon 1984:45–46; 50–51; 61–63). It sometimes appears that the mass media sets the agenda because the first time that many of us become aware of an issue is when it appears in the news. But the chances are good that political discussion about the issue has occurred among political leaders or private organizations and perhaps in specialized professional journals and newsletters.

Variations on Outside and Inside Strategies

Herbert Jacob suggests that political activists select the strategy they think will work best, but also that outside and inside strategies are poles on a continuum with elements of each in most policy-making situations (1988). Free choice cannot fully account for the use of outside and inside strategies, for a particular strategy may not be available due to many other political conditions.

Policy content. The outside and inside forces strategies seem best for promoting distinctive types of policies. Policies that require substantial and new public expenditures or that sharply deviate from past policies are likely to be controversial regardless of the strategy selected. An inside strategy probably cannot work if opposing groups pounce on a new issue and link it to a broader set of public worries. For example, creating the right to divorce in the first instance was much more controversial and required much more time than adding the no-fault reforms of the 1960s (Jacob 1988).

Robert L. Savage argues that an innovation is "fragile" if it is likely to provoke organized opposition, and legislators distance themselves from it in order to avoid political exposure and uncertainty. The adoption and diffusion of fragile policies may require many years. In contrast, an innovation that is not controversial may spread rapidly among different jurisdictions even without a particular organization or government agency promoting adoption (Savage 1983–84; also, Bingham 1976; Clark 1976). Legislators are eager to promote legislation that is important or salient to the public, but that is not opposed by powerful groups, such as a war on crime or drugs, etc. In contrast, issues that are crucial to powerful groups but have low public salience, such as increased professional regulation of doctors, lawyers, and real estate agents, or arcane tax provisions, are least likely to attract legislative interest (Price 1985).

As will be described more fully in the following chapters, the right to die moved from low public salience in the 1950s and early 1960s to higher public awareness in the early and mid–1970s. However, it also has aroused the opposition of very powerful and well-established interest groups, which object to government endorsement of the right to die, either through living will laws or judicial policy. Consequently, in the early years bill sponsors often found supporting the living will to be a lonely road, but with rising public interest and awareness, other groups have endorsed government involvement and enactment of living will laws has occurred more frequently. All the evidence indicates that right to die laws have been enacted only through highly competitive outside strategies.

Clearly, bill sponsors cannot simply choose a strategy. If they could the inside strategy always would be the preferred path since it is the quickest and least costly route to law. Instead, the content of policies frequently thrusts a strategy upon a sponsor and for controversial or fragile policies an outside strategy always is required.

Sponsors.   The social characteristics and political positions of sponsors also are important for determining whether issues are likely to get on the agenda. Supporters of radical change frequently lack routine access to government and are cast in the role of outsiders, forcing them to elect an outside strategy. Equal rights for blacks and women, prison and mental institution reform, property tax equalization, AIDS research and treatment, and many other controversial policies pit minorities or other nonelites and underdogs against established interests and the status quo.

In contrast, respected professional elites or well-placed political leaders who seek major changes from existing policy are apt to be more successful. Highly visible and politically secure leaders with safe Congressional or state legislative seats may take on "fragile" but high public salience policies, such as civil rights, since they have sufficient reserve political capital to withstand the heat of opposition and the stature to attract new support for challenging the status quo (Price 1985:569).

Ideology.   If general consensus exists on the acceptability or legitimacy of policy change and there is little risk in innovation, opposition is unlikely. But if groups have strongly held fundamental beliefs which lead them to reject the new policy, or they deeply fear unknown consequences or implications of change, opposition is guaranteed. The issue will expand beyond the narrow definition given it by professionals, attract wider interest from other groups, and become a controversial issue on both the mass and professional social agendas. These are the nemeses of an inside strategy. Extreme controversy based on conflicting ideologies may prevent new ideas from becoming innovations for a very long period, if ever.

Socioeconomic and political context.   The pioneering innovation research indicated that populous, urban, and affluent states generally adopt innovations early (Walker 1969), and it is possible that new ideas and demands get on government agendas in these states early as well. If this is the case, the same social, economic, and political contextual variables that explain innovation account for agenda setting. But recent innovation research, discussed below, suggests that the process is not so simple. Some innovations sweep the nation quickly, but others percolate slowly, and certain states never adopt particular policies. It is likely, therefore, that similar items may be placed on many government agendas at about the same time, but some fail to become innovations due to political obstacles within various states.

Including state contexts in research on agenda setting will help to account for differences in the importance of particular issues in the states and, subsequently, why innovation varies by type of policy. If, for example, liberal morals policies never reach the agenda in conservative states, or they die on official agendas for lack of support (Fairbanks 1980), we need to identify the reasons and processes which explain how they became items on the agenda but fail to become innovations. Instead of simply labeling such states as nonadopters or innovation laggards, linking state contexts to earlier processes of agenda setting would add to our knowledge of innovation and produce a more complete model of state policy-making.

Previous innovation. Innovation stimulates policy emulation, but agenda-setting processes may differ between early and later adopters. For a proposal to gain a hearing and acceptance, proponents must "soften up" their audience (Kingdon 1988:137–45). They need to accustom various publics to hearing about an idea and alternative policy proposals and accept the likelihood of change. Talking about and publishing ideas, listening to opinions, anticipating objections, weighing the technical feasibility, impact, and cost of a program, and persuading skeptics are required before a proposal will receive serious consideration.

The amount of softening up needed to get a proposal on the agenda and adopted as policy is likely to vary considerably depending upon the amount of controversy surrounding the issue. Issues that do not upset the status quo and arouse opposition are likely to need little advance work and are adopted easily. Others, such as the right to die, need careful nurturing, patience, and plenty of preparation and persuasion to obtain sufficient support for enactment.

40

Policy sponsors in the first state to adopt a controversial innovation probably must do much more softening up than is necessary in states that adopt similar or identical policies later on. For the later adopters the first innovation may legitimize a policy and make it easier for sponsors to get it on the government agenda. In particular, policy sponsors in later adopting states that are in the same region or sphere of policy influence as the early innovators may find it much easier to elevate a problem onto the governmental agenda than sponsors in states that do not identify with the early leader. For example, if New York were the initial policy leader, we would expect to find other northeastern states as well as California, Alaska, and perhaps a few other typical early innovators adopting similar policies. But many midwestern and southern states may pay little heed and policy sponsors in these states may have a much more difficult time persuading legislatures, courts, and governors to adopt an innovation. As mentioned earlier, California's first living will law was largely copied by other western states the year following its enactment, but widespread adoption of living will laws did not come until much later.

Innovation and State Politics

If it were possible to neatly separate parts of the political process, innovation would begin where agenda setting ends, but the two clearly are connected. Most research on policy innovation assumes earlier agenda setting, but it rarely inquires into that process. Since studies of innovation take place after substantial diffusion and adoption has occurred, there is no need to discover how issues were placed before the government in the first place. Tracing the pattern of policy diffusion can stand on its own as a separate research enterprise. But to understand how particular issues emerge, evolve, and are adopted it is essential to begin to forge links between agenda setting and innovation.

An innovation is defined as any policy, idea, or procedure that is new to a potential adopter (Rogers 1962; 1983; Savage 1985; Walker 1969; Gray 1973; Eyestone 1977). This does not mean that each adopter creates a brand new or unique policy, but that it adopts

41

a type of policy that is new to it. In the case of living will laws, California created and enacted the nation's first living will law and other states followed later. Since California forged the first law the following adopting states perhaps are not as creative as California, but they are considered innovative in varying degrees depending on when they adopted a living will law.

While the degree to which a state is considered innovative genererally has been defined by the date it adopts a particular policy or a group of policies, the process of innovation is much more complex. For example, although California enacted the first living will law, some of the ideas for this first law came from others. The law included certain provisions found in other states' earlier living will bills and model living will laws proposed by various national organizations. But other provisions were those of the bill sponsor and interest groups that influenced the final law. Innovation also is complicated because the contents of similar laws adopted later by other states differ in various ways from the earliest laws, giving some of the later adopters a measure of creativity due to the new content of the innovations that they put into place. I shall refer shortly to this aspect of innovation as reinvention, which is a new way of looking at the process of innovation.

Nearly every social and behavioral science has conducted innovation research. From anthropology, education, and speech communication, to rural sociology, political science, and others, researchers have investigated how new ideas, administrative procedures, and policies spread among professionals and other practitioners, organizations, and governments. Research on the spread of governmental policy innovations has focused mostly on diffusion among the fifty states, with concentration on state legislatures, although there are a few studies of the diffusion innovations among state supreme courts.

Theories of State Policy Innovation

There are three approaches to the study of political innovation in the states. Although each has a different focus, the major emphasis has been on the characteristics of the states as adopters rather than on the characteristics of the innovations.

The Decision to Adopt

By far the largest amount of research examines the dates that states adopt a number of given, presumed uniform innovations. Typically, researchers group a large number of varied policies and assign the states an average adoption score for all policies. These scores are then correlated with numerous indicators of state characteristics such as wealth, urbanism, education, political party competition, and many others. Generally, this research has uncovered that the wealthiest, most urban, and industrial states are more likely to be early innovators.

This general approach has been refined through the discovery that not all policies diffuse the same way, and that states that are early innovators in one policy field sometimes are late adopters or nonadopters in others. In addition, the ranking of adopting states varies by historical period and by political institution (Gray 1973; Savage 1978; Canon and Baum 1981; Glick 1981; Savage 1985). For example, New York has been a leader in civil rights and energy conservation, but is just above average in adopting education innovations. California is high in education, but average on civil rights. New Mexico is high on energy conservation but nearly last in consumer protection. Overall, California and Minnesota have been policy leaders since the nineteenth century while Oklahoma, a policy leader in the 1800s, has steadily slipped to become an average innovator in the late twentieth century. State supreme courts that are leaders in tort reform, such as those in California and Hawaii, sometimes lag in having modern methods of judicial administration. Finally, states that have innovative supreme courts sometimes have reluctant legislatures.

However, not all is chaos or chance in the diffusion of new policies, for certain states tend to rank high in most innovations. California, Colorado, New York, New Jersey, Oregon, Pennsylvania, Massachusetts, Wisconsin, and several others tend to be early innovators most of the time, but beyond the first dozen typically early leaders, there is great variation among the states as to when they adopt particular new laws and procedures.

Interstate communications. The mechanics of state decisions to adopt innovations rest on two levels of communication among public officials. The first is horizontal interstate communications in which parallel decision makers in different states provide information and ideas to each other concerning new policies. State legislators, legislative staff, and lobbyists frequently are in contact with their opposites in other states in order to learn of new ways for coping with common problems. Governors and their staffs communicate as well, and they discuss common concerns at annual meetings of the National Governors Conference. State officials who view their counterparts as equals or as appropriate models are likely to adopt each other's policies, although national and regional leaders, such as California, Wisconsin, and New York, are likely to feed and legitimize innovations for second and third tiers of innovators in different parts of the country.

Communications among courts probably are more indirect. News of novel cases is likely to stimulate similar litigation in other states, and it is likely that novel cases appear first in states with complex and diverse societies—again, California, New York, and other populous states. Judges are likely to become aware of particular decisions from other jurisdictions mainly when they have to decide a similar case. They and their staffs learn of new decisions through the written briefs of opposing attorneys and when they begin to search for precedents in support of written opinions.

While states interact, the timing of a particular state's decision to innovate is believed to rest mainly on its internal characteristics and regional affiliation. As indicated earlier, states that rank high in urbanization, total population, education, wealth, and other characteristics are the most likely to innovate early. Neighboring states and others in their region may follow and in time, when a certain percentage of states have adopted an innovation, others are likely to get on the bandwagon and the pace of innovation picks up.

National communications. A second explanation for innovative state policy adoptions rests on vertical communications between national organizations and/or the federal government and the states. Major national events or federal policy become widely visible through the news media or direct communications and stimulate innovation in many states at approximately the same time. One or several major events that indicate an innovation is spreading rapidly frequently encourages many late adopters to join the mainstream. Prominent national events may occur because of the cumulative impact of early state innovations, but the national events become critical themselves in tipping many later adopting states simultaneously toward innovation.

The tendency toward simultaneous innovation among state legislatures is reminiscent of innovation in the United States Congress. There, a "time is right" or "it's in the air" effect signals that political compromises and bargains have been reached, and all interested parties want to be in on the official act for fear of being left out of influencing the content of a law (Kingdon 1984; 147–48). In a similar way significant external forces signal that innovation "is in the air" nationally, and many state legislatures tip toward innovation at about the same time.

The concept that many states respond the same way to external systemwide events is similar to *rapid point source diffusion*, which has been applied to state reactions to innovations of the federal government. In rapid point source diffusion, the federal government adopts policies that require or encourage state participation in order for them to receive federal funds, for example, for highway construction, social welfare programs, and support for environmental protection, or which provide desirable models for the states to emulate, such as child abuse reporting laws (Eyestone 1977; Nelson 1984; Regens 1980; Welch and Thompson 1980). If federal funds are at stake, or there are other clear benefits and few costs involved with adopting a policy (i.e., it is not controversial or "fragile"), most of the states quickly adopt the innovation.

While lacking the power of federal law and grants-in-aid—and involving more than a single source—national organizations frequently make proposals for state policy innovations and attempt to influence the content of statutes in similar ways in all of the states. They frequently distribute identical sets of policy guidelines to supporters or affiliated state organizations, and, while state groups largely are responsible for lobbying in each legislature, they rely on national guidelines furnished by national organizations in negotiating state laws. National organizations that have been prominent in shaping living will laws are the Committee on Pro-Life Activities of the National Conference of Catholic Bishops, the National Conference Commission on Uniform State Laws, Concern for Dying, and the Society for the Right to Die.

Along with the impact of highly visible events, state innovation may occur in response to an issue's increasing presence on national social and political agendas. Changing agendas often precede and contribute to national events, but they also correlate over time with individual state decisions to adopt a policy. In particular, the rising volume of publications in the mass and professional media and increases in the frequency of appellate court cases may contribute to state legislative decisions to adopt living will laws. These trends usually are not distinctive to an individual state, but reflect broad social developments affecting the entire nation. Early experimenters create new laws without much regard to the general or growing visibility of the issue on the social agenda, but other states wait until the trend is well established and accompanied by policy recommendations by major national organizations.

The Extent of Policy Innovation

Another, but less common, approach to state policy innovation examines the extent of adoption of a particular innovation, usually at a single point in time. This research assesses the penetration of a policy or the degree a particular innovation is used by identical adopting units—such as school districts, sheriff's departments, judicial administrators, etc. This approach has certain advantages over the time of adoption approach. In a study of criminal justice reform, George W. Downs (1976:39) noted:

> Although [the adoption/nonadoption] method of scoring produces an interesting ordering of adopting units, it does not differentiate between "superficial" and "deep" adoption—that is, it reveals nothing about the extent to which the innovation has been employed, and frequently it is the determinants of this extent that are really of interest.

An early study that examined the extent of innovation is the classic article by Zvi Griliches (1957) on farmers' planting of hybrid corn. Rather than indicating whether they had adopted the innovation, he gathered the percentage (extent) of the farmer's acreage planted in the new crop. Recent research has examined the percentage of offenders in community-based correction programs; the percent of state money spent on criminal justice programs; state adoption of centralized court management; the use of computers in public housing authorities; and prefabricated housing for the poor (Gray and Williams 1980; Bingham 1976; Downs 1976; Glick 1981).

These studies indicate that discovering how extensively an innovation is used may require reevaluating the conclusions reached in the adoption/nonadoption studies. For example, if an early innovator does not employ its innovation very much or very often, its relative standing as a policy leader has to be tempered in view of the possibly greater use of the innovation by subsequent adopters. The early leader may be a "superficial" innovator while the later adopters are more deeply committed to the new policy. However, few studies have considered both dimensions at the same time or for the same policy.

The extent of using an innovation is most relevant for studying government operations or programs designed to implement a policy, such as in education, law enforcement, or environmental protection. It is less relevant to permissive policies or grants of rights—such as the right to die—which individuals may use at their own discretion. The extent of use of this type of innovation rests on citizens' decisions to use available policies, not on government decisions to employ a particular innovation. This does not mean that the extent to which citizens use permissive policies, such as living wills, is unimportant, but only that it is not a measure of a government's tendency to employ innovations in its own operations.

Policy Reinvention

Related to the extent of adoption is the likely "reinvention" of an innovation by adopting units during the period of diffusion. This concern suggests there is linkage between the date of adoption and the evolving content of policy. Everett Rogers, a leading authority on the theory of innovation, distinguishes "reinvention" from extent of adoption this way: reinvention is the modification by a user of a core innovation during the diffusion process, whereas extent is the degree of adoption of a "constant" innovation. An illustration is found in the changing goals and methods of airplane hijackers as they learned about previous hijacks through the mass media. Successful hijacking dramatically declined when the media, urged by the Federal Aviation Administration, stopped reporting details of the crimes (Rogers 1983:175; 183).

Jill Clark and others also suggest that policies vary in scope, stringency of controls, and level of governmental control during the diffusion process. For example state education accountability legislation, which concerns public controls over how well schools are educating students, varies according to state or local control and the number of students affected. Homestead tax exemption laws vary from exemptions for all homeowners to various limitations, such as exemptions for the elderly only or circuit breaker policies linked to the ability to pay. State regulation of lobbyists varies from strict regulation and full financial disclosure to no regulation (Allen and Clark 1981; Clark and French 1984; Clark 1985).

Research on policy reinvention strongly suggests that the content of many similar laws, policies, and procedures varies in important ways, and they are likely to affect citizens differently according to where they live. As in the previous discussion of the extent to which an innovation is used, studies of policy reinvention indicate that if states or other adopting units do not embrace a uniform policy, the early/late adoption dimension is but a partial indicator of a state's level of innovativeness.

There is so much more to learn about how innovation occurs. For example, previous research indicates that state officials look to each other for information and experience when embracing previously adopted innovations. Consequently, late adopting states may enact laws that take into account the consequences of early innovations, and create new twists on old policies that possibly are more effective in coping with social problems. Although late adopters do not score high on date of adoption measures, they may be more innovative than the earlier adopters if their policies contain new approaches for dealing with social problems and are more closely geared to current conditions. Even when states adopt proposals of the National Conference Commission on Uniform State Laws (NCCUSL) states frequently produce their own variations on policy, and the adoption of a presumed uniform law does not actually produce uniform policy (Jacob 1988:87).

There are two ways that reinvention may occur. Following Rogers, change is likely to occur during the period of initial adoption of legislation, but it also can occur when early adopters amend their initial legislation. Amendment may be thought of as reinvention through renovation, since early adopters modify their own previously enacted policy. However, the content of many initial reinventions and renovations are similar and can be viewed as two components of the reinvention process.

Agenda Setting, Innovation, and the Right to Die

Most previous research on agenda setting and innovation has tended to view these processes as separate dimensions of politics. My research combines the two by examining the emergence of the right to die as a social and political issue and the diffusion and changing content of legislative and judicial policies over time.

Approaches to Research

Case studies. The little agenda-setting research that has been done at the level of state politics has been case studies of single issues and/or single states. They have not emphasized variations in the innovative behavior of the states nor differences in the content of their policies. There are several reasons for the prominence of the case study approach. First, air pollution, child abuse, divorce, and certain other problems generally became prominent as national concerns, and new policies were stimulated by a few national sources and/or the federal government. Subsequent innovations spread very quickly among the states, and their policies appeared to be very similar. Consequently, variations among the states and their policies were not the primary concern. Second, as discussed earlier, research on agenda setting requires gathering large amounts of varied information from many sources in order to piece together the movement and evolution of issues into policies. Most of the necessary data is not recorded in public documents, the census, or standard reference books, but requires interviews and access to public and private files, and sifting through hundreds or thousands of documents. This makes extensive comparative research very difficult to accomplish.

The main advantage of the case study approach to agenda setting is that it produces considerable information about how various issues emerge and become the subject for government action. But we cannot easily generalize the findings to other states or to other issues.

Aggregate research.   In contrast to research on agenda setting, most prior research on policy innovation tends to be studies of large aggregates of policies and the patterns of diffusion among all fifty states. The only data needed to measure innovation is the date when states adopted particular laws or judicial doctrines. Generally, the large aggregate studies provide a fairly clear image of the state characteristics that are associated with decisions to adopt innovations, and we can identify the states that usually are leaders and followers.

The main disadvantage is that this type of research cannot provide in-depth information about many other interesting and important aspects of innovation. We lack information about the substantive content of particular policies; the processes of change or reinvention which occur during the period that new states adopt an innovation; the political processes which shape various policies and the interactions among political institutions which occur in forming policy; and the states' commitment to a policy, including the possibility that states may disinvent or repeal innovative policies adopted earlier (Downs and Mohr 1976; Eyestone 1977; Menzel and Feller 1977; Clark 1985).

Combining approaches.   Instead of opting either for a case study or a broad aggregate approach, my research on the right to die combines elements of both. First, I focus on state level agenda setting since right to die proposals and policies were not stimulated by major national events, but developed independently in many of the states. However, increasing concern with the right to die and significant national events appear to have influenced many late adopters to enact laws and particular judicial policies at about the same time, which makes national events relevant later on. Therefore, I shall provide some detail about agenda setting and innovation in three different but illustrative states, but I also will examine the influence of national trends and events on all of the states. It is not possible to do detailed research on agenda setting in all fifty states, but I have gathered considerable information about the diffusion and content of policies for all fifty states in order to make broad comparisons.

Since my research examines a single issue that I explore in detail for three states it is partly a case study. From another perspective, however, it is an aggregate study since I have gathered data on legislation and court decisions for all of the states, not just one or a few. This makes it possible to bridge several approaches to policymaking including how issues get on governmental agendas, the chronology of policy innovation, changes in the content of policies over time, and the correlates of state political behavior. This strategy puts the research within the context of comparative state politics while retaining the advantages of looking intensively at the politics associated with one social issue in a few jurisdictions.

In addition to investigating how the right to die emerged as a social and political issue and became policy in the United States, my research emphasizes several aspects of policy development and innovation that have not been investigated very deeply in the past. First, I focus on the political processes responsible for agenda setting and innovation, and the interactions among the different branches of government in shaping the content of this policy. Second, as in previous innovation research, I examine the chronological adoption of living will laws and state appellate court decisions in all adopting states.

I go further, however, and investigate the reinvention of policy during the period that new laws and decisions were being put into place. I examine the content of laws adopted by the late innovating states and amendments to early laws made by the first adopters. I also expand research on judicial innovation by looking at changes in the content of judicial policy over time, the disproportionate impact that certain courts have had on shaping the content of judicial right to die rulings, and the effects of judicial decisions on legislative innovation.

3 The Rise of the Right to Die Issue

The recent drive to enact living will laws and other right to die measures has a long social and political history in the western world, and the issue has been on the American agenda for decades. However, the right to die was not produced by a mass social movement. A few specialized groups have long promoted public awareness and interest in the right to die, but the issue did not substantially enter the mass social agenda until the early 1970s, preceding the Quinlan case in New Jersey and the first law in California.

Looking to the past to earlier writings and events, it is tempting to construct a neat and logical ordering of early ideas and actions that led inevitably to Quinlan and beyond. Some commentators have assumed, for example, that New Jersey's Quinlan decision caused California to enact a living will law. But this is an oversimplification, and the history of the right to die is much richer and more complex. It is not a single straight line but several separate paths, some more heavily trod than others, but all having rough boundaries, detours, and unanticipated intersections. Instead of a straight march to the present, separate streams of activity collided over the right to die decades ago and they continue to influence lawmaking today.

This chapter has three major sections that focus on separate aspects of the rise of the right to die issue. The first examines the early social agenda and attempts to enact legislation. It also focuses on the principal supporters and opponents of the right to die. The second section examines the emergence of the right to die in the professional and mass media over four decades and the role of each in elevating the issue on the social agenda. The final section follows changes in public opinion since polling has been done on the right to die.

The Early Agenda

Many early observers trace the origins of modern discussion and political conflict over the right to die to Great Britain in the 1870s, when various intellectuals proposed voluntary active euthanasia for the hopelessly ill (Kamisar 1958). In 1935, following several decades of debate and writing on euthanasia, a group of British doctors, Protestant theologians, teachers and prominent intellectuals, and writers formed the Voluntary Euthanasia Legislation Society in order to propose a bill to Parliament permitting voluntary euthanasia for seriously ill patients over age twenty-one. The bill had elaborate procedures and safeguards to ensure that a patient was suffering great pain from terminal illness and was requesting death, and to guard against killing the patient without clear consent (Kamisar 1958). However, the bill was easily defeated and voluntary active euthanasia did not reach Britain's governmental agenda again until well after World War II. Similar bills also were defeated in 1950 and 1952.

In 1938 a similar group of Americans formed the American Euthanasia Society in New York, modeled on the British organization. Most of its board of directors and advisers were composed of university professors in the social, behavioral, and natural sciences, but several of the advisers were English members of the British Euthanasia Society. The American group put a voluntary active euthanasia bill before the New York legislature even though the Society anticipated opposition from the Catholic church and many lawyers and doctors. However, opposition was so strong that it did not reach the governmental agenda: no legislator would agree to sponsor it (*New York Times,* 1 January 1938:21; 27 January 1939:21; 14 February 1939:2; Society for the Right to Die 1988).

Until the end of World War II proponents of legislation did not distinguish between active euthanasia and the withdrawal of treatment (passive euthanasia), probably because medicine had not yet gained enough sophistication to do much to keep the hopelessly ill alive or alleviate pain effectively for extended periods. Patients also were as likely to die at home as in hospitals, which limited opportunities for extraordinary treatment. Therefore, early writing about euthanasia generally distinguished between voluntary active euthanasia for ending the suffering of patients in great pain from cancer and other terminal diseases, and active involuntary euthanasia for the severely retarded, physically deformed, or the hopelessly ill young who were suffering, but could not express their wishes concerning living and dying.

Outside Strategy

The early advocates of euthanasia legislation developed very limited outside strategies. Intellectual and medical elites with few ties to political parties or individual legislators merely proposed bills and expected legislatures to embrace what the supporters believed were rational and obviously needed measures. The Society did little to soften up other elites or the public by disseminating information through the mass media, which perhaps may have made it somewhat politically safer for other groups and legislators to endorse a proposal and work for enactment. An indicator of the Society's lack of visibility is that only three very brief articles about the Society and its political activities appeared in the *New York Times* before 1940, and only five others appeared about the organization or its successors (Concern for Dying and the Society for the Right to Die) between 1941 and 1975.

Hoping for the enactment of euthanasia laws probably was futile in any case since public support was modest. In the late 1930s various polls indicated that between 37 and 46 percent of Americans favored voluntary active euthanasia for the hopelessly ill. The lowest support was produced by questions that included the term "mercy death," whereas questions with less emotionally charged language produced higher levels of approval (Humphry and Wickett 1986:18). Therefore, while a small specialized elite concentrated in New York City supported voluntary active euthanasia, many other elites and most of the public opposed it, and legislators avoided it as an obvious political liability.

Modest support for euthanasia was not due to a lack of public interest, however. Individual cases of extreme personal suffering and mercy killing cases occasionally appeared in the news, and the issue evoked empathy and identification with both sufferers and their killers. The earliest polls on euthanasia in the 1930s revealed that only about 15 percent of the public did not have an opinion on euthanasia. That number dwindled to 7 percent in 1950 and it has decreased to 4 or 5 percent in the most recent polls. In contrast, polls on many complex issues, such as foreign policy and defense strategy or policies in their early stages of exposure or development, often produce large numbers of "don't know" responses, sometimes as high as 60 percent. Unless an issue has been covered heavily in the news, is very controversial, or has some personal relevance, few people have a basis for forming and holding an opinion (Erikson, Luttbeg, and Tedin 1980:19–25). Therefore, for advocates of the right to die, the political problem has not been one of arousing an uninterested public, but in shifting public opinion from opposition to support and formulating policies that the public would accept.[1]

Controversial proposals. Although the bills offered by the early euthanasia societies were limited to voluntary active euthanasia for the terminally ill, some supporters believed that euthanasia for the severely retarded and the physically deformed was even more important. In 1939 Dr. Foster Kennedy, president of the American Euthanasia Society, argued that euthanasia would shorten the suffering of "born defectives" and would relieve families of severe financial and psychological stress. Therefore, in his view, voluntary active euthanasia for the seriously ill would be only the first of new legislation that would recognize the value of reducing human suffering (*New York Times,* 14 February 1939:2).

But support for euthanasia for the severely retarded and disabled has been much less acceptable than for the terminally ill. A 1941 poll conducted by the Euthanasia Society of all doctors in New York state indicated that few physicians supported involuntary euthanasia for "congenital monstrosities, idiots and imbeciles," but a large majority did support euthanasia for terminally ill adults who requested it (Kamisar 1958; Humphry and Wickett 1986).

Therefore, the Society decided to limit its future proposals to active euthanasia requested by seriously ill adults. It offered another bill to the New York legislature in 1941 but again it failed to find a sponsor. In 1946 the organization expanded its outside strategy by securing support from over 50 prominent Protestant ministers and more than 1,500 physicians, most of whom signed a petition supporting voluntary euthanasia legislation. But mass and other elite support still did not exist and again no legislator would offer the bill. The organization suffered a similar defeat in 1950 after proposing a bill in New Hampshire following the widely publicized trial of Dr. Hermann Sander, who was acquitted of killing a terminally ill cancer patient with an injection of air, despite admitting his guilt and having recorded the event in the patient's medical record (*New York Times*, 3 January 1950, Sec.7:1). The Euthanasia Society dropped its efforts to win support for voluntary active euthanasia in 1952.

Following World War II national and state health officials, state medical societies, and Catholic clergy denounced euthanasia legislation. Public support also was lower than before. In 1947 a Gallup poll on euthanasia asked: "When a person has a disease that cannot be cured, do you think doctors should be allowed by law to end the patient's life by some painless means if the patient and his family request it?" Even though the emotionally charged *mercy death* term was absent in this question, only 37 percent answered "yes." This is nearly 10 percent less than public support evidenced through similar polls in the 1930s (Humphry and Wickett 1986:36). Either the Euthanasia Society and its few supporters had not substantially influenced public opinion or, more likely, the Holocaust and World War II stifled possible shifts in favorable opinion.

Expanded Agenda and New Conflict

Despite the horrors of World War II, interest in medical treatment issues and proposals for voluntary euthanasia did not fade. The prospect of a slow and painful death caused by terminal illness or serious injury intensified during the 1950s due to the growing ability of medicine to treat illness and prolong life. This new dimension to the process of dying also had new implications for the proper role of physicians. Political conflict and discussion concerning the withdrawal of treatment did not replace voluntary active euthanasia as a political issue. Instead, it added new items to the social agenda, but the new conflicts followed familiar political lines.

Proponents of the early active euthanasia bills believed that the Catholic church would be the main opponent but that "liberals" would support the policy (Kamisar 1958:411). However, Nazi *involuntary* euthanasia and extermination programs discredited political organizations and proposals that employed the term euthanasia in any form. The scourge of Naziism on the euthanasia debate has lasted a very long time. In the 1970s and 1980s the Catholic church and other opponents frequently linked living will bills to early proposals for involuntary euthanasia for the severely retarded and disabled in order to discredit them. Any legislation has been considered a wedge or the first step on the slippery slope to legalized mercy killing, and the most intense right to life opponents graphically use the Nazi link. In agenda setting nearly all new concerns and ideas grow and evolve from the old, creating links between contemporary issues and past beliefs and events, but for the right to die the past has been very heavy baggage.

Catholic influence.   More than any other group, Catholic theologians have grappled for centuries with circumstances under which the general obligation to maintain life may be breached without intentional killing. Euthanasia and the means of preserving life were explicitly pondered in the mid–1500s (Kelly 1979). Ironically, Catholic moral theologians at one time were more willing than other religious thinkers to permit individuals to forego certain extreme life-saving treatments. The Catholic church has required the acceptance of medical treatment that may do a patient some good, but it also has recognized that some life-prolonging measures may place too great a burden on the individual. Before modern medicine and anesthesia, Catholics believed that extreme measures—such as amputation to save a life, which came with extreme pain, likely infection, and disfigurement—may be more than a person should have to bear. Distinctions among medical treatments have changed with technology but the general issue has long been a similar one.

The main contribution of twentieth century Catholic writers to contemporary thinking about the right to die is their updating of the difference between ordinary and extraordinary medical treatment and concern over the double effects of treatment, particularly the use of pain-relieving drugs that have valuable benefits but also may shorten life (Kelly 1979:244–74; Weir 1989:218). Although Catholic writing in the 1950s suggests that passive euthanasia sometimes is acceptable (because it implies the withdrawal or withholding of extraordinary medical treatment), the Catholic church has not provided specific guidelines for patients or doctors, and it has opposed legislation because it fears that law inevitably will lead to government-sanctioned active euthanasia.

Challenges to orthodoxy.   Catholic dominance in medical ethics was explicitly challenged in 1954 by Joseph Fletcher, a Protestant minister and professor of theology and medical ethics and a director of the Euthanasia Society. His book, *Morals and Medicine: The Moral Problems of the Patient's Right to Know the Truth; Contraception; Artificial Insemination; Sterilization; Euthanasia,* concerned the ethics of medical care rather than the usual discussions of personal ethics for doctors, which typically had dealt with bedside manners and doctors' personal appearance and habits. Fletcher and others state that it was the first modern work on medical ethics other than the extensive writings of Catholic theologians (Fletcher 1954; Weir 1986:220). Although extensive medical writing on the right to die did not begin until the late 1960s, discussed below, Fletcher's book and articles in medical journals were among the earliest writings on euthanasia, and they contributed to enlarging the scope of professional and popular writing on the right to die.

Critical of Catholic writings, Fletcher argued that ethical treatment has to be derived from the perspective of "personalism" or the unique characteristics of each individual and that individualism and freedom obtained by human control over circumstances "are the heart and muscle of morality" (Fletcher 1954:xii and 26). Fletcher's view is similar to the Renaissance emphasis on individualism (as opposed to community and organizational control) found in the writings of philosophers, poets, and statesmen during the sixteenth and seventeenth centuries. In that era Sir Thomas More, John Donne, Francis Bacon, and others argued that physicians owed dying patients an easy way out of their slow death, or that terminally ill and suffering patients be helped to commit suicide (Humphry and Wickett 1986).

To Fletcher, constantly expanding medical technology requires that people take control of life rather than submitting to traditional and ancient ways dictated by religious beliefs and a fatalistic view of the power of biology over behavior. On euthanasia, Fletcher (1954) objected to the traditional view

> that the disposition of life is too sacred to be entrusted to human control. . . . In the personalistic view of man and morals . . . person-ality is supreme over mere life. To prolong life uselessly, while the personal qualities of freedom, knowledge, self-possession and con-trol, and responsibility are sacrificed is to attack the moral status of a person. . . . It is a false humility or a subtle determinism which asks us to 'leave things in God's hands.' (174, 191, 215)

Contrasting the voluminous Catholic literature written for Cath-olic doctors, nurses, and hospitals with the lack of other guides for medical ethics, Fletcher observed: "Were medical workers and non-Catholics to expend the care and concern we have seen in the studies of the Roman theologians, how much might be gained for man's moral stature and for the claims of mercy and well-being!" But reli-gious moralists must discard useless "dogmas which contribute to the stultifying influences of customary morality" (Fletcher 1954: 224–25).

It is not surprising that Fletcher's harsh criticism of Catholic teaching on medical treatment and euthanasia convinced various Catholic theologians and ethicists that the book should be banned from libraries and withheld from Catholic readers (Weir 1989). Fletcher continued to endorse voluntary active euthanasia in 1973 when the distinction between active and passive euthanasia was be-coming more common. In his view withdrawing and withholding treatment already was widespread but was not sufficient to deal with human suffering (Fletcher 1973).

In 1957 Catholic writing concerning the distinction between ordinary and extraordinary treatment and the dilemma of double effects became official policy of the Church through an allocution of Pope Pius XII. As before, the Pope stated that Catholics needed to accept ordinary, but not extraordinary treatment, and that great care needed to be taken regarding the use of painkilling drugs lest the patient lose consciousness and be unable to perform necessary duties and/or prepare for death. The Pope acknowledged modern medical technology when he concluded that patients need not be resuscitated or maintained on ventilators when unequivocal determinations of death have been made.

Church policy has been updated several times including a statement by Pope Paul II in 1980, in which he stated that patients may refuse even ordinary medical treatment when death is imminent and treatment is futile. He also seemed more accepting of painkillers even if patients were reduced to semiconsciousness. But as before, the papal statement is vague and general and it has not settled the issue for Catholics or others. In the United States the National Conference of Catholic Bishops, Committee on Pro-Life Activities, has issued several sets of guidelines to state Catholic conferences on right to die issues and state legislation, but state Catholic organizations have adopted conflicting positions toward government policy.

Growing agenda. Following the 1957 Vatican declaration on euthanasia, a somewhat larger trickle of journal articles was published concerning death and the right to die. However, more important than the number of articles, the public discussion expanded beyond Catholic ethics and the dissents of a few Protestant theologians and others who sought euthanasia legislation (Weir 1989). It is unlikely that the Vatican announcement caused others to take up the issue. Rather the Pope's directive was part of a growing reinforcing cycle of concern and attention about the right to die. For instance the issue already was beginning to reach the medical agenda since the Pope issued his declaration at a conference of anesthesiologists as an answer to a set of questions submitted by a prominent Catholic physician. In turn the visibility of the Vatican's official statement generated more interest and awareness of the issues of terminal care, and the professional audience concerned with medical ethics and the process of dying began to grow. A few journal articles, prominently

Yale Kamisar's, "Some Non-Religious Views Against Proposed 'Mercy-Killing' Legislation" (1958), and later new books, including Elisabeth Kubler-Ross's best seller, *On Death and Dying* (1969) and Paul Ramsey's *The Patient as Person* (1970), enlarged professional and popular awareness of the issues.

Besides new publications, increased social and political activity on behalf of the right to die and related medical concerns also underscored the growing salience of the issue. In 1967 a Chicago attorney proposed a model living will to the Euthanasia Society, and in the following year a Florida physician-legislator put the nation's first right to die proposal before a state legislature (chapter 4). The founding of the Hastings Center in 1969 and the Kennedy Institute of Ethics at Georgetown University in 1970 also reflected increased interest in research and writing about bioethics and policy (Weir 1989). By the early 1970s the right to die had begun to emerge as an important social and political issue.

Narrow or General Interest

Early writings of Catholics and others and the political activities of the Euthanasia Society may give the impression that the right to die was a widespread, constant, and burning social issue. Certainly the advocates and opponents of euthanasia felt intensely about it and the supporters sincerely hoped for legislation, but membership in the early euthanasia societies was small and concentrated in New York City and their meetings were not held in public halls but in the homes of activists. Public support also was modest and politicians avoided the issue or hotly condemned proposals for legislation. Therefore, broader assessments of the dimensions of the right to die agenda are important.

Two ways to examine the place of an issue on the social agenda are through the publication of articles in newspapers, popular magazines, and professional periodic literature, and through changes in public opinion. Analysis of these sources over time indicates when and how extensively the right to die has spread to the professional and mass agendas. It also is possible to relate publications and polls to the major social and political events concerning the right to die. Together, this analysis provides a more complete picture of the early development and growth of public attention to the issue than can be obtained through a review of the handful of early elite publications and announcements.

Professional and Mass Media

The mass and professional literature reflect the social agenda in different ways. As discussed in chapter 2, professional elites generally lead in defining new social issues. Various professionals—doctors, lawyers, university researchers, and others—frequently are the first to perceive and transform isolated incidents and events into social problems, and to do research and present findings at professional conferences and publish in professional journals. Some of their work attracts additional professional awareness and gradually contributes to the professional agenda. Other professionals pick up leading ideas and theories and do additional research and writing and in time—sometimes almost immediately as in the case of new medical discoveries published in the leading medical journals—journalists summarize and popularize the research in the mass media. The visible experts receive telephone calls from reporters, and authors appear regularly on television and radio news and talk shows.

Publications in professional and mass literature provide several important indicators of agenda setting and policy adoption. First, tabulating articles indicates when an issue began to emerge as a prominent social issue. Government did not begin to adopt right to die policy until 1976, but since the issue has received government attention only through outside strategies—in which substantial external pressure is necessary before government creates policy—it is likely that the volume of literature on the right to die began to increase well before 1976.

Identifying the timing of specific sets of publications also reveals the relative importance of an issue to various groups and their role in setting the social and governmental agendas. Since the right to die is a medical treatment issue that affects people individually rather than large numbers at the same time, it also is likely that the right to die reached medical agendas earlier than other agendas and that medical events and literature provided the subject material for the mass agenda.

Finally, analyzing the volume and trends in publication reveals how various publics react to government enactments and reinforce agenda setting and policy adoption through additional publications. Combined with the previous discussion of the early emergence of the right to die, we can obtain a more complete understanding of when and how the issue emerged as an important social and political concern and how it relates to the adoption of policy.

I have examined the frequency of publications on the right to die in professional and mass media from 1950 to 1990. This is an ample period since previous research indicates that the right to die was not widely discussed until the late 1950s. In addition, I will discuss the subjects and content of the articles published throughout this period. To tap the relevant professional literature I have included publications in medical, legal, religion, and social science and humanities journals through the *Index Medicus,* the *Index to Legal Periodicals,* the *Catholic Index,* the *Religion Index,* and the *International Index* and its successors, the *Social Science Index* and the *Humanities Index.* For the mass literature I have counted articles in the *New York Times* and the *Reader's Guide to Periodic Literature.*[2] The results of this examination are presented in three graphs (figures 3.1, 3.2, and 3.3): one for the medical, legal, and social science and humanities professions; a second for Catholic and other religious publications; and a third for news articles appearing in the *New York Times* and the popular mass-circulation journals and magazines.

Emerging Interest

Overall the three graphs are similar. Although the right to die had been important to various religious and intellectual elites for many years, the issue did not have a substantial impact on professional and mass agendas until the late 1960s and early 1970s. A few more articles appeared in the early 1960s than in the previous decade, which suggests that the Vatican statement in 1957 may have stimulated some increased discussion, but significant increases in publication did not occur until later.

Major peaks in all literature occurred in 1975–1976 when the

FIGURE 3.1 *Articles in*
Professional Literature, 1950–1990

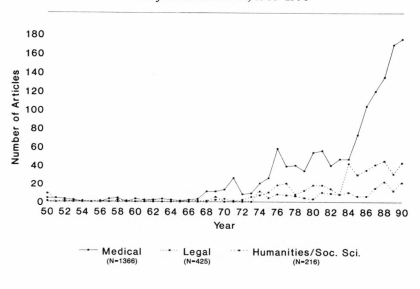

Medical
(N=1366)　　　Legal
(N=425)　　　Humanities/Soc. Sci.
(N=216)

FIGURE 3.2 *Articles in*
Religious Literature, 1950–1990

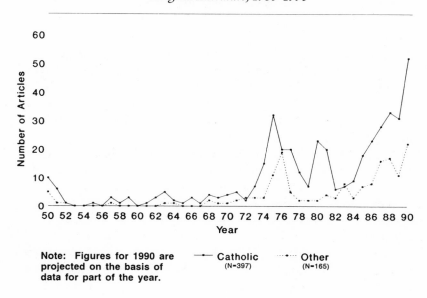

Note: Figures for 1990 are
projected on the basis of
data for part of the year.　　　Catholic
(N=397)　　　Other
(N=165)

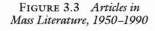

FIGURE 3.3 *Articles in
Mass Literature, 1950–1990*

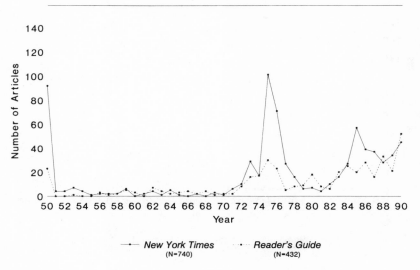

Karen Quinlan case began and the New Jersey Supreme Court made the nation's first official policy regarding the right to die. Most literature declined somewhat after this case and it did not begin to emerge again until the 1980s. Although the Quinlan case has received more media attention than any other event, and probably made more Americans aware of the right to die than in any other period, the graphs demonstrate that the issue did not suddenly appear with this case. Before the Quinlan case other significant social and political events had begun to accumulate that aroused growing media attention.

Table 3.1 lists the major events in the rise of the right to die issue. In 1967, before publication of any of the literature began to increase beyond previous consistently low levels, the Euthanasia Society received a new proposal calling for living wills and a doctor-legislator in Florida proposed the first right to die legislation. The following year, when the volume of medical literature first began to increase, Harvard Medical School and others proposed that death be defined as brain death—reflecting the ability of medicine to artificially extend circulation and respiration. No longer would the

TABLE 3.1 *Major Events in the Right to Die*

1957	Pope Pius XII issues Catholic doctrine distinguishing ordinary and extraordinary means for sustaining life.
1967	Living will proposed to Euthanasia Society.
	Euthanasia Educational Council is formed.
	Dr. Walter F. Sackett proposes "right to die with dignity" amendment to Florida Constitution.
1969	Hastings Center established to consider bioethics issues.
1968	Harvard Medical School issues proposed definition of death based on symptoms of irreversible coma. Other definitions are offered by three organizations. Kansas enacts first definition of death law to include absence of spontaneous brain function.
1970	Dr. Walter F. Sackett proposes first living will bill to Florida legislature.
1971	Kennedy Institute on Ethics at Georgetown University established to consider bioethics issues.
1972	United States Senate, Special Committee on Aging, holds public hearings on right to die.
1973	American Medical Association opposes formal living will but endorses discussion between doctors, patients, and families concerning care for the terminally ill and the withdrawal of extraordinary measures when death is imminent.
	American Hospital Association proposes 12-point Patient Bill of Rights, including the right to reject treatment.
1974	Euthanasia Society becomes the Society for the Right to Die.
1975	Society for the Right to Die proposes model living will bill.
	American Bar Association endorses definition of death to include cessation of brain function.
	Quinlan case begins in New Jersey trial court.
1976	Quinlan appeal decided by New Jersey Supreme Court.
	California enacts nation's first living will law.
	Harvard Medical School guidelines for treating hopelessly ill patients are published in *New England Journal of Medicine*.
	American Medical Association opposes judicial or legislative policy in the right to die and declines to issue its own guidelines.
1977	Forty-two states consider living will bills; seven states enact laws.
	National Conference of Catholic Bishops distributes "Resource Paper on Death and Dying" to state Catholic conferences, and opposes living will laws and definition of death laws as unnecessary.
	Massachusetts Supreme Judicial Court decides Saikewicz case, the nation's second landmark case in the right to die.
1978	Yale Law School drafts model living will bill.
	Conference Commission on Uniform State Laws adopts uniform brain death statute defining death as cessation of all functions of the brain, including the brain stem.
1980	Pope John Paul II issues Declaration on Euthanasia opposing mercy killing but permits greater use of painkillers to ease pain and the right to refuse extraordinary means for sustaining life.
	Delaware and Florida Supreme Courts issue first judicial calls for comprehensive right to die legislation.
1981	Prominent Catholic academics propose reconsideration of Church opposition to living will laws as a way of limiting expansive judicial policy.
1982	American Medical Association endorses withdrawal of treatment in hopeless terminal cases including cases of permanent coma.
1983	National Conference of Catholic Bishops restates its opposition to definition

TABLE 3.1   *Contd.*

	of death statutes but encourages Catholic involvement in legislative debate to ensure its influence in legislation.
	President's Commission for the Study of Ethical Problems in Medicine and Biomedical and Behavioral Research issues report "Deciding to Forego Life-sustaining Treatment," and endorses brain death statutes, living wills, and other advance directives and the withdrawal of treatment in hopeless cases.
	Three state supreme courts decide right to die cases.
1984	National Conference of Catholic Bishops does not endorse legislation but issues legislative guidelines to be used in influencing living will bills that are likely to pass.
	National Conference Commission on Uniform State Laws drafts uniform living will law.
	Seven states enact living will laws; six appellate courts decide right to die cases.
1985	New Jersey Supreme Court is the first court to state there is no distinction between ordinary and extraordinary medical treatment and permits the withdrawal of all forms of medical treatment, including food and hydration, from an incompetent elderly nursing home patient expected to die within one year.
	Thirteen states enact living will laws.
1986	American Medical Association endorses withdrawal of all medical treatment, including the artificial administration of food and hydration, from dying patients and those in a permanent coma.
1987	Six appellate courts decide right to die cases, all involving food and hydration.
1988	Missouri Supreme Court denies the right to withdraw treatment from Nancy Cruzan, who was then in a permanent vegetative state.
1990	U.S. Supreme Court grants appeal from Missouri decision (its first right to die case), upholds state power to require clear evidence of patients' wishes, and encourages use of advance directives.

natural stopping of breathing and heartbeat be satisfactory definitions of death.

While there are general parallels among the literature, the emergence of the issue on each agenda varies, and professional and mass
literature have performed differently in bringing the right to die
before the general public and political decision makers. In the 1950s
and 1960s much of the literature concerned mercy killing cases and
the ethics of voluntary active euthanasia, but later the agendas enlarged substantially as various professionals and the public began to
differ over the ethics of prolonging life through improvements in
medical technology.

Professional agendas.   Significantly, publications in medical literature increased first, several years before similar increases in Catholic

and other religious literature, legal literature, and the mass media. The social sciences and humanities literature began to increase about the same time that publications in other professional literature began to rise, but the right to die has not been very important to these groups.[3]

In 1967 and 1968 the right to die appeared more frequently as a medical topic with explicit recognition of the power of medical science to prolong the lives of dying patients and the ethics of doing so. The titles of new articles revealed the ethical concerns: "Euthanasia: A Growing Concern for Physicians," a symposium on "The Right to Live and the Right to Die," "When Should Patients be Allowed to Die" (by Joseph Fletcher and others), "Legal Aspects of the Decision not to Prolong Life," and "When do we Let the Patient Die?"

Many articles titled "The Right to Die" and "Death with Dignity" appeared in 1970 and beyond although the headings "right to die" and "death with dignity" did not appear in any periodical index until 1978, well after the "right to die" had become a frequently used phrase. Almost all articles were found under the heading "euthanasia."

A scattering of legal articles on euthanasia and living wills appeared prior to 1970—with a few innovators calling for legislation—but the legal agenda has largely reacted to events and social change. Increases in legal literature did not substantially occur until 1973 and 1974, following additional public proposals for living will laws. A comparison with the trend lines for the other literature also indicates that the right to die did not become a significant part of the legal agenda until several years after the medical and Catholic literature began to increase and the mass media enlarged its coverage.

Just as the medical literature approached the right to die from its distinctive professional point of view—concentrating on recent medical technology and the ethics of withdrawal—the legal literature concerned issues that fit well within the traditions of legal analysis—legal liability for active euthanasia and the withdrawal of treatment, the legal rights of patients to refuse treatment, and the prospects for legislation. By 1977 legal literature was analyzing court cases and the application of the right to privacy and California's new law, and several writers proposed new general rules for withdrawing treatment and ways to improve legislation.

As discussed earlier, Catholic literature always has outnumbered other religious groups' publications on the right to die. The graphs of religious literature show that while the early volume of Catholic literature was low it exceeded the nearly nonexistent literature from all other religions. Generally, Catholic writers approached the right to die from traditional moral and ethical perspectives and evaluated the right to die as conflicting with the need to preserve life. However, as legislation was proposed and adopted, Catholic literature expanded to include analysis of court decisions and legislation and their relation to Catholic moral positions.

Mass agenda. The mass agenda is particularly important in politics because many legislators and other officials do not consider an issue important until it appears frequently in the newspapers, news magazines, and other popular periodicals (Cobb and Elder 1972:91–92; Kingdon 1973:206–207; Nelson 1984:51–58; Burstein 1985:83). This is doubly important for controversial issues such as the right to die, which require outside strategies in order to get policy enacted. The various professional literature is not likely to be visible to most officials. Few are likely to be interested in the medical or religious journals, and even lawyer/legislators or their staff do not routinely scan many law reviews to see what is new. They are likely to consult the professional literature only when they already have become aware of a problem through the mass media and want to learn more about it. Therefore, moving an issue from the professional onto the mass agenda is an important step in attracting official attention.

This does not mean that the mass literature sets the government agenda. As discussed in the following chapter, individual legislators brought the right to die to state legislatures before there was extensive media coverage, but the mass literature reflects the issues that are on the public agenda. Equally important, articles in the popular press stimulate constituency letter writing, which makes legislators more aware of new public concerns. The growing volume and regularity of literature also encourages a wider group of legislators, who previously were only vaguely aware or casually interested in the issue, to support new policy.

The mass agenda reflects the impact of all professional agendas as well as news events on popular writing. Over time the mass literature has covered a wide range of right to die issues, and it reflects changes in problems and perspectives in different periods. In the 1950s the mass agenda was concerned primarily with mercy killing cases, but later a broader range of interrelated right to die issues began to appear. Evidence exists that other advances in medicine began to sensitize Americans to changes in medical science, the practice of medicine, and their potential impact on individuals.

From 1950 to 1972 the *New York Times* concentrated almost entirely on individual mercy killing cases as news events with only a scattering of articles on other topics, such as a public euthanasia debate held in Great Britain on BBC TV in 1959. Between 1972 and 1974, however, many death-related issues began to converge and the media substantially enlarged its coverage to include much more than mercy death.

Articles on many new subjects appeared in the news, including the following: medical and hospital association debates and resolutions on patients' rights; Florida legislative consideration of new right to die legislation; thanatology—the new study of the dying process, and marantology—aiding death with dignity; changes in hospital methods for caring for dying patients, new definitions of death, death and heart transplants; polls of medical doctors; university and medical school seminars on death and dying; cryonics— freezing the dead to await future medical miracle cures; and book reviews on these and related subjects. In 1974 NBC broadcast a television special on the right to die that covered the ability of new medical technology to sustain life, mercy killing, and living wills. By the time of the Karen Quinlan case, which accounted for the dramatic increase in news coverage in 1975 and 1976, the *New York Times* already had begun to cover a wide range of right to die issues.

In contrast to the emphasis on separate news events in the *New York Times,* the *Reader's Guide* includes a greater variety of articles on the right to die. Mercy killing cases accounted for a substantial portion of all articles in the 1950s, including fourteen of twenty-three on the 1950 Sanders case, but much of the other literature in the popular journals was based on earlier medical publications or was written by doctors, which further indicates professional medical literature led the mass literature in setting the general public agenda.

In 1956, for example, *Time* summarized an article published previously by a medical doctor in a regional medical journal on the conflicts between the evils of active euthanasia and the ethical problems in sustaining life in hopeless cases. The following year the *Atlantic Monthly* published an article by a widow who described in detail the futile life-sustaining treatments given her terminally ill husband over several days before his death, including repeated surgery, inadequate pain relief, intravenous feeding, oxygen, and multiple medications. Although the technology discussed in this article now appears routine or even dated, her complaint about the process of providing extensive but futile treatment is very similar to those heard today.

The intensity and concern surrounding the withdrawal of futile treatment could only increase with further advances in medical technology and related changes in the practice of medicine. The curve in the *Reader's Guide* literature reveals a slight rise in publications in 1959 and, like the *New York Times,* most of these articles covered the British euthanasia debate and mercy killing cases in Great Britain. However, in 1960 *Harper's Magazine* published a broad symposium titled "The Crisis in American Medicine," which explicitly linked several medical issues that affect patient control of their treatment including the politics of medicine; the decline of the art of medicine and advances in medical technology; increased specialization and depersonalization in medicine; the cost of medical research; predictions concerning the organization and administration of hospitals of the future; and the right to die. The right to die section was written by Joseph Fletcher, famous for his revolutionary book on medical ethics published a few years before.

Another short-term rise in the popular literature came in 1962 and 1963, and many of these articles reported on proposals for active euthanasia linked to severe birth defects caused by the then new drug thalidomide prescribed for pregnant women as a sleep aid mainly in Europe, but also in the United States, Australia, and various other countries. Also around 1960 a few articles appeared that concerned the psychology and metaphysics of the dying process. Although Elisabeth Kubler-Ross's influential book *On Death and Dying* was not published until 1969, *Time* reported on other early religious and psychological inquiries into the meaning of death and the process of dying.

The convergence and mutual reinforcement of developments in medical technology and public concern with the right to die is illustrated by the thalidomide tragedy. That event contributed directly to the right to die literature in a very limited way since only a few articles published in 1962 and 1963 concerned active euthanasia for severely deformed babies. But the thalidomide tragedy itself was very heavily covered in the news and contributed to sensitizing medical professionals, the public, and government officials to the possible harmful effects of certain new medical discoveries.

In 1962, when the thalidomide tragedy was discovered and first made public, forty-eight articles appeared in the *Reader's Guide* and ninety-nine were published in the *New York Times*. The number of articles published on thalidomide that year is equal to or exceeds those published in 1975 on the Karen Quinlan case, which marks the largest number of mass media publications on the right to die. Most of the thalidomide articles reported on the distribution of the drug, the number of people affected, and its physical effects, although mercy killing charges against several Belgians also received some coverage. Many other articles reported on the need for greater government regulation of the distribution of new drugs, including calls by President John F. Kennedy for new federal laws.

Once thalidomide was withdrawn from the market and suits for compensation had begun, the issue began to fade. The number of articles on thalidomide decreased sharply to 20 in the *Reader's Guide* and 10 in the *New York Times* in 1963 and 1964 and the issue disappeared soon thereafter. But while the thalidomide event was not directly a right to die concern, it accentuated the cumulative impact of modern medical technology on the public. The mercy killing aspects of the tragedy also are related to early concerns about active involuntary euthanasia. The extensive news coverage given thalidomide and other individual medical misfortunes contributes to viewing modern medicine both as a benefit as well as a problem on the public agenda, and it reinforces the growing public interest in the broader issue of the right to die.

After Quinlan

Although the right to die was increasingly visible by the early 1970s, the Karen Quinlan case made the issue very prominent and the right to die became a permanent agenda item ever after. Events and writing took off in the states and among national organizations (table 3.1). California's adoption of the first living will law in 1976, seven additional adoptions in 1977, and the Massachusetts Saikewicz case also kept the issue before the professional and mass publics, although coverage was down from the high levels of 1975–1976. Coverage in the medical literature did not decline as much, however, and it quickly rose again. With few exceptions, most other literature remained above the pre–1970 lows when there were many years with no publications on the right to die. Following 1976 at least several articles were published each year in each set of literature.

Publications rose sharply again in the mid–1980s, a period characterized by much heavier and concentrated political activity. Leading the way for change in state policy the American Medical Association in 1982 for the first time endorsed the withdrawal of treatment in hopeless, terminal illnesses and cases of permanent vegetative state. The following year the President's Commission endorsed living wills and other advance medical directives and the Catholic church signaled future changes in its own policies. Significantly, the President's commission was not originally charged to consider the right to die but added the issue to its agenda because members believed it needed to be analyzed along with others. In 1984 the National Conference Commission on Uniform State Laws proposed a model living will law (an NCCUSL study committee had existed since 1980).

In 1983 three additional appellate courts decided right to die cases, followed in 1984 by six more court decisions and living will laws in seven states. In 1985 thirteen more states enacted living will laws—the largest number in a single year. The New Jersey Supreme

Court also made another ground-breaking decision, this time ruling that there is no distinction between ordinary and extraordinary medical treatment, and that the artificial administration of food and hydration may be withdrawn (*In Re Conroy*). The Cruzan case is the most recent event that has contributed to maintaining attention to the right to die, and media coverage shows increased attention over 1989 levels. However, coverage of this case does not stand out when compared with the attention paid to the right to die over many previous years.

Medical agenda dominates. While there are similarities in the shape of publication curves and links to political events, the attention given the right to die after 1976 has not been the same for all agendas. Similar to its early rise in the 1960s, the medical literature reached much greater heights by 1980 and it soared after 1984, indicating a high and permanent concern in medicine with terminal care treatment issues. The mass literature began to ascend again in 1983. In contrast to the medical and popular literature, the religious and legal literature lagged somewhat and appeared to react to events and new policies. Nevertheless, the right to die was firmly on these agendas as well by 1984 and 1985. The number of publications in Catholic periodicals in the late 1980s was nearly equal to the number of publications in 1975 and articles in legal periodicals were much greater than before.

As before, the medical literature provided many news events and commentary to the mass literature. Summary reports of articles appearing in the major medical journals, discussions of health and science issues, mercy killing cases, personal medical tragedies, interviews with doctors and hospital administrators, along with political developments in courts and state legislatures all were discussed in the popular literature in the 1980s. The number of articles in the *Reader's Guide* in the late 1980s was almost equal to the number of articles published at the time of the Quinlan case. Overall, from 1972 forward the right to die had became a permanent item on the social agenda preceded by a few years by heightened attention in the medical literature.

Medical Treatment and Individual Rights

The professional and mass literature strongly indicate that the rise of the right to die issue—particularly recent emphasis on the withdrawal of treatment—is largely due to changes in medical technology and the practice of medicine. However, the increase in publications and wider use of the term *right to die* in the late 1960s and early 1970s also may be partly due to the revolution in civil rights and liberties, which sensitized Americans to growing claims of personal freedom and autonomy.

From 1964 to 1968 Congress passed civil rights laws that banned race and sex discrimination in employment, public accommodations, housing, voting, and programs receiving federal assistance. The Supreme Court substantially expanded the rights of criminal defendants throughout the 1960s and the right to privacy, which later became the basis for New Jersey's Quinlan decision and other right to die cases, was established by the U.S. Supreme Court in 1965 in a case involving a state ban on contraception devices and drugs and the dissemination of family planning information (*Griswold v. Connecticut*).

Although other state and federal court decisions between 1965 and 1976 refused to grant patients' rights to refuse medical treatment, usually on religious grounds (Humphry and Wickett 1986:230–37), and there is no explicit link between the right to die and other civil rights policies, the right to die began to emerge as a more visible political issue at about the same time the federal courts and Congress were heavily engaged in making new policy in constitutional rights and liberties. The growing emphasis on the withdrawal of treatment would not have become an issue if medical technology had not advanced to a point where life could be extended significantly through artificial means, but the move to individual rights may have prompted greater awareness and sensitivity to the right to be free from unwanted medical care.

Public Opinion

In addition to professional and mass literature as indicators of the social agenda, opinion surveys also reflect public concerns. However, polls do not set the social agenda since pollsters typically ask about issues only after they already are being widely discussed or following events that stimulate public reaction. Asking about issues that are not yet visible produces a large number of "don't knows," and responses to unfamiliar issues are dubious and unreliable indicators of public sentiment. Therefore, the social and governmental agendas already are likely to be well defined and established and the public is likely to have various points of view concerning the issues before polls appear. While polls do not set agendas, they reinforce public awareness and interest in an issue when survey results are published as part of the news. Public opinion also can influence policymakers when opinion leans heavily in one direction and is expressed and publicized repeatedly so that policymakers have little difficulty understanding the public's views.

I shall examine public opinion on the right to die in two ways. First, I have examined all available polls that included questions on the right to die.[4] Although there is a lag between agenda setting and polling, examining when and how often polls have been done and the number and type of questions included in them provides information about which issues become significant at particular times and how they relate to public events. Second, I will examine what people have thought about right to die issues and the effect of these opinions on policy.

Timing of Polls

Except for two Gallup polls in 1947 and 1950 on voluntary active euthanasia for the terminally ill, no other polls on the right to die were taken until 1973. Figure 3.4 shows the number of polls done annually on the right to die from 1973 to 1990. Polling was spotty in the 1970s with several years with one or no polls conducted. Polling became more frequent in the 1980s when surveys began to appear every year and, allowing for annual variations, they have become more frequent than in the previous decade. Although the number of polls sharply increased in the 1980s, a comparison of the frequency of polls, the publication of professional and mass literature, and events and policy-making indicates that polling lags well behind other forces that set the social and governmental agendas.

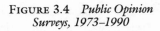

FIGURE 3.4 *Public Opinion Surveys, 1973–1990*

(N=53)

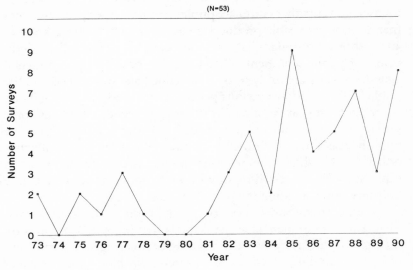

As discussed earlier, professional literature became more plentiful in the late 1960s and the mass literature began to cover the right to die more heavily in 1972. Mass literature, especially newspaper coverage, soared in 1975 as it focused on the Quinlan trial case. However, polling increased only slightly between 1975 and 1977, then stopped until 1981. Polling increased again in 1982 and 1983 following the trend of legislative adoptions and judicial decisions that began in 1981. It increased again only after the growing number of court cases and laws of 1984 and 1985. Additional court cases in 1986 and 1987 also stimulated additional polling in 1987 and 1988. Like publications in the various media, polling increased again in 1990, most likely in reaction to the Cruzan case.

Most polls on the right to die have included only general questions unrelated to particular events, possibly because individual state court decisions, legislation, or interest group activities are not likely to be especially visible to most of the public. An exception occurred in 1985, however, the year in which polling reached its peak. On January 17, 1985, the New Jersey Supreme Court made its important food and hydration decision. The Harris and Gallup Polls were in the field the following week with several questions concerning approval of this specific decision, and the poll results were released and published in March and April of that year.

Changing Issues

The focus of public opinion surveys has shifted slightly over the years, and reflects changes in the social agenda and events. The distribution of right to die survey questions is presented in table 3.2. The figures are the percentage of questions from major subject areas that have appeared in surveys since 1973. Nearly 60 percent of all questions have concerned two core issues: approval of voluntary active euthanasia and approval of the withdrawal or withholding of medical treatment and food and hydration.

There have been no questions concerning active involuntary euthanasia for the mentally retarded or severely disabled. Just as the early supporters of euthanasia have given up on this issue, it is not now a significant part of the social agenda. Additional questions have concerned the rights of patients to commit suicide in the case of terminal illness or extreme pain, the right to assisted suicide, and occasional others concerning duties to preserve life and the responsibilities of doctors to follow a patient's written instructions. Questions regarding the withdrawal or withholding of food and hydration, in particular, have been asked infrequently and only since

TABLE 3.2   *Questions on Right to Die Surveys, 1973–1990*

Subject	Percentage of Questions (N = 146)
Active voluntary euthanasia	22
Withdrawal of treatment	37
Withdrawal of food and hydration	3
Right to suicide	11
Right to assisted suicide	3
Anticipated behavior	19[a]
Other	4
Total	99[b]

[a]All but four of twenty-eight questions on behavior were included in a single 1990 survey.
[b]Rounded.

1985, but the issue received most attention in 1990. The right to suicide and assisted suicide have received sporadic attention over many years but interest in this issue also has increased recently, which reflects recent efforts to legalize assisted suicide in California and Washington state and the cases of assisted suicide in Michigan. The core issues, however, are voluntary active euthanasia and the withdrawal of treatment.

Paralleling the earliest political conflict on the right to die, pollsters asked more questions on voluntary active euthanasia from 1947 to 1983 than on all other issues. But since 1985, there have been more than twice as many questions on the withdrawal of treatment than on voluntary active euthanasia, and nearly three-quarters of all questions concerning the withdrawal of treatment have been asked since 1985. This parallels New Jersey's innovative Conroy decision concerning the withdrawal of all forms of life-sustaining treatment, including food and hydration, and similar decisions which followed quickly in other states.

As the withdrawal of treatment has become a more complex issue as a result of new court cases and legislation, the polls increasingly reflect the variety of issues involved. Before 1985 surveys included only an occasional question on the right to refuse medical treatment, but beginning in 1985 the number of polls and the number of questions in each poll has increased sharply. Several polls have included six or more related questions about specific treatment situations or policies, including treatment for persons in a permanent comatose condition, the withdrawal of artificially administered food and hydration, evidence of a patient's wishes, and the quality of a patient's life.

A 1990 poll conducted for the Times Mirror Corporation of Los Angeles asked respondents twenty-four questions concerning how they would react to various hypothetical situations involving themselves and family members. The list of questions included: who should make decisions for unconscious patients; the types of illnesses and degree of disability and dependence that might lead an individual to wish to terminate treatment; communications among family members concerning their wishes regarding medical treatment; and whether respondents had living wills or other written instructions.

Persistence of voluntary active euthanasia. Although polls concentrate now on the withdrawal of treatment, questions on voluntary active euthanasia continue to appear regularly. At first the continued prominence of voluntary active euthanasia in recent polls seems difficult to explain, since this proposal never received serious governmental consideration and active euthanasia continues to be a crime, and because the Society for the Right to Die and Concern for Dying have given up on it as a political objective in favor of living wills and the withdrawal of treatment. In terms of changing political events, poll questions on voluntary active euthanasia seem out of date.

However, there are two explanations for the sustained prominence of voluntary active euthanasia in the polls. The first is a strategic behavioral science consideration. The early appearance and longevity of questions in surveys sustains their future importance as polling items. Since the phrasing of questions affects the answers the public gives, asking identical questions over many years is the most reliable way to track changes in opinion. Therefore, polling organizations have an incentive to keep particular items active. Questions on voluntary active euthanasia were among the earliest ones asked regarding the right to die, and the Gallup question that has been asked since 1947 has been part of the General Social Survey of the National Opinion Research Center since 1977. NORC has asked this question every year or two, and this set of identical questions has provided the best available data for assessing changes in public opinion on voluntary active euthanasia over several decades.

But polls other than the General Social Survey have only recently been done, and they too include questions on active euthanasia. Therefore, continuity in the phrasing of questions is not the only reason why active euthanasia still is so conspicuous in the polls. A second explanation lies in the high visibility of mercy killing cases. Mercy killing is not the same as voluntary active euthanasia since many killings are committed without patient request or consent—typically an elderly husband shoots his terminally ill and unconscious or Alzheimer's disease-stricken wife. But the cases almost always exhibit wrenching long-term personal suffering and sacrifice and financial ruin (Humphry and Wickett 1986:133–42). They

81

evoke sympathy for both killer and victim and perpetuate interest in the legalization of voluntary active euthanasia, which some believe might eliminate the compelling need that desperate people feel for killing their hopelessly ill spouses.

The number of mercy killing cases has increased dramatically in recent years, which keeps the issue on official judicial agendas and in the headlines and reinforces the pollsters' incentive to ask the public for its views. Following a surge in the 1950s, mercy killing cases declined until the 1980s. Humphry and Wickett found that the frequency of mercy killing cases increased from a mere eight between 1960 and 1979 to nearly thirty between 1980 and 1985 (1986:135). Others believe there may be many other unreported cases (Meisel 1989:62–63).

The overwhelming majority of all news reporting on local trial courts focuses on brutal or unusual crimes (Drechsel 1983), and mercy killings in particular attract heavy coverage because the issues are controversial and elicit strong emotions and reader involvement. The outcomes also are controversial, especially when a defendant receives an unusually long prison sentence for murder, such as the life sentence given Roswell Gilbert for shooting his Alzheimer's disease-stricken wife in Florida in 1985. Most defendants are convicted of lesser crimes and are not imprisoned. (Governor Bob Martinez ordered the ailing Gilbert released in 1990.) Therefore, even though no state has legalized active euthanasia, mercy killing cases occur regularly, they appear to be increasing, and they provide a continuous stream of interesting and unusual news stories—keeping public interest high in active euthanasia. The news media reacts to unusual cases and portrays many of them so vividly and extensively that the issue is bound to remain on the social agenda. In turn, asking questions about active euthanasia and reporting on the degree of public acceptance reinforces public attention to the issue.

Changing Opinion

Since most surveys have concerned voluntary active euthanasia and the withdrawal or withholding of treatment, I shall track changes in opinion mainly toward these two issues. The Gallup and Harris surveys have asked different questions on these issues, but each polling organization has used the same question over many decades. As explained earlier, such continuity increases confidence that changes in public opinion are due to changes in public sentiment toward the issues rather than the wording of different questions. Public support for active voluntary euthanasia and the withdrawal or withholding of treatment are summarized in table 3.3. Each of these areas of public opinion will be discussed separately below.

The right to die has been a salient issue in all of the polls. The group of respondents who profess to have no opinion almost always has been less than 10 percent and frequently is under 5 percent. Nearly all polls allow only for yes/no, or agree/disagree responses, which do not indicate how intensely or deeply people feel about their opinions. However, two national polls done in 1985 and 1986 that did provide for a greater range of responses revealed that large majorities felt strongly about their views. Of those agreeing that terminally ill patients ought to have the right to demand that treatment be withdrawn, 58 percent in one poll and 75 percent in another strongly agreed, whereas only 22 and 17 percent answered with the milder "agree."

Voluntary active euthanasia. Since the Harris and Gallup polls have asked different questions on voluntary active euthanasia, each provides somewhat different evidence of public opinion. Overall, however, changes in the direction of opinion have been similar. On voluntary active euthanasia, Gallup and the General Social Survey have asked: "When a person has a disease that cannot be cured, do you think doctors should be allowed by law to end the patient's life by some painless means if the patient and his family request it?" (This is the same question discussed earlier that Gallup has asked since 1947.) The question explicitly refers to legalized voluntary euthanasia *allowed by law,* and euthanasia is described as *ending the patient's life.*

In contrast the Harris Poll has asked: "Do you think the patient who is terminally ill, with no cure in sight, ought to have the right to tell his doctor to put him out of his misery, or do you think this is wrong?" In this question there is no clear reference to legalized voluntary euthanasia except the vague term, "the right to tell his doctor" and euthanasia is described more coarsely as "putting the patient out if his misery"—perhaps creating an image closer to destroying sick or injured animals than administering a lethal dose of drugs to a terminally ill or comatose patient.

Although there are differences in the poll results, support for voluntary active euthanasia has steadily increased with a mirror image of changing support from the 1940s to the present (table 3.3). In 1947 and 1950, only 36 to 37 percent of Americans responded positively to the Gallup question, and support increased to a bare majority of 53 percent by 1973. But by 1977, following the Quinlan case and the early adoption of living will laws, public support had climbed to 60 percent. It increased further to approximately 65 percent in 1985 and 69 percent in 1990. As measured by the Gallup question, public opinion has shifted over forty years from two-thirds opposed to legalized voluntary active euthanasia to more than two-thirds in favor.

The Harris question has shown less public support. In 1973 only 37 percent approved of voluntary active euthanasia as phrased by Harris, contrasted with Gallup's 53 percent. In 1977 the Harris question produced 49 percent approval while Gallup showed 60 percent. But the gap between the Gallup and Harris results has narrowed in recent years. The latest 1985 Harris figures indicated 61 percent support for "putting him out of his misery," lower than Gallup's 65 percent, but a much smaller difference than had existed

TABLE 3.3   *Public Support for Voluntary Active Euthanasia and the Withdrawal/Withholding of Treatment*

	Voluntary Active Euthanasia		Withdrawal of Treatment	
	Gallup[a]	Harris[b]	Harris-family[c]	Harris-patient[d]
1947	37%	–%	–%	–%
1950	36	–	–	–
1973	53	37	–	62
1977	60	49	66	71
1981	–[e]	56	73	78
1985	65	61	80	85
1990	69	–	–	–

[a] ". . . end . . . life . . . if patient and family request it."
[b] ". . . patient . . . tell doctor to put him out of his misery. . . ."
[c] ". . . family . . . tell doctors to . . . let patient die. . . ."
[d] ". . . patient . . . tell doctors to . . . let him die. . . ."
[e] No figures are available for Gallup in 1981. However, a 1982 Gallup survey showed that 61 percent of the public supported voluntary active euthanasia in that year.

earlier. Since the right to die has been on the social agenda for a long time, people probably have become more aware and knowledgeable of the issues and may feel more strongly about their position and wording differences may not affect responses as much as before.

Although a large majority approves of the general principle of voluntary active euthanasia, the public is less supportive of implementing it in specific medical situations. Three questions asked of the same sample in 1990 produced very different responses: "Do you think doctors should be allowed to administer lethal injections or provide lethal pills to a terminally ill patient who is: (1) conscious and requests it (yes, 48 percent); (2) unconscious but whose family requests it (yes, 43 percent); (3) unconscious but has left written instructions in a 'living will'"? (yes, 57 percent). Similar differences were found in other polls using nearly identical questions. It seems that a written request when the patient is so ill or comatose that they cannot communicate carries greater weight with the public than other circumstances.

Very few people approve of doctors administering euthanasia under other rules and without a clear patient or family request. The following question has been asked periodically between 1977 and 1985: "Would you approve of ending a patient's life if a board of doctors appointed by the court agreed that the patient could not be cured?" A mere 11 percent approved in 1977 and approval has dropped continuously since then to 4 percent.

Since one-third of the public opposes voluntary active euthanasia, and support declines under specific medical scenarios, it is unlikely that changes in public policy to permit voluntary active euthanasia will be adopted soon. However, defendants convicted of murder or manslaughter in mercy killing cases probably will continue to receive leniency as judges and juries stretch between the formal law and informal justice dictated by the facts and extenuating circumstances of individual cases.

Withdrawing or withholding treatment.   Support for ending treatment for the terminally ill has steadily increased since it was first measured in 1973 (table 3.3). As before, specific levels of support vary according to the questions asked, but the overall trend in all surveys is up sharply. The earliest polls on withdrawing or with-holding treatment were Harris surveys that asked:

All doctors take an oath saying they will maintain, restore, and pro-long human life in their treatment of patients. It is now argued by some people that in many cases people with terminal diseases (those which can only end in death) have their lives prolonged unnecessar-ily, making them endure much pain and suffering for no real reason. Do you think a patient with a terminal disease ought to be able to tell his doctor to let him die rather than to extend his life when no cure is in sight, or do you think this is wrong?

A second question was:

There have been cases where a patient is terminally ill, in a coma and not conscious, with no cure in sight. Do you think that the family of such a patient ought to be able to tell doctors to remove all life-support services and let the patient die, or do you think this is wrong?

The first question concerns the patient's right to request an end to treatment and the second focuses on the rights of families when patients are unable to make their own wishes known. Support for patients' rights always has exceeded support for family decision making, but both eventualities have been supported by ever-increasing percentages of the population.

In 1973 62 percent of the public supported a patient's right to end treatment, about 10 percent more than said yes to Gallup's vol-untary active euthanasia question. But immediately following Quin-lan and California's living will law, support for ending treatment climbed to 71 percent. Support for family decision making was not measured in 1973, but in 1977 66 percent approved. By 1981 pub-lic support for patient and family decision making had increased to 78 and 73 percent respectively. In 1985 85 percent of the public supported a patient's right to end treatment and 80 percent ap-proved of family decision making for unconscious patients.

Polls conducted by various other organizations show similar in-creases. Support has climbed from 77 percent for patients' rights in 1984 to 91 percent in 1988. Public support for family decision making has increased from 70 percent in 1983 to 84 percent in

1986. Support for the withdrawal of food and fluids, if requested by terminally ill patients, or by families in the case of comatose patients, has been measured occasionally since 1985. Support for this also is generally high with an average of 73 percent in favor. Unlike support for active euthanasia, which has increased only a few percentage points since the mid–1980s, support for the withdrawal of treatment has steadily climbed with only 10 to 15 percent of the public opposed to a patient's and/or family members' rights to end treatment. Clearly, a national consensus on withdrawing treatment in hopeless cases has been reached.

Although support for the withdrawal of treatment is high overall, there are variations according to region of the country and the social characteristics of the population. A 1985 Gallup Poll found support highest in the west and midwest with 90 percent of westerners and 80 percent of those in the midwest in favor of permitting withdrawal. Approval in California has been very high for a number of years. In 1975, for example, 87 percent of Californians agreed that "incurably ill patient(s) have the right to refuse medical treatment that may prolong his/her life." This figure increased to 93 percent in 1983. Individuals of higher socioeconomic status also are more likely to approve ending treatment. Whites, college graduates with professional and business careers, and Republicans are 6 to 12 percentage points higher in approval than nonwhites, clerical, sales and manual workers, and Democrats. Age also produces a difference. Eighty percent of individuals younger than 65 favored the withdrawal of treatment compared with 68 percent of persons age 65 and older. Religion, however, has little effect. Despite heavy opposition to governmental policy from the Catholic church, there are very few differences between Catholics and Protestants regarding the withdrawal of medical treatment. Most of the Catholic laity holds opinions sharply different from the official church position.

Suicide.   Another issue that has been examined since the 1970s is the right to suicide. Opinions regarding suicide have been tapped since 1977 through the following question: "Do you think a person has a moral right to end his or her life under these circumstances: when this person has a disease that is incurable?" Like other right to die opinions, support for suicide in the case of terminal illness has increased—from 38 percent in 1977 to nearly 50 percent in 1990. Opinions regarding the right to assisted suicide have been obtained through various questions from 1987 to 1990. Approval ranges from a low of 31 percent to a high of 53 percent. Clearly, suicide and assisted suicide fall well below the levels of approval given to the withdrawal of treatment and to voluntary active euthanasia.

Public Opinion and Public Policy

Public support of the right to die has been highest for the withdrawal of treatment, and approval jumped from 62 percent in 1973 to 71 percent in 1977, following the Quinlan case and the early adoptions of living will laws. But most living will laws were not enacted until 1984 and 1985, well after public approval had moved to the 80 percent level. With public support already high in 1977, and revealing 7 percent increases every ensuing four years, it seems surprising that legislation came so late to most of the states. But there are a number of reasons why public opinion did not put the right to die on government agendas earlier or translate into public policy more quickly.

First, except for the early polls in the 1940s and 1950s, public opinion on the right to die was not measured until 1973, and then it was not measured often. With a few exceptions in the later years, the polls also did not tap the intensity of the public's views. Since public officials had no systematic way of determining public opinion until polls were taken regularly and frequently, and few polls reveal the depth of feeling, politicians are unlikely to feel secure about public opinion on this issue.

Another impediment to the impact of polls on right to die policy is that nearly all polls are based on national samples of the population, not the states. Typically, only about fifteen hundred people or less are included in national samples. Cautious inferences can be drawn about regional or social group differences from these polls, but the samples are much too small for extracting reliable state level information, and it is impossible to identify public opinion at the level of individual state legislative districts, where representatives are most likely to be interested in public opinion.

Savvy politicians also are aware that the wording of questions affects the size of majorities. Seemingly minor changes in wording can shift substantial portions of the public from one side to another (Erikson, Luttbeg, and Tedin 1980:252–53). Relying on polls as an indicator of public desires also is dangerous because most voters do not cast ballots according to an official's stand on a single issue unless that issue is very visible, has the appearance of a long-term crisis, or sustains public interest over a long time. Although it is a significant concern, the right to die cannot compete for attention with abortion, drugs and crime, a troubled economy, or a war.

Public opinion also cannot translate directly into policy because the expression of an opinion does not produce specific policy proposals. There is a large chasm between public support for a general statement regarding the withdrawal of treatment and creating a specific living will bill or other legislation. Legislation has to be crafted by individual legislators and interest groups, and those engaged in face-to-face lobbying and bill writing have much more effect on shaping policy than the reporting of passive opinion holding by the general public.[5] Well-organized and vocal opponents delayed adoption of living will laws in most states for many years following the emergence of strong public support for the withdrawal of treatment, and some states still have no legislation.

Despite inaction in some states, public opinion probably is tied to policy-making in a continuous cycle of mutual reinforcement. Public opinion research strongly documents that the public frequently takes its cues from public officials, and that public support for policy increases following government announcements and action (Weissberg 1976). In turn, a developing public consensus reinforces and encourages policy-making (Page and Shapiro 1983). Although the right to die polls are national ones, when public opinion overwhelmingly favors a policy, it may favor the odds of further political action.

The web of cause and effect relationships between national measurements of public opinion and other national events on state political action is complex and probably impossible to uncover precisely. When an issue becomes so visible and salient that "everyone is talking about it" (Kingdon 1984:76;147–49), many activities occur at the same time, indicating a broad and growing presence of an issue on the public agenda. Public opinion already was heavily in support of permitting the withdrawal of treatment in the early 1980s, and publications in professional and mass media were increasing once again since their high levels in the mid–1970s. Prominent national organizations also began to endorse similar policies soon thereafter, and state governments increasingly enacted living will laws. In part public opinion responded positively to early court decisions and laws and later, a nearly unanimous public certainly signaled continued approval for the right to die. Growing public support may have encouraged national organizations to favor the withdrawal of treatment and more states to enact laws.

Similar one-sided support is lacking for other right to die proposals. While 65 percent favor the general principle of voluntary active euthanasia, approval decreases for each specific situation in which it might be implemented—which underscores the problem in viewing public opinion as a source of specific policy. The traditional opponents to living will laws and judicial policy permitting the withdrawal of treatment object even more strenuously to these proposals. These proposals are unlikely to achieve official status in the foreseeable future. The right to die will be limited to the withdrawal of treatment, including food and hydration, from terminally ill and permanently comatose patients.

Conclusion

Although there was no governmental action concerning the right to die until 1976, the issue had been on the social agenda in several forms for many years. The Karen Quinlan case did not suddenly create public interest, but it was largely responsible for the subsequent take-off in public awareness and additional governmental policy-making. Following the Quinlan case, the right to die became firmly established as a significant political issue and public policy.

New concerns about the withdrawal of treatment added to earlier interest in voluntary active euthanasia as medical technology advanced and new procedures made it increasingly possible to prolong life in the face of death. New issues did not supplant the old since mercy killing cases continued to occur and new problems underscored the potential of sophisticated medical technology both for good and ill. Instead many issues, including recent interest in assisted suicide, remained visible and added to professional and public awareness and concern about medical care for cases of terminal illness and other hopeless medical conditions.

As research on other issues has demonstrated (Nelson 1984), professional agendas lead the mass agenda. The right to die first became visible in the medical literature, and some of the early articles in the mass media summarized medical writing or were written by doctors. As the other professional agendas began to emphasize the right to die as well, they too became the basis for new literature in the mass media, and the right to die gradually accelerated as a social issue with many medical, legal, ethical, and philosophical dimensions.

Polling on the right to die came much later than its visibility on professional and mass agendas, and most early polls concentrated on traditional concerns with voluntary active euthanasia. Interest in the withdrawal of treatment came much later, after government policy already had been adopted, and the most recent polls have explored alternatives in treatment decisions in much more detail than earlier surveys.

Although polling was spotty until the 1970s, and did not increase substantially until a decade later, early public opinion polls on the right to die indicate that most of the public had strong views about euthanasia and related issues. Early support for voluntary active euthanasia was low, but it has climbed so that about two-thirds of the public now supports a general policy of voluntary euthanasia. However, the public is divided on the details of implementation. In contrast, support for the withdrawal of treatment is much higher, which probably is a reaction as well as a stimulus to government policy in this aspect of the right to die.

This chapter has described and analyzed the growth of right to die agendas in broad terms and has examined the expansion of the volume and coverage of literature and polling at the national level. The following chapter focuses in greater detail on the development of the right to die on the political agendas of three states and the movement of the issue to government policy-making.

4 Three Paths to Innovation

This chapter examines the origins, development, and enactment of right to die policy in California, Florida, and Massachusetts. These states were selected because each reveals different patterns in agenda setting and innovation. California enacted the nation's first living will law in 1976; Florida had the first right to die proposal before a state legislature, but delayed enacting a living will law until a second wave of innovation swept many of the states in the mid–1980s; and Massachusetts, usually an innovative state, did not enact any legislation until 1990 and opted for a durable power of attorney law, not a living will statute. Late action in Massachusetts is not due to the recent addition of the right to die to the state's political agenda. Instead, the issue has been on the legislative agenda for years, and the Massachusetts Supreme Judicial Court has made several important right to die decisions.

State agenda setting and innovation is not limited to the behavior of a single institution, although each may have its own distinctive agenda. The right to die has been the primary concern of state courts and legislatures, and their separate agendas frequently have influenced each other's policies. Governors generally have not made living wills part of their program. However, governors are very important due to their power to veto legislation, and the right to die has had varied success in the states due to this single, but critical decision. So much public attention has focused on legislative lobbying, debate, and negotiation regarding living wills that a governor's veto decision sometimes seems almost anticlimactic, but the governor's office is a separate place and opportunity for supporters and opponents to win the day.

The data for these case studies include interviews with bill sponsors and principal supporters and opponents of legislation, analysis of the content of state laws and amendments and court decisions, and information derived from the files of political organizations in the three states. I have also closely examined legislative archives for information on the flow of legislation and the roles of various participants.

California: The First Law

Since California enacted the nation's first living will law in 1976, a few months after the Quinlan decision, it appears that this innovative and widely reported court case caused California to take up the issue and create innovative legislation. But there is no clear cause and effect between these two events. First, the origin of the California law predates the Quinlan case by several years, and Karen Quinlan's vegetative state was not addressed by the California law. Not only was she a young woman who had not and probably would not have executed a living will, she was not suffering from a terminal illness, as required by California's and most other living will laws.

Powerful Sponsor

Senator Barry Keene, the Democratic majority leader of the California Senate, is seen by all observers and political participants as the person most responsible for California's living will law and later right to die legislation. Senator Keene became interested in living will legislation several years before his election to the Assembly.

An attorney, Keene had been asked to search for a way to end the medical treatment being given a neighbor's wife for terminal cancer. The neighbor and his wife had agreed that, in the event she became terminally ill, neither of them would allow her to be "hooked up to machines" to prolong the inevitable. But when the husband visited his wife in the hospital, she was in the exact medical circumstances

that both of them had vowed to prevent—she was tied with re-
straints to prevent her from pulling out nasogastric and ventilator
tubes. Keene searched the law for a remedy, but found none. The
rights and duties of doctors and hospitals were unclear and the
dying had no clear rights or way to refuse life-sustaining medical
treatment. Then, in 1972, Keene encountered the same situation
when his mother-in-law developed cancer and faced a similar life-
prolonging medical regimen. Despite having signed a medical directive to limit treatment, no law required doctors or hospitals to
honor it.

When Keene was elected in 1974, he took the living will to the
legislature. It was his own special, self-assigned project to get legislation enacted which would give the dying the right and power to
control their own medical treatment. But a freshman legislator in a
two-party competitive state—where party organization and disci-
pline exercise some control over its members—normally would
have difficulty getting new legislation on the legislative and decisional agendas.

But Keene was no ordinary freshman senator. Very early in his
legislative career, he and four other newcomers had cast the deciding votes to elect the speaker of the assembly who repaid the favor
by appointing the five to chair various legislative committees. Keene
chose the Committee on Health and the speaker assured him that
Keene's new living will bill would be referred to Keene's committee,
and that the issue would receive a hearing and leadership support.
Quickly, Keene proposed a bill in 1974 that simply stated "every
person has the right to die without prolongation of life by medical means." The proposal was immediately opposed by the California Pro-Life Council (CPLC) and the California Catholic Conference (CCC).

Outside Strategy

Keene's 1974 bill was easily defeated because he did little advance
preparation to win support for it, hoping his insider status might
be enough to get the bill through. But his next effort to enact a
living will law in 1976 was dramatically different. Instead of simply
offering a new proposal, Keene embraced an outside strategy. He

anticipated disagreement and conflict, and in the intervening two years he and his staff softened up many supporters and opponents. Nevertheless, CPLC remained opposed. In its view, any government policy that suggested limitations on life-sustaining medical treatment was the "first step on a slippery slope" to active euthanasia and extermination of undesirables. Extreme opponents demonstrated loudly near Keene's office, hung him in effigy, and compared him on handbills with Hitler. At a committee hearing opponents placed a copy of William Shirer's *Rise and Fall of the Third Reich* on the witness table. Ideological commitment to their right to life position would prevent the CPLC from ever compromising on right to die legislation.

Building consensus. Keene's main approach was to negotiate with two well-organized and powerful groups that were willing to compromise—the Catholic clergy and the California Medical Association (CMA). The CCC was much more flexible and pragmatic than the CPLC for several reasons. The first is political context. The California bishops and the director of the Conference, Auxiliary Bishop John S. Cummins, recognized that the California public was a mixed and divided polity, and that many California Catholics were much more liberal than those in other parts of the nation. As mentioned in the previous chapter, polls in California on the withdrawal of treatment draw almost universal support and Catholics and Protestants do not differ greatly on this issue. Catholic leaders also professed to have no doctrinal opposition to the concept of a living will since the rejection of extraordinary medical treatment in hopeless cases had been endorsed, albeit in vague and general terms, by Pope Pius XIIth in 1957. Consequently, some limitations on medical treatment in hopeless cases was not unreasonable to the California hierarchy. In contrast with the CPLC, the CCC was much less motivated by ideology.

As one avenue to the Catholic hierarchy, Keene dispatched a member of his committee staff, who also was a Catholic priest, to the bishop in Keene's district. His mission was to persuade the bishop that Keene's legislative proposal would be a modest one and to ask his support. The bishop agreed, but would not publicly endorse the proposal for fear of conservative Catholic criticism. In ad-

95

dition to the CCC, the administrators and staff of Catholic hospitals recognized the value of the living will since, as in other facilities, Catholic hospitals had much ad hoc and inconsistent decision making regarding treatment for the terminally ill. But the CCC and the Conference of Catholic Health Facilities preferred health matters to be handled privately—between doctor and patient without government involvement or sanction.

More compelling than Catholic attitudes and ideology toward living wills, however, were CCC calculations regarding Keene's political strategy and his chances for legislative success. At the heart of the Conference's position on the living will bill was its belief that Keene's bill might pass the legislature. Not only had Keene demonstrated his commitment to the issue and he was well positioned to get it enacted, he enlisted the support of the prestigious CMA. Once CMA support seemed likely, the CCC declared itself neutral on the legislation—if it could get crucial amendments. The alternative was to risk legislative defeat, and perhaps get a law that it found very intrusive. The CCC also believed it was important to maintain access to Keene for future policy-making, since it seemed clear that Keene would be an important player in the legislature.

Despite its neutral stance on the living will law in return for compromise, the CCC and Bishop Cummins were harshly criticized in personal correspondence and through the newspapers by the National Conference of Catholic Bishops, Committee on Pro-Life Activities. It believed the CCC should have resisted the living will bill in a legislative fight, and that California Catholics were accepting euthanasia. Their position forecast the battles over living will laws in other, later adopting states.

Keene accepted many amendments required by the CCC in trade for dropping its opposition. These amendments included making living wills inapplicable in the case of pregnancy; including a declaration against active euthanasia; requiring extensive witnessing provisions; requiring two physicians to certify a diagnosis of terminal illness; making a living will valid for only five years from the date of signature; and requiring a fourteen-day waiting period following a diagnosis of terminal illness before a valid living will can be made. Like the CCC, the CMA initially opposed the bill until it too received concessions that removed serious sanctions against doctors for not complying with the terms of a living will. In all, the bill was amended nine different times before it was passed by the legislature.

Keene recognized that the amendments severely limited the bill—he even has used the term crippling—and he acknowledged that it was much less than he hoped to accomplish. But, citing competing and hostile interest groups and reluctant legislators who feared having to vote on a controversial bill, Keene believed that compromise was necessary to get any law enacted and that this law was better than no law. Although California's Natural Death Act was the first of its kind in the nation it remains the most restrictive living will law.

The CMA generally was much more receptive to a living will law than the Catholic church. Two developments in medicine converged with Keene's agenda and made the association receptive to the law. First, the executive director of the CMA recognized the need for legislation, for he personally had intervened in his father's medical treatment to prevent the process of dying from being protracted. It also was abundantly clear to the CMA that while modern medicine had the power to prolong life, the consequences required attention. The tendency to use the new machines and technology in hopeless situations needed to be checked.

Second and most important, the CMA saw the living will as a partial solution to a separate problem—sharp increases in the early 1970s in medical malpractice insurance premiums and perceived increases in incidents of medical liability. Allowing patients to designate the conditions under which life-saving medical treatment should be withdrawn presumably would remove some of the discretion from doctors and reduce their liability for terminating life support. The CMA thought the living will bill might help this problem, and with amendments excluding legal liability for doctors who refused to comply with a living will, the bill could do no harm. Thus the living will bill became a possible solution to a separate problem perceived by one group affected by the bill, but it was a unique problem that Keene and other supporters had not anticipated nor included as part of their rationale for the new law.

Mass media.   During negotiation with the CCC and the medical association, Keene sought widespread public support for the living will bill. He distributed news releases to newspapers statewide, and the media heavily covered the legislative debate. In Keene's terms, he and the media used each other well: the media had not created the issue nor put it on the public agenda, but the media loved the controversy surrounding the right to die, for it kept reader interest high. In turn, media coverage encouraged people to write to Keene and other politicians—letters which Keene could use to argue that the people were in favor of his bill. Many newspapers and radio and television stations across the state also supported the legislation in editorials, some early in the process, others later in the year. But most important, media coverage was continuous throughout 1976 and kept the issue before the public.

Window of opportunity. As discussed earlier, the Quinlan case was not responsible for California's living will bill. The living will had been on the public agenda for several years and Senator Keene and the CMA were concerned with the issue, although from different perspectives, before the Quinlan case became news. But Karen Quinlan's plight created a window of opportunity for the living will bill. The case gave Keene additional publicity and heightened public and elite interest in the legislation. It is possible that the living will bill would have passed without Quinlan, given longstanding interest in the issue and the converging values of interest groups, but Quinlan clearly was an asset that heightened concern and interest and made support for the bill much more compelling. The timing for new law seemed right.

The legislation easily passed. Nevertheless, Democratic governor Jerry Brown did not immediately sign it. A letter-writing campaign by the CPLC sent a stream of mail to his office opposing the bill, but this stimulated supporters as well. Organizations representing the elderly and retirees, medical, nursing, health and hospice associations, many individual Protestant churches, and Jewish organizations all supported the bill. Governor Brown announced that he had delayed signing the bill so that all interested groups and individuals had an opportunity to express their support or opposition or other concerns about the bill. However, there is no indication that he was undecided or strongly considered not signing it.

Agenda Maintenance

The enactment of the Natural Death Act (NDA) in 1976 did not end public concern or governmental agenda setting in the right to die. First, California's innovation had a tremendous impact nationally. The following year, seven states enacted similar living will laws—all but two were in California's western regional orbit—and sixty-one living will bills were introduced in forty-two states (Society for the Right to Die 1988). In California the issue did not fade partly because the NDA had limited effect. First, neither executives at the CMA nor California physicians, whose views were obtained in various polls, indicated that the NDA had solved the crisis in medical malpractice insurance or affected doctors' fears of liability. The CMA also felt the impact of another new converging issue— the rise in health care costs for terminal care. A CMA executive referred to studies showing that more money is spent on health care in the last six months than during the rest of life. It was an issue discussed at medical cocktail parties—it was in the air—and advance medical directives were now seen as one way of shortening this period of costly, but futile, medical care.

The heavily amended NDA also had little or no impact on medical decision making in terminal cases. Relatively few citizens executed living wills, and the law did not work well for those who tried to use it. The required fourteen-day waiting period following a diagnosis of terminal illness made the law unusable to half or more patients who lapsed into permanent comas before they were diagnosed as terminal. There also was considerable disagreement among doctors regarding when death is imminent and the conditions under which they would withhold treatment. Nearly half of doctors surveyed said that death is imminent only within twenty-four hours or less; another 30 percent said within one week or less; the answers of the others varied between two weeks and six months or less. Over 75 percent of the doctors also said that they would continue to give treatment to a patient who most probably could not be saved regardless of a patient's oral or written request not to be treated (*California Natural Death Act* 1979).

The Natural Death Act also did not cover care of persons in a permanent vegetative state. The permanent vegetative state had been raised by supporters of the living will law, but it was too controversial to be included. Therefore, despite enactment of a law that seemed to solve a problem and that took the living will temporarily off the decisional agenda, problems associated with medical decision making in terminal care and other hopeless situations had not gone away. The right to die would be back.

Judicial innovation. While the issue was temporarily off the legislative agenda, the right to die began to appear on judicial agendas. Between 1983 and 1988, four California (intermediate) Courts of Appeals had cases dealing with medical treatment for patients both with and without living wills, but whose medical conditions were not covered by the statute. The number of appellate cases in California is second only to the number of cases decided in New Jersey. The courts ruled that the NDA was not exclusive policy governing patients' rights and that the courts could extend these rights.

In the state's first appellate case, which involved murder charges against two doctors for removing life-support systems, the court condoned the withdrawal of artificially administered food and hydration from a permanently comatose patient who had not been diagnosed terminally ill and who, therefore, was not covered by the law (*Barber v. Superior Court*). The judges also criticized the NDA as inadequate, especially the fourteen-day rule for executing a living will.

Other California cases dramatically illustrated limitations of the statute in two similar situations. First, a seventy-year-old mentally competent and conscious patient with multiple incurable problems, but who had not been diagnosed as terminally ill, had been refused his wish to discontinue treatment despite having signed a living will and a durable power of attorney form (*Bartling v. Superior Court*). The second case was that of paralyzed Elizabeth Bouvia who had objected orally and in writing to forced feeding (*Bouvia v. Superior Court*). The courts ruled in both cases that the withdrawal of life-sustaining treatment was not limited to terminally ill or comatose patients, but could be requested by any patient who simply wanted no more treatment. In a third appellate case, the judges held that court-appointed custodians could act on behalf of permanently unconscious patients without prior judicial approval (*Conservatorship*

of Drabick). The early California decisions cited New Jersey's Quinlan decision most heavily; the later cases cited a much longer string
of cases from several states.

The judges in the Bouvia case expressed their exasperation with
the doctors, lawyers, and hospitals when they wrote: "We do not
believe that all of the foregoing case law and statements of policy
and statutory recognition are mere lip service to a fictitious
fight. . . . The right of a competent adult patient to refuse medical
treatment is a constitutionally guaranteed right which must not
be abridged." Even the right to suicide probably is the "ultimate
exercise of one's right to privacy" (*Bouvia v. Superior Court*, 304
and 306).

These appellate court decisions received enormous publicity and
reinforced public awareness that the right to die was far from
settled. The self-imposed starvation case of Elizabeth Bouvia in particular, which was heavily reported in the media nationwide, received very heavy coverage in California. Between 1984 and 1986
101 stories on Bouvia and other cases appeared in the *Los Angeles
Times,* nearly ten times the number of all other stories on the right
to die. This number is exceeded only by the number of articles appearing in the *New York Times* in 1975 and 1976, when the Quinlan
case received its greatest attention in the mass media. The state
courts were very important in keeping the issue before the public
and in demonstrating through their own decisions that there were
major limitations in the NDA and, although they did not openly
call for new legislation, the judges made it clear they would make
their own policy to meet these additional problems.

Amendment and new legislation. In 1979 Senator Keene introduced a bill to amend the 1976 law, but it received no consideration,
possibly because it came soon after the original law and contradicted
a pledge he made to the CCC not to seek amendments until there
was experience with the 1976 statute. But in 1983 he introduced a
different, but related medical treatment bill—the durable power of
attorney for health care. As described in chapter 1, this law permits
an individual to direct that health care decisions be made by another
designated person if the individual executing the durable power of
attorney is unable to make decisions for him or herself. The source

of this law was a previous statute unrelated to the right to die. In 1981 the California legislature had revised and expanded the general durable power of attorney used in financial and real estate matters, and Keene said it gave him the idea to apply it to health care as well. Like the living will, Keene's durable power of attorney for health care law was the first of its kind in the nation.

In contrast to living will bills, the durable power of attorney law was enacted easily, without any of the vitriol or numerous amendments associated with the living will law. The durable power of attorney for health care was considered a routine, noncontroversial extension of a policy already in place. But there were other reasons it had wide support. The CMA favored it because it reduced doctors' responsibility and legal liability further by passing the burden of decision making on to nonmedical personnel, typically family and friends. Both the CMA and the CCC favored it because it kept medical decision making between doctor and patient, without government-established rules or guidelines for decision making.

The bill also was simple and straightforward for, unlike the NDA, it left medical conditions and other technical requirements unspecified. It contained no provisions concerning pregnancy, waiting periods, diagnoses, etc., which require interpretation and invite conflict, but left all medical contingencies open. And it was a document that healthy individuals, or those who were seriously ill but not yet comatose or diagnosed terminal, could execute. Finally, the state bar association saw the durable power of attorney for health care as an extension of their role in estate planning. It appeared to be a solution to many problems without any political costs.

In 1987 Senator Keene introduced a comprehensive amendment to the NDA. By this time, the issue had deeply penetrated the mass and professional agendas in California and throughout the United States, and there were many new state and national pressures for upgrading California's very limited law. The issue was very much in the air everywhere and support for change was widespread.

By the end of 1985, when active consideration for revision began to form in California, thirty-four states and Washington, D.C. had enacted laws that were more facilitative of the right to die than California's, and the Society for the Right to Die urged improvements in California. In 1986 the National Conference Commission on Uniform State Laws produced a model living will law with provisions that were much more facilitative than those in California's law. That same year, the American Medical Association endorsed withdrawing all forms of treatment from the terminally ill, when death is imminent, and from those in a permanent comatose state.

In California many forces converged. Early in 1986 the Hemlock Society, then based in California, proposed amendments to the 1976 law that would have included "aid in dying" and it urged Keene to include it in a revised bill. (He declined.) That same year the CMA and the Los Angeles County Medical and Bar Associations issued guidelines for the withdrawal of treatment. The California Gray Panthers and other seniors' organizations also urged Keene to introduce the law proposed by the NCCUSL. Newly formed organizations also favored change, such as California Health Decisions, which called itself a grass-roots citizens' action project to educate the public about dilemmas caused by high-tech, high-cost health care. Finally, California and other courts were producing policy that went much further than the NDA.

Keene's amendments would have added "a permanent unconscious condition" as a circumstance for which a living will is valid; required doctors and medical institutions to comply with a living will or transfer the patient to another physician or facility (failure to transfer would be a criminal misdemeanor); simplified the forms and witnessing requirements; and removed the fourteen-day waiting period and the five-year renewal requirement. In many ways the 1987 amendments would have brought California's law much closer to the more facilitative laws already adopted by other states. The bill failed to pass in 1987 because there were many amendments left and the session ended before compromises among the CCC, CMA, and others were reached.

In 1988 a bill that included many of the provisions of the NCCUSL law was introduced by another member of the Assembly. However, it received little attention, probably out of deference to Keene's preeminent position in this field. The CMA also indicated to the bill sponsor that it had worked with Keene in the past to iron out differences in legislation and it planned to do so in the future.

Keene reintroduced his bill in January 1988; it was amended on six occasions through August 1988 and passed at the close of the session.

The list of supporters and opponents were nearly identical to those in 1976. Again the CCC was convinced it could not oppose the bill. California's diverse and liberal society led the CCC to believe that an amended bill would be better than more extreme alternatives, specifically the assisted suicide proposal endorsed by the Hemlock Society. While Keene's new bill was being considered, the Hemlock Society attempted to place its assisted suicide proposal on the California ballot as a popular initiative, since the legislature and most groups refused to support it. While it failed to obtain the necessary signatures, the appearance of the suicide proposal convinced the CCC that it could not object to Keene's much milder bill.

Although compromise got the bill through the legislature, Jerry Brown was not the governor. Despite heavy support for Keene's bill, conservative Republican Governor George Deukmejian vetoed the law, consistent with his own ideology, buttressed by an active letter-writing campaign by religious fundamentalists and prolife supporters in the Committee on Moral Concerns and the CPLC (Schaeffer 1988).

California's 1976 law remains unchanged and revision may not be possible unless the state elects a liberal governor whose views are similar to a majority of the legislature and the interest groups that have supported Senator Keene's compromise proposals. Nevertheless, the right to die has been a nearly constant item on the California public and governmental agendas.

Florida: First Proposal, Postponed Adoption

As in California, the right to die was placed on Florida's governmental agenda by a novice representative, Dr. Walter Sackett of Miami. Representative Sackett had been a family doctor for several decades before he ran for the state legislature in 1966 at age sixty. He introduced his first measure in 1967 and he is credited by state lobbyists and national organizations with being the first to place the issue on the governmental agenda anywhere in the United States.

Similar to Assemblyman Keene, Dr. Sackett reported that his interest in the right to die developed from frequent personal experience and, in his view, the needlessly tragic final days of many patients who were kept alive by respirators, antibiotics, and other procedures. He believed legislation was needed to protect the terminally ill and their families from unwanted and futile treatment (Sackett 1971).

Weak Sponsor

But, unlike Keene, Dr. Sackett was a powerless, freshman backbencher. He impulsively proposed an amendment to the Florida constitution from the floor of the legislature during a special 1967 amendment session. Florida's bill of rights would have included the short phrase "the right to die with dignity." The proposal was debated heatedly in the House for one hour and then voted down. However, several members approached the doctor and urged him to bring the issue up again in a future legislative session. He reintroduced the same proposal in 1969, but sensing little support, withdrew it. In 1970 he introduced the first living will bill.

Dr. Sackett received national attention for his early involvement and promotion of right to die legislation, and in 1972 he was invited to testify at hearings before the United States Senate Special Committee on Aging, chaired by the late Senator Frank Church. He also gained national notoriety for his provocative appearances on *60 Minutes,* and the Phil Donahue and Dick Cavett talk shows.

Outside Strategy

Dr. Sackett's early bills were short, simple documents that included several items found in the living will laws of most states. With two witnesses, adults may specify the nature of medical treatment during the final days of a terminal illness; medical personnel are not liable for complying with a living will; and a resulting death does not constitute suicide. However, Sackett's bill's also contained extremely controversial provisions that guaranteed that an outside strategy would be required, but also that it probably would fail.

But it is difficult to determine if he actually had a strategy for getting his bills through the legislature other than simply filing them and hoping for the best. Instead of courting and softening up the opposition, Sackett appeared oblivious to the subtleties of the political process, and his bills almost seemed designed for conflict and failure.

Controversial proposals.   In addition to allowing competent adults to determine medical treatment during a terminal illness, Dr. Sackett proposed that hopelessly retarded patients who were wards of the state, completely out of touch with reality, indigent, and without relatives, be allowed to die if they contracted any illnesses—including infections—that, if left untreated, may lead to death. Three staff physicians would have to agree that the patient's life was meaning-less, and the decision would be certified by a judge. Sackett believed that this was one of the most urgently needed elements of right to die legislation, both to end the lives of patients "whom some would have difficulty in recognizing as human beings," and to save the state millions of dollars (Sackett 1971:331).

These proposals ignited advocates for the disabled and retarded, right to life organizations, and the Florida Catholic Conference (FCC), but heavy lobbying against the bill was unnecessary since the proposals were so extreme they died in house committees in the three successive years that Sackett filed them. Equally important, no organization representing a large number of Florida citizens supported Sackett's bills. Sackett was armed only with a statement of support from the American Euthanasia Foundation (a little known and unfortunately named Florida group that distributed living wills in return for membership fees), a few letters from constituents, and polls published in out-of-state newspapers showing that a majority of Americans favored right to die legislation. The recorded house committee sessions are punctuated with the exasperated groans of fellow legislators when Sackett introduced his early bills for discussion and vote. Dr. Sackett gradually was cast as a loner and an outsider and his status diminished in the legislature.

In 1973, Dr. Sackett introduced a revised living will bill that did not explicitly mention the hopelessly retarded, but it provided for three physicians to make decisions regarding treatment for the terminally ill who were incompetent and who lacked relatives. Again, finding no support, Sackett agreed to substantial revision, leaving only a living will for competent adults. Sackett buttressed his previous arguments for legislation by pointing to an increasing number of contradictory Florida trial court decisions concerning the removal of life-support systems from the terminally ill. No cases had yet reached the state appellate courts, but there was growing evidence that the issue was on the public agenda and had approached the judicial doors of the governmental agenda as well.

The FCC lobbied against this revised version, but the House Judiciary Committee approved the bill and sent it to the floor. The bill initially failed, but with Sackett lobbying individual representatives, it passed on a motion to reconsider by a close vote of 56 to 50. The bill also passed a Senate committee, but it died on the calendar a week before the end of the legislative session. The FCC takes credit for persuading conservative Senate leadership to block the bill.

Sackett's greater success in 1973 may have caught the opposition off guard. All of his previous bills were so extreme they died without a fight, but the 1973 bill was a very mild and limited one, and although it would have instituted new and controversial policy for Florida and the nation, it was much more palatable than Sackett's earlier proposals. There was little lobbying from the opposition, and it appeared that the narrow bill might some day be successful. But support for the bill galvanized and motivated the Catholic church and many conservative Florida legislators who saw living wills as a threat to life or contrary to their religious beliefs. California's diversity and liberalism contrasted sharply with Florida's greater homogeneity and conservatism.

No consensus. In preparation for the 1974 legislative session, the FCC came armed with documented opposition from the National Conference of Catholic Bishops and newspaper articles depicting situations in which doctors and families voluntarily ceased life-support systems for the terminally ill, which supported the FCC view that legislation was unnecessary. But significantly, the National and Florida Associations for Retarded Children vehemently opposed the bill. In their view, even though Sackett's latest living will bill was limited to competent adults who voluntarily executed living wills, his previous bills calling for withholding medical treatment for the mentally retarded and his statement that he would accept a limited version of his bill as "a first step," convinced them that this was dangerous legislation. Undermining his own cause Sackett continued to speak about the merits of his earlier proposals for curtailing treatment for the severely retarded. Also after the 1973 legislative vote the American Medical Association announced its opposition to living wills, and encouraged traditional doctor-patient/family interactions as the proper setting for making treatment decisions.

Similar limited bills were introduced by Sackett or others between 1975 and 1982 with identical results. The bills died in house or senate committees or on the floor, and a constitutional amendment was defeated in 1976 despite repeated references to Quinlan and new support from another doctor-legislator who previously had opposed all of Sackett's measures. Like Sackett and Keene in California, Dr. Richard Hodes changed his mind on living wills as a result of close personal experience—he had participated in a decision to end life support for a close friend who had suffered a massive brain hemorrhage.

With the exception of the state's Department of Health and Rehabilitative Services, which began to support living will legislation in 1981, organizations could not be found to endorse the bills. But the FCC, the Florida Association of Retarded Citizens, and later, the Florida Association of Retired Persons and various right to life organizations all lobbied against the bills. The FCC characterized Sackett's proposals as mercy killing and similar to Nazi policies on euthanasia for the mentally and physically deformed. Repeatedly, living wills were described as the "first step on the slippery slope to active euthanasia" for the elderly and other unwanted groups. The FCC always operated in a professional and courteous manner, but extreme right to life groups on the fringe of the legislative process injected emotionalism and bizarre ideas into the battle, linking living will legislation to a declining respect for life in America, the injection of birth control drugs into the nation's water supplies, cannibalism which would result from using the bodies of those selected to die to feed the hungry, and more.

Dr. Sackett was defeated for reelection in 1976 by a younger challenger—an uncommon event in state politics since most legislators win reelection, often running unopposed. Sackett was depicted as a one-issue legislator with photographs in local newspapers showing him napping during legislative sessions. The living will fell to others. Nevertheless, he performed a very important function in agenda setting by keeping the right to die before Florida government. Even though his controversial bills were defeated, and he was the only person in the state visibly supporting legislation, his tenacity attracted media and public attention and kept the issue on the decisional agenda, and, in time, the right to die became official policy.

Agenda Maintenance

With one exception, all the later living will bills were introduced by various liberal Democratic legislators from south Florida—principally representing St. Petersburg, Tampa, and the Miami area. Like Sackett's proposals, their bills also were unsuccessful until new political events began to converge and impinge on political conflict over the right to die. Gradually they altered the political equation. Most important, like Sackett's bills, they kept the issue before the public and on the legislative agenda.

Probably most significant were decisions of the Florida appellate courts. Cases similar to the ones cited by Dr. Sackett in his early legislative testimony reached state intermediate courts and the supreme court by 1980. A second source of political influence developed from the legislature's enactment of a definition of brain death statute, similar to those being enacted in other states in the 1970s and 1980s (Blumberg and Wharton-Hagen 1988).

Judicial innovation.   In 1980 the Florida Supreme Court ruled that a competent, conscious, terminally ill patient had the right to refuse continued medical treatment and it recognized a patient's right to die with dignity. Seventy-three year old Abe Perlmutter was suffering from amyotrophic lateral sclerosis ("Lou Gerig's disease"), and he was being maintained on a respirator (*Satz v. Perlmutter*). This decision was the first in the nation to deal with the enormous practical difficulty that competent patients have in refusing medical treatment, a right long recognized in common law.

This decision was only the fourth state supreme court case in the nation involving the right to die. Regarding agenda setting and innovation, the court demanded that the state legislature act, or the court would resolve disputes on a case-by-case basis. It was the first and is one of the few state supreme court decisions to demand comprehensive legislation.

The court castigated the legislature when it said, quoting the opinion of the intermediate appellate court: "Abe Perlmutter should be allowed to make his choice to die with dignity, notwithstanding over a dozen legislative failures in this state to adopt suitable legislation in this field." The court added:

> It is the type of issue which is more suitably addressed in the legislative forum, where fact finding can be less confined and the viewpoints of all interested institutions and disciplines can be presented and synthesized. In this manner only can the subject be dealt with comprehensively and the interest of all institutions and individuals be properly accommodated. Nevertheless, preferences for legislative treatment cannot shackle the courts when legally protected interests are at stake. . . . Legislative inaction cannot serve to close the doors of the courtrooms . . . to . . . citizens who assert cognizable Constitutional rights. (359)

The legislature paid little heed to this warning, but the case further legitimized the right to die and gave supporters new ammunition. Legislative staff who prepared background reports on future bills began to heavily emphasize Perlmutter, especially its warnings about the lack of legislation. Instead of listing out-of-state court cases and living will laws, staff reports would increasingly be enriched with Florida cases.

Living will legislation received its major boost from the Florida courts in 1983 in the state's first case dealing with the rights of a legally incompetent, comatose, terminally ill patient who had executed a living will (*John F. Kennedy Memorial Hospital, Inc. v. Bludworth*). A Florida intermediate appellate court ruled that living wills provide evidence of a patient's intent and should be given weight by the trial courts, but also that the legal guardian of a comatose, terminally ill patient with a living will must apply to a trial court for authority to remove life-sustaining procedures. This ruling followed the reasoning of the Massachusetts Supreme Judicial Court in *Superintendent of Belchertown State School et al. v. Joseph Saikewicz,* which was decided in 1977 and is the nation's second appellate right to die decision. (This case is discussed more fully below in the analysis of the right to die in Massachusetts.)

The decision was immediately appealed to the Florida Supreme Court, but its ruling was not announced until May 24, 1984, two days after the Florida legislature passed a living will law. This was too quick for the law to have affected the court's written opinion and, in fact, the reverse process occurred. As will be discussed shortly, the court was widely expected to legalize living wills, and it motivated interest groups and legislators finally to act on their own.

Brain death. Besides being helped by the Florida court cases, the road to a living will law was smoothed by the legislature's decision in 1980 to redefine death as brain death, rather than the traditional definition which relied on the continued functioning of the circulatory and respiratory systems. Since these systems could be maintained through artificial means, a new definition of death was needed so that equipment could be removed from brain dead patients.

The FCC was involved in this issue as well and sought a definition that required total brain death. But the issue was handled as a technical modification of existing law. There is no record of support or opposition or committee testimony. Despite the routine nature of this bill, action on brain death spilled over into living wills. Bill sponsors distinguished between " 'pulling of the plug' which might ethically occur in cases of terminal unconsciousness and also in cases of brain death, but this is not the same thing." The legislature's bill file also included references to Perlmutter; *A Guide to Living Wills,* produced by the Society for the Right to Die; and the Quinlan case. Therefore, even though brain death and the withdrawal of treatment were stated to be different issues, discussion of the brain death bill included the idea of withdrawing medical treatment from the terminally ill or the permanently unconscious, and created linkage between the two policies.

111

Legislative Innovation

In preparation for the 1984 legislative session, committee staffers prominently presented the Florida intermediate appellate court ruling in the Bludworth living will case, and they summarized the main points of an amicus curia brief to be filed by the Florida Hospital Association when the case formally was placed before the Florida Supreme Court. The Florida Hospital Association was the first prominent, mainline, Florida interest group to support living will legislation. Its brief emphasized the need for legislation to remove the threat of criminal and civil liability from medical personnel and institutions that complied with a living will, and it linked medical costs to the right to die by including an estimate of the daily cost of maintaining terminally ill patients on life-support systems.

In September 1983 the lobbyist-lawyer for the FCC wrote to the clerk of the supreme court asking for an expedited decision in the case, which the court ignored. Later, the Conference also submitted an amicus brief to the supreme court, not arguing for reversal of the lower court—which seemed unlikely given the court's previous decision in Perlmutter—but for a narrow and limited decision. It urged the court to avoid a sweeping statement of policy, to limit its decision to this case only, and to avoid basing its decision on a constitutional right to privacy. Joining with the hospital association, the Conference urged that judicial approval not be required in each case before life-support systems could be withdrawn, but to keep the decision-making process with families and doctors.

The purpose of seeking a quick court decision was to give the FCC an opportunity in the 1984 session to obtain legislation limiting the impact of the court decision. But since the court refused to be rushed—and was likely to legalize living wills, but in an unknown way—court delay was perceived as silent pressure on the legislature and interest groups to draft legislation rather than wait for a judicial unknown. The FCC reluctantly abandoned its opposition to legislation and cooperated with bill sponsors to get the most limited living will law possible.

Two additional sources of influence affected the FCC attitude toward legislation. First, it perceived that public and professional support was steadily increasing for a living will law. For example, even though the Florida Medical Association never endorsed a bill, a growing list of doctors testified in favor of legislation each time a bill was filed, adding prestige to the proposals. Second, in the view of Catholic academicians, state courts increasingly were producing policies that promoted the right to die at a level well beyond that which state legislatures probably would approve if state Catholic conferences lobbied for restrictive provisions and participated actively in bill drafting (Paris and McCormick 1981). In the view of the FCC, Florida fit this description well and the FCC reconsidered its position early in 1984. The National Conference of Catholic Bishops indirectly endorsed this view later that year, not by calling for legislation, but by issuing a list of desirable legislative provisions for any state in which a living will law seemed likely to pass.

The executive director of the FCC communicated with Catholic dioceses in other states in order to locate laws that had been successfully influenced by the Catholic church. Florida relied heavily on Virginia's law, enacted in 1983, which the Virginia diocese sanctioned as an acceptable compromise between supporters and opponents. Important to the Florida Conference were a statement of intent supporting life; a requirement that sustenance (food and hydration) be provided to all patients; application of the law to terminal patients only; language against mercy killing; and nullification of a living will in the case of pregnancy. All of these provisions were included in Florida's law.

However, supporters were able to include procedures for withdrawing treatment from an incompetent terminally ill patient who had not executed a living will. Court-appointed guardians or another person previously designated in writing by the patient could make decisions on the patient's behalf; the patient's spouse and others were rank ordered in priority as having the authority to make treatment decisions in consultation with attending physicians. In the end, the FCC was officially neutral toward the law and there were no opponents.

As anticipated, the Florida Supreme Court legalized living wills, but the decision went further than the new state living will law and maintained the distinction between legislative and judicial streams of policy regarding the right to die. Since the policy of the two branches was different, additional political conflict and litigation was likely.

In addition to supporting living wills, the court allowed a patient's custodian to make decisions on behalf of an incompetent patient who had not executed a living will and to do so without prior court approval. But, the court policy also applies to terminal patients and those in a permanent vegetative state, whereas the state statute was limited to those who had been diagnosed terminally ill. The supreme court heavily cited the Quinlan decision of the New Jersey Supreme Court and a very similar Washington state decision (*In the Matter of the Welfare of Bertha Colyer*), which permitted the withdrawal of a respirator by a patient's family without prior court approval. This policy is different from that in Massachusetts, which the lower court had emphasized. Other restrictive provisions found in Florida's living will law were not addressed by the supreme court. In the absence of legislation, judicial policy would have left the use of living wills much more open and flexible.

Continuing Agenda

The living will issue did not end with the 1984 law. As in California, the law did not solve all of the problems, and new issues quickly reached the courts and kept the issue on the social and governmental agendas. The 1984 Florida act *excluded* the following treatments from the definition of life-prolonging procedures that could be terminated: "the provision of sustenance (food and hydration) and medication or performance of any medical procedure deemed necessary to provide comfort care or to alleviate pain." Presumably, if a procedure was not required to provide comfort care, it could be removed. However, it is unclear whether "deemed necessary to provide comfort care or to alleviate pain" covers artificial feeding and hydration *and* medicine and medical procedures, or whether it applies *only* to medicine and medical procedures, making it illegal under any conditions to withdraw artificial feeding and hydration from a terminal patient.

The courts. A case involving artificial feeding and hydration was brought to a Florida trial court in 1985. Thomas Corbett wanted artificial feeding and hydration stopped for his seventy-six-year-old wife, Helen, a nursing home resident who had been in a persistent vegetative state for three years following a massive stroke. Doctors agreed that there was no chance she would regain cognitive brain function. The trial court agreed that the feeding and hydration should be removed, but that it could not be done because the Florida living will statute prohibited the withdrawal of sustenance.

As in many other right to die cases, the patient died shortly before the trial court decision was announced, technically making the case moot, but the husband appealed because the issue was an important one which needed to be clarified. In April 1986 the intermediate appellate court reversed the decision of the trial court and stated that artificial feeding was similar to other medical procedures used to keep patients alive and all could be withdrawn under the Florida statute (*Corbett v. D'Alessandro*). The state supreme court declined to hear an appeal by the state.

A similar case, but with somewhat different circumstances, was brought before another trial court in the same judicial district in 1988. Suffering from a massive stroke, eighty-nine-year-old Estelle Browning previously had signed a living will that included a request for no artificial feeding, but she nevertheless was being kept alive through feeding tubes. However, she was not terminal and she appeared to lapse into and out of consciousness, although one physician described her condition as a permanent vegetative state. All agreed she was incompetent and unable to communicate. While in the nursing home, Mrs. Browning suffered massive chronic complications including serious bed sores, vomiting, bleeding, and other problems.

The trial court ruled that it could not order the withdrawal of artificial feeding under the statute since the patient was not terminal, but the appellate court ruled that while the statute did not provide a solution, Florida's constitutional right to privacy permitted a guardian to make decisions on behalf of the patient. Moreover, this court went further than others when it ruled the patient does not have to be terminal or in a vegetative state. Important for agenda setting, the court included a call for legislation and urged that treatment decisions be made with input from family, friends, doctors, hospitals, and others who may have information about the wishes of an incompetent patient. The intermediate appellate court also certified the issue to the state supreme court, which agreed to decide the case (*In re Guardianship of Browning v. State of Florida*). However, the case was not decided until September 1990, many months after the Florida legislature amended the 1984 living will law.

Legislature. These intermediate appellate court decisions put the food and hydration issue back on the legislative agenda. In 1987 liberal Democratic south Florida legislators proposed an amendment specifying that sustenance needed for comfort care or to alleviate pain shall be administered, but also that sustenance was a medical procedure which could be withdrawn if a patient wishes. The FCC lobbied vigorously against the bill and it was defeated in the House by a few votes. Conservatives on the Senate Rules Committee kept the bill from receiving consideration in that chamber. However, despite continued opposition from the FCC, a similar amendment passed in both houses of the legislature in 1988. The difference seems to have been due to the personal crusade of a south Florida nurses aide who organized a letter writing and telephone campaign to contact each state legislator on the need for the food and hydration amendment. No one since Dr. Walter Sackett worked so diligently to enact a right to die measure. The amendment would have made the living will law consistent with court opinions.

However, as in California, Governor Bob Martinez, a conservative Republican, vetoed the legislation. Ironically, in view of the supreme court's denial of a review of the earlier Corbett case, the governor stated that the amendment came too soon since the state supreme court had not yet ruled on this issue in the pending Browning case. More likely, however, the governor was acting according to his own publicly aired right to life beliefs and his perceived conservative constituency. Florida Right to Life was credited with organizing a massive letter-writing campaign opposing the amendment.

In 1990 the same group of legislators again introduced a similar food and hydration amendment. But, as amended in compromise with Republicans and conservative Democrats, the bill permits the family of the patient with a living will to block a doctor's order to disconnect feeding tubes for an undefined "reasonable" period of time. This time Governor Martinez signed the bill. The FCC did not oppose the amended bill since, similar to its view regarding the enactment of the 1986 law, it was a limited change that did not go as far as the intermediate appellate court decision in the Browning case, which it expected the state supreme court soon to affirm.

As anticipated, in 1990 the Florida Supreme Court approved the intermediate appellate court decision in Browning (*In re Guardianship of Estelle M. Browning*). Citing a long list of similar decisions accumulating in other states as well as its own precedents, it declared that the right to privacy included freedom from unwanted medical treatment and that this right was not limited or qualified by distinctions between major or minor, ordinary or extraordinary, life-prolonging, or other categories of treatment. It affirmed that all seriously ill patients had the same rights to refuse medical treatment under all circumstances, be they incompetent and unconscious, competent and capable of communicating their wishes, or incapacitated in some other way. Surrogate decision makers do not need to obtain prior judicial approval before making treatment decisions for incompetent patients who previously had expressed their desires either orally or in writing. Living wills or other advance directives are to be followed. The court concluded with a hope that the decision would spur individuals to express their wishes concerning final medical treatment clearly and completely. The FCC viewed the decision as extreme and dangerous.

The Browning decision does not address the 1990 legislative provision allowing a patient's next of kin to negate a decision to withhold or withdraw artificially administered food and hydration for a period of time. This provision seemingly conflicts with the judicially granted power of a patient or his or her surrogate to make decisions that carry out the patient's previously expressed wishes. Future litigation may test this provision.

Administrative agencies. Legislative and judicial struggles over defining the right to die have spilled over into the state administrative agenda as well. Following the 1986 Corbett case and the defeat of the 1987 legislative amendment, the state Department of Health and Rehabilitative Services (HRS) began to review its policies regarding the feeding of nursing home residents. Prior to Corbett, state licensure law required that all nursing home patients be provided adequate nutrition, including the artificial administration of food and fluids, if necessary. Refusal to accept feeding would result in the discharge of the patient. The director of licensing and regulation formed a study group that included several HRS staffers as well as nursing home and FCC lobbyists. These groups were identified by HRS as a result of their routine lobbying of HRS personnel on a variety of health issues. The FCC was prominent in getting the group organized, setting its agenda, and in getting specific rules adopted.

The study group proposed a new policy regarding food and hydration, which went into effect in 1988. The new rules permit the withdrawal of feeding if the patient is terminal and death is imminent, language similar to the state's living will law. Family or judicially appointed guardians may make decisions on behalf of unconscious terminally ill patients. Conscious patients who are terminal may refuse food and fluids but HRS is to be notified when a patient has refused to accept sustenance, and the rules provide various procedures to encourage them to accept nutrition and hydration.

However, the new rules do not cover patients in a persistent vegetative state nor do they define when death is imminent. Certain HRS staff members believed that death is imminent when it is expected to occur within sixty days, but the FCC lobbyist believed that death is imminent when it occurs within a few days. In his view, the new HRS policy was designed only for patients in their final days; people in a vegetative state were not covered.

The FCC dominated the formulation of the nursing home rules. Nursing home organizations, such as the Florida Association of Homes for the Aging, are divided on the right to die and are reluctant or are unable to take firm positions on this or other right to die issues. The right to die also is only one of several of their concerns.

Nursing homes frequently are organized according to religion, and there is no agreement among them on the right to die. Jewish nursing homes are sensitive to policies that smack of early withdrawal of care or euthanasia since some residents had relatives who died during the Holocaust. Catholic nursing homes adhere to the position of the FCC and view withdrawal of food and fluids as a step toward active euthanasia. Protestant denominations also are divided. Consequently, the nursing home organizations avoid controversy and concentrate on clarifying governmental policy for individual nursing home residents. This leaves the policy-making field open to well-organized, internally cohesive, and well-funded groups, for whom the right to die is a core part of their political mission—particularly the FCC.

Neither HRS officials nor private organizations have sought to define when death is imminent, leaving some terminally ill and other unconscious patients in nursing homes and hospices subject to required artificially administered food and fluids under HRS rules. However, the Browning decision stimulated HRS staff and attorneys, and nursing home and FCC lobbyists to begin once again to consider forming a new study group to revise feeding and hydration policy.

No last word. The struggle for the last word on the right to die shifts back and forth between the courts and the legislature, and recently has involved the bureaucracy as well. Judges generally have expanded patients' rights to control their own treatment while conservative legislators and interest groups seek to limit it. The power of administrative agencies to make rules for nursing homes also has encouraged lobbyists who generally have been successful in the legislature, but not the courts, to lobby the executive branch. Administrative agencies are very important because they translate the broad language of legislation and judicial opinions into rules for the day-to-day implementation of general policies, and they ultimately control how government policies are put into effect by individuals and institutions under their jurisdiction. The right to die increasingly has become relevant to all segments of state government.

The strategy of the FCC, which has been the most prominent force in Florida's right to die politics, is to resist enlarging the right to die until expansive judicial policy is expected. Then, the FCC compromises on legislative measures that do not go as far as the appellate courts. However, when threatened by expansive legislative amendment, as in 1987, the FCC seeks to limit its impact by lobbying administrative agencies for restrictive rules.

Overall, the right to die has expanded and is continually being reinvented in Florida, not in smooth continuous steps but as a result of sporadic battles in all three branches of government. Conflicts over the legislature's 1990 food and hydration provision, HRS rules concerning the feeding of nursing home residents, and expansive judicial interpretations of individuals' rights are likely to enter the trial courts and the right to die will remain on Florida's agenda.

Massachusetts: Active Agenda, Limited and Late Innovation

The right to die reached the Massachusetts governmental agenda through the personal interest of various legislators. One of the early sponsors was motivated by a 1977 court case in his own district involving a brain dead teenager injured in an automobile accident who was being maintained on life-support systems. The county medical examiner had refused to permit their removal due to concern for the legal rights of the motorist who had caused the accident.

Bills have been introduced in every legislative session since 1975, and they have passed the House of Representatives several times since 1983. However, nearly all bills have died in Senate commit-tees. One that went to the floor was defeated 24 to 9. As in other states, the Massachusetts Catholic Conference has been the main and the most powerful opponent to the right to die—so powerful, in fact, that the right to die in Massachusetts is largely a story of the Catholic church and its key spokesman in the state senate.

With consistent and predictable defeats, it perhaps is surprising that the issue has remained on the governmental agenda, for when policies are routinely rejected, proponents sometimes give up and go on to other issues. But the right to die has remained on the agenda partly because of a steady stream of appellate cases (their number is equaled only in a few other states). Consequently, al-though living will bills did not become law, the courts made deci-sions that provided news stories and support for those seeking to keep the issue on the legislative agenda. Increasingly, the courts have been an alternative forum for obtaining governmental policy sup-porting the right to die, and they have affected the political position of the Catholic church.

Judicial Innovation and Agenda Maintenance

Heightened interest in the right to die was spurred by an innovative 1977 Massachusetts Supreme Judicial Court decision (*Superintendent of Belchertown State School et al. v. Joseph Saikewicz*). In the nation's second state supreme court case on the right to die, the Massachusetts court permitted a state hospital to withhold leukemia treatment from an elderly, severely retarded patient. But, unlike the New Jersey Supreme Court in Quinlan, the court required state trial courts to retain final decision-making authority regarding withdrawing or withholding treatment from incompetent patients. Court-appointed guardians would have to petition the courts for treatment decisions in each case.

The Saikewicz decision caused much concern among doctors and lawyers (Doudera and Peters 1982) and motivated some, including faculty of the Harvard Medical School, to testify in favor of living will bills. A living will law was needed, in their view, to allow people to plan in advance and to eliminate the cumbersome, costly, and emotionally devastating need to go to court.

In 1978, six months after Saikewicz, a Massachusetts court of appeals ruled that resuscitation could be withheld from an advanced Alzheimer's patient, and that not all cases involving medical treatment for the terminally ill or comatose needed to be taken to court (*In re Dinnerstein*). But it provided few guidelines for making such decisions. In 1980 the state supreme court permitted the withdrawal of kidney dialysis from an elderly and senile patient, but it too was vague concerning which cases required judicial intervention (*In re Spring*). Each of these decisions relied primarily on the supreme court's previous policy in Saikewicz, although the court was seeking ways of modifying that ruling.

Then, in 1986, the supreme court ruled on ending the artificial administration of food and hydration to a patient in a permanent vegetative state, but who was not elderly or terminally ill. Paul Brophy, age forty-five, suffered a massive brain hemorrhage as a result of an aneurysm. Following surgery, he did not regain consciousness. However, he could breathe on his own and was being kept alive through an implanted stomach tube. His wife sued to have the feeding stopped. Recognizing a substantial right to privacy and the power of guardians to act on behalf of patients, the court ordered the feeding stopped and Brophy died within a few days (*Brophy v. New England Sinai Hospital, Inc.*).

This time the Court ignored the issue of determining which medical cases required prior judicial involvement, and the Massachusetts court joined the mainstream of most other courts that have permitted the withholding or withdrawal of treatment without requiring judicial intervention or other cumbersome procedures. It relied heavily, not on its own prior cases, but on the innovative New Jersey decision (*In re Conroy*) decided the previous year which permitted the withdrawal of artificially administered food and hydration.

All these cases—but especially Brophy, because it was an early case dealing with food and hydration as medical treatment—were reported in the news media continuously as they moved through the court system. Between May 1985 and December 1986, thirty-seven news articles on court cases appeared in the *Boston Globe*—twice as many as all other right to die news stories, and witnesses testifying before the state legislature referred to these cases as evidence of the need for comprehensive legislation.

While the Massachusetts courts have made innovative decisions that contributed to maintaining the right to die on the governmental agenda, unlike those in California and Florida, they have not called for legislation. The Massachusetts judges have limited their opinions to the facts of the individual cases, and their policy statements regarding judicial intervention required to withdraw treatment have been vague. Also, none of their cases have involved living wills nor have they endorsed them in their opinions. They have allowed judicial and legislative agendas and policy to remain separate and apart.

Various lawyers, medical school faculty, and other commentators in Massachusetts have argued that living wills are valid due to the trend in judicial policy, but others claim that without legislation doctors and medical institutions are not required to follow patients' wishes. The lack of clear guidance from the courts and explicit and urgent calls for legislation may contribute to the Massachusetts Senate's refusal to enact a law. One Senate opponent said that he opposed living will bills and preferred, instead, to have the courts make decisions on a case-by-case basis (*Boston Globe,* 23 September 1986, 25).

Legislature: Powerful Sponsor, Powerful Opponent

In 1980 Representative Richard Voke, Chairman of the House Ways and Means Committee and a prominent legislative leader, took up the right to die as his personal agenda. Until recently, he has filed legislation every year. Reportedly, Representative Voke's mother was a registered nurse who became very interested and concerned about the right to die due to her long experience in hospital nursing. A representative of the Massachusetts Catholic Conference gives Voke the major credit for getting the bill through the House. If the bill had been introduced by a less senior legislator, its chances of success would have been reduced.

Although there are parallels between Representative Voke's steadfast sponsorship and political power and Senator Keene's influence in California, interest group support in Massachusetts has been sporadic and divided and Representative Voke has not been able to move the Catholic conference. In 1985 the state medical association indirectly endorsed living wills by issuing guidelines for withdrawing treatment, but they have not worked for legislation. The state hospital association endorsed legislation in 1983, but also has not campaigned for enactment. Other groups have registered support over the years, including the Silver Haired Legislature, the state director of Elder Affairs, and others, but there is no evidence of a long-term, orchestrated political campaign to get the living will bill through the legislature. Sometimes group support has been revealed only in letters of endorsement to legislative committees, and even then with hesitation or objection to particular provisions.

The main explanation for the lukewarm and erratic support is the pervasive influence of religion on social issues. With its large Catholic population, many health care and other organizations are divided along religious lines, and Protestant and Catholic members are unable to agree on a living will measure. In addition, while certain groups, such as nurses and social workers, are sympathetic to living will legislation, their organizations are preoccupied with issues that are more salient to their members, leaving active support

123

for living wills to unspecified others. When living will bills are routinely defeated, these groups in particular move on to other concerns.

Recently, the Massachusetts Council of Churches added the living will and durable power of attorney for health care to its legislative agenda. Since it is a Protestant organization, it can avoid religious divisions within its ranks, but its main opponent will be the Catholic conference, which makes the right to die an explicit Catholic-Protestant issue.

Outside Strategy

There is no evidence that medical or other professionals ever controlled or tried to limit debate over the right to die. Instead, the issue quickly tapped the deeply held religious beliefs of ready opponents. Since the late 1970s Boston area radio and television stations generally favored living will laws through editorials, but they also have had open forums for listeners to call in and they have invited various medical experts to appear on talk shows. Some endorsed living wills, but others, representing Catholic or Protestant fundamentalist right to life views, raised emotional arguments against them.

While they are vocal, outspoken fundamentalist Protestants are not a significant force in Massachusetts politics. In contrast, the Catholic church has direct access and enormous influence in the legislature, and all observers and participants agree that it is able to block or postpone legislation that it opposes. Its access is assured by several factors. First, the Catholic constituency of Massachusetts is the second largest in the United States—the population is over 50 percent Catholic, second only to Rhode Island. Its size alone guarantees that state officials will pay close attention to Catholic policy positions. Of course, many members of the legislature are Catholic and are sympathetic to church preferences. The Boston diocese is the largest in the state and the Catholic conference largely transmits its conservative point of view to the legislature. Also, unlike the California Catholic leadership, the Massachusetts hierarchy is much more uniform, cohesive, and consistent in championing conservative Catholic positions.

The main obstacle to the living will in the legislature has been Senate President William M. Bulger. Senator Bulger and Representative Voke both are Catholics, but Senator Bulger represents a working-class and socially conservative south Boston district. He is reported to directly represent church interests in the legislature. Generally, there have been many political conflicts between House and Senate leaders, and Representative Voke and Senator Bulger have had their share. Recently, Representative Voke has urged other representatives to sponsor the living will in order to remove the stigma of his close connection to the bill.

Senator Bulger has been Senate President for a decade, and he is an experienced and adept politician and parliamentarian. The Massachusetts Senate president has substantial control over committee assignments and chairmanships and has indirect power, therefore, on the flow of legislation. He has appointed loyal supporters to committee chairmanships, which earn legislators an extra $7,500 per year, and opponents and reformers seem unable to round up support for measures that Senator Bulger opposes. A former senator has described his political clout and style this way:

> The positive exercise of power he reserves for those who are loyalists . . . so it's not that he kills your bill. He just . . . leaves you to try to shepherd it through, and by and large, most people know that unless you've gotten a green light somewhere, it's not going to go anywhere. So, you shepherding it through is pretty much a dead-end process. (*Boston Globe,* 21 September 1988:1)

Despite continued rejection, various participants in Massachusetts living will politics have believed that legislation would pass one day. One factor is growing popular and professional support for legislation, both among Catholics and Protestants. As in the rest of the nation, polls in Massachusetts indicate a division of opinion among the Catholic laity on controversial issues, and reveal that the Catholic rank and file is not a cohesive unit that uniformly supports the conservative positions of the Church. A majority of Catholics and non-Catholics alike have opposed various restrictions on abortion, for example. The Massachusetts Catholic church also lags behind other state Catholic organizations and the National Conference of Catholic Bishops on living will laws. As discussed earlier, the National Conference has signaled its reluctant acceptance of living will laws. Some observers also believe that Senator Bulger has become more receptive to legislation as a result of the recent death of his mother.

Outsiders to insiders. Early in 1989 spokespersons for the Massachusetts Council of Churches observed that a proxy decision maker for health care bill might pass more easily since it is a fresh idea and an alternative to the living will, which had been on the agenda for more than a decade. The Catholic church has shown no signs of changing its position on the living will and supporters are growing weary of unending losing battles. Also, as in California, the proxy is a simpler idea that easily could be adapted from the general durable power of attorney that is used for many personal financial matters. Finally, a new proposal might be the vehicle for a new political coalition that avoids conflict along religious lines.

Later in 1989 representatives of the Massachusetts Council of Churches, the family of Paul Brophy, and associations representing nurses and the elderly began to organize an effort to enact a proxy law. But the bill remained in committee at the end of a busy legislative session that concentrated on Massachusetts's battered economy and state budget deficit. The group renewed its campaign in 1990 and a law was passed in December.

This time Senator Bulger invited the outsiders to come inside by agreeing not to block the bill if the supporters also agreed not to alert the mass media to their campaign and to keep their lobbying low-key and quiet. This strategy allowed legislation to pass while not advertising that Bulger had changed positions or creating an image that he had been defeated by old supporters of the living will. The participants appear to have abided by this informal agreement, for only two articles appeared in the *Boston Globe* on the proxy bill. Both were published after the house and senate had resolved differences on the bill, and they announced agreement and touted an "unusual show of unity" among the usual combatants (*Boston Globe*, 28 June 1990, 29:2; 10 August 1990, 19:3).

Senator Bulger's shift also occurred because the Catholic bishops reluctantly agreed not to oppose the bill. There were several reasons for their new posture. First, as in Florida, the Catholic church viewed the Massachusetts's Supreme Judicial Court's decision in Brophy, which permitted the withdrawal of artificial feeding and hydration from an individual who did not have a living will, as a very threatening decision. Legislation of some sort was viewed as a way of heading off additional ominous judicial policy. Second, the proponents of living wills had not abandoned their efforts to enact legislation and there was evidence that their support was growing. The Church recognized that a living will bill might pass one day despite its steadfast opposition. Third, the U.S. Supreme Court announced its Cruzan decision in June while the proxy bill was in committee, and the house passed it the same day. The Church interpreted Cruzan as calling for state policy regarding evidence of patients' wishes, and it seemed that legislation of some sort would soon be inevitable. By the time of Cruzan, the right to die had so permeated the social agenda that even the powerful and conservative Massachusetts Catholic hierarchy believed it no longer could flatly refuse to accept some form of legislation.

The Catholic church preferred the health proxy bill to the living will because the health proxy came closest to reflecting Catholic policy on the right to die. Unlike the living will, in which an individual states his or her preferences regarding various forms of medical treatment, the proxy or durable power of attorney for health care allows and encourages communication and dialogue concerning medical treatment between an individual and his representative, who presumably would be family or very close friends. The Church has maintained that health care decisions ought to be kept private, between patients, family, and doctors, and the health care proxy permits that.

Continued Catholic influence. Although the Catholic church accepted the proxy bill, it obtained crucial amendments in the senate to the house version. These amendments limit the options of proxies and secure continuing Catholic priorities. Most other state health proxy or durable power of attorney laws allow a person to simply designate another to make health care decisions in the event the person is unable to communicate his or her own wishes. No special limitations are imposed on the kinds of treatment decisions that might be made. The Massachusetts law, however, allows the attending physician to decide which treatments are necessary "to provide comfort care or pain alleviation." Similar provisions in living will laws often have been interpreted to require the artificial administration of food and hydration.

The law also allows doctors, nurses, other health workers, and medical institutions motivated by religious beliefs or religious policies to refuse to honor the proxy, although patients are required to be transferred to other facilities that will abide by the proxy's decisions. If another institution is unavailable or unwilling to accept the patient, the medical institution is required to obtain a judicial ruling on the impasse before taking further action. These provisions permit health care providers motivated by Catholic or other religious beliefs to avoid withdrawing treatment, and treatment decisions likely will be delayed while judicial proceedings are begun to resolve the conflict. Finally, in contrast with the house version, which eliminated legal liability for *complying* with a proxy's directions, the law absolves health care providers from all legal liability and discriminatory and punitive action for *refusing to comply* with a proxy's directions. Therefore, the law's emphasis is on allowing health care providers to resist a proxy's decisions rather than on an assumption that they will be carried out.

If comfort care is interpreted to mean the artificial administration of food and hydration as well as other remedies, the new statute conflicts with Massachusetts judicial policy, which permits the withdrawal of all treatment including food and hydration. Additional disputes are bound to arise when individuals challenge the limitations of the proxy law in court. The policy-making process will continue and the right to die will remain on the Massachusetts agenda.

Conclusion

The right to die is not routine policy that can be put into place through an inside strategy. Living will laws have been controversial in all three states, and well-established, conservative interest groups that routinely monitor the flow of legislation have vigorously opposed all proposals. The only exception in these case studies is the durable power of attorney law in California, which passed easily because it avoided the detail of living will legislation and was made to appear an extension of existing law.

Contrary to one theory of agenda setting, political conflict was not responsible for getting the issue on the government agenda. Rather, individual legislators, whose personal experience sensitized them to the right to die, submitted all bills. Interest groups tried to keep the issue off the agenda by arguing that legislation was not needed and by linking living will laws to active euthanasia and other much broader—and sometimes bizarre—social concerns. However, once a living will law seemed likely to pass, interest groups worked to be sure that their priorities were represented in the law. California's earliest law, Florida's later legislation, and the recent Massachusetts proxy law all reflect demands from powerful groups for the most limited legislation possible.

The political skills and tenacity of policy sponsors are crucial in agenda setting and innovation. Despite early defeats, bill sponsors in all three states tried repeatedly to enact living will laws. Senator Keene was successful more quickly in California, but others in Florida and Massachusetts have played a critical role in keeping the issue on the agenda. There is no evidence that policy sponsors in these states coordinated their strategies with national organizations or with their counterparts in other states. No clear policy or communications network existed. National organizations, particularly the Society for the Right to Die, were mentioned by many participants as sources for information, but state politicians and local groups were largely on their own in getting laws passed. Bill sponsors also sometimes were aware of the activities of legislators in other states, but they were not part of a national effort to enact living will laws.

The ideology of policy sponsors and opposing interest groups also is critical. In an outside strategy, keeping control of an issue is very difficult for bill sponsors. California's skilled and pragmatic sponsor, who carefully softened up and compromised with the opposition, contrasts sharply with Florida's more impulsive and extreme advocate; and in Massachusetts, a liberal committee chair with substantial support in his own legislative chamber ran into an equally or more powerful and steadfast conservative opponent in the other house. Only additional signals that right to die legislation was in the air motivated the conservative Catholic church to modify its opposition in these two states.

State political contexts may temper the ideology of the participants. In California the general population and the Catholic church was not as homogeneous as in Florida and Massachusetts, and although the California Catholic hierarchy preferred no legislation, it did not believe that it could control policy-making. It quickly saw the need for compromise to get the most limited law possible. In contrast, Florida's generally conservative political environment created few popular or professional pressures for a living will law, and in Massachusetts the Catholic church is a major power in state politics. The Catholic conferences in these two states had little reason to compromise their ideology and cooperate on legislation. Both Catholic conferences finally shifted positions only for strategic reasons related to the direction of state court and U.S. Supreme Court decisions.

Right to die policy is not the sole domain of state legislatures, and interaction between legislatures and courts is very important in agenda setting and innovation. The courts are alternatives to legislatures as sources of governmental policy and their decisions have as much or even more impact as lawful mandates for behavior. Individuals and groups use courts and legislatures differently depending on where they believe they can win what they want. Since they are much more insulated from lobbying and other political pressures, judicial decisions sometimes run contrary to the desires of otherwise powerful groups; yet their potential impact as alternative sources of available policies has to be taken into account by opponents.

Interest groups and individuals who lack access or fail to win in the legislature frequently go to court or sponsor the cases of others in order to have another chance at winning. Alternatively, groups and representatives who block legislative lawmaking may change their strategy when faced with court decisions that accomplish what they have been trying to stop in the legislative branch. Then they turn to the legislature or the bureaucracy to limit or undo what the courts have put into place.

Although the right to die was on the public and governmental agendas before major court decisions appeared, state appellate court innovation has contributed mightily to agenda maintenance and placing pressure on legislatures to enact right to die policies and to keeping the issue before the public. In California the legislature acted first, but intermediate appellate courts heard cases with new issues that emphasized the deficiencies of legislation. The timing of the New Jersey Supreme Court's Quinlan decision, coming a few months before the enactment of California's law, also created a window of opportunity for the bill sponsor. In Florida courts placed pressure on a reluctant legislature by promising its own living will and related right to die policy. However, in Massachusetts, courts did not link judicial decisions to legislation. They placed no explicit pressure on the legislature to enact a law, although the state supreme court's expansive food and hydration decision was viewed by Catholic lobbyists as a reason to accept legislation.

The case studies also provide insight into the links among the states in agenda setting and innovation. Significantly, California's law had an enormous impact on agenda setting in other states. The year following enactment, seven other states adopted living will laws, sometimes closely copying the California legislation, and most other states considered living will bills. Since these other enactments occurred so soon after the California law was passed, the amount of softening up necessary for getting these bills through the legislature probably was much less than what was needed to get California's law on the books. In time, policy-making in other states also had a reciprocal effect on innovation. By the time California passed its revised but vetoed living will bill, many states had enacted laws that were much more progressive or facilitative of the right to die. These laws, plus the policy positions of national interest groups, influenced the content of California's proposed revisions. Florida's living will law reflects the current state of policy in the 1980s and the influence of national trends in judicial policy-making. Consequently, there is interaction between the political context and events and personalities in a particular state and national political trends on innovation.

However, while early agenda setting seems to speed up agenda setting and innovation elsewhere, agenda setting and innovation are not interchangeable concepts or the same behaviors. The case studies reveal that the right to die was on the public and governmental

131

agendas in California, Florida, and Massachusetts at about the same time, but innovation in this policy was very different in the three states. Once items are placed on the agenda, agenda maintenance, careful strategy, ideology, and political context are all important in moving a proposal toward policy adoption.

5 The Right
to Die
in Court

In the previous chapters I discussed the origins and rise of the right to die as a social and political issue, and how right to die policy developed and evolved in three states. In this and the following chapter I look broadly at the development of right to die policy in all the states, first through an examination of state judicial policy, where the right to die received its earliest official recognition, and next in state legislatures. Together these two chapters survey the overall patterns of policy innovation in the states and the factors that are associated with state government decisions to create right to die policies.

Although I treat courts and legislatures separately, policy-making in the two institutions is politically intertwined, and I shall refer to the connections between courts and legislatures as well as the influence of national political events in both of these chapters. I have found no states in which governors have put the right to die on the governmental agenda. Therefore, as discussed in the previous chapter, the role of governors is largely limited to approving or vetoing legislation.

I examine courts first because court decisions frequently have motivated interest groups and state legislatures to act. Some courts have created right to die policies because legislatures have failed to act, and in several early decisions courts called for comprehensive legislation as a more systematic way for dealing with the right to die. As discussed in the previous chapter, the Florida legislature appeared to take action only when the state supreme court was prepared to create its own living will policy after having called for legislation in several written opinions. The Massachusetts legislature delayed action until the lengthy accumulation of judicial policy—particularly the U.S. Supreme Court's Cruzan decision—spelled out the future of the right to die more fully. In California, however, the state legislature enacted a living will law before a right to die case reached the appellate courts. Then, however, courts interpreted the law and substantially expanded the scope of the right to die. As more and more states enact living will and durable power of attorney for health care laws, the courts have more opportunities to expand the scope of their decision making to include the interpretation of state statutes.

As discussed in chapter 2, political theories of agenda setting and policy innovation offer fragmented images of the policy-making process. The two often appear as separate and isolated parts of the political system, rather than linked segments of a continuous stream of political activity. In a dynamic and comprehensive model of the political process, however, political demands from the mass and professional agendas are converted into innovations, and new policies constantly generate new pressures for fresh solutions to old and new problems.

However, research on the adoption and diffusion of policy innovations also tends to ignore much of the policy-making process. Instead of portraying a continuous process of early policy-making and later reformulation, innovation research usually examines the initial adoption of a presumed uniform policy and its diffusion among states or local governments, or on how deeply a particular innovation has penetrated government at a particular point in time. Researchers have given little attention to the likely alteration of policy during the diffusion process by other governments, later revisions or renovations by the early adopters, and resulting variations in the content of policies among governments that adopt a particular type of policy.

In this chapter I show that many state courts have made policies in the right to die and, although the broad outlines of judicial policy are similar, the courts have distinctive orientations to withholding and withdrawing treatment. There is no uniform policy for the nation or one model for future court decisions. These varied judicial policies also have different consequences for citizens of each of the states. Courts that decided right to die cases soon after New Jersey's landmark Quinlan decision created somewhat different policies that are reinventions or modifications of New Jersey's core innovation. Moreover, while New Jersey and the other early innovators are among the courts generally identified as the most innovative or the leading state supreme courts, their decisions have had unequal impacts on following courts. Most later adopting courts followed New Jersey's lead, but others did not and these cases have created policy alternatives. Finally, in a later second wave of reinvention the state courts substantially broadened the right to die beyond its original scope. Continuous reinvention of policy during diffusion underscores the view that the chronology of the adoption of new policies is but a partial view of the policy-making process.

I have identified and coded data through 1990 from all state supreme court decisions and the few decisions of intermediate appellate courts in states in which the highest court has not heard a case in this field. The decisions of intermediate appellate courts are included because they represent the final appellate judicial authority on this issue in certain states. In addition to the date of each decision, which is used to examine the chronology of diffusion, I analyzed the content of each majority opinion to obtain explicit policy statements concerning the rights of patients and families.

In addition, since the diffusion of policy depends upon communications among courts, I also have identified and counted all citations to previous right to die precedents and the amount of space devoted to each one. I also have identified precedents that were considered binding by the courts by noting explicit statements in majority opinions where a previous case or cases heavily influenced a later majority to adopt its decision. These measures are used to establish the policy linkages among courts, their impact on each other, and differences in the development of judicial policy.

This chapter has four main sections. The first examines the chronological diffusion of innovations, the influence of national events on the flow of litigation, and the relationship of early innovation in the right to die to other studies of judicial leadership and innovation. The second section explores policy reinvention during

135

the diffusion process and the importance of precedent as an indicator of a court's policy leadership. The third examines the role of interest groups in litigation, and the fourth surveys the links between courts and legislatures.

Diffusion of Judicial Innovations

The structure of judicial institutions presents a unique problem to the study of the chronology of judicial innovations. Unlike most studies of the diffusion of legislative policy, the leading study of judicial innovation found little relationship between judicial innovation in dozens of tort policies (liability and damage cases) and variations among state social and political characteristics (Canon and Baum 1981). The authors suggest that this reflects the idiosyncrasies of policy-making opportunities that are unique to the courts. Unlike legislatures, courts are passive institutions and they must wait for problems to come to them via litigation. Since people bring cases as it suits them, and not the courts, the subject matter of court cases and subsequent judicial policy is largely beyond the control of judges. Consequently, happenstance and chance lead people to court in one state but not in another, and the social and political context surrounding the courts has little impact on generating judicial business.

Legislatures and administrators, in contrast, are able to be much more active and purposeful in policy-making. Upon becoming aware of innovations in other states with which they identify or feel they have something in common, they may decide to put a similar item on their official governmental agenda. When a certain number of adopters, usually about 30 percent, have embraced a particular innovation, others get on the bandwagon quickly and rapid take-off occurs in the rate of state adoptions (Rogers 1962; 1983). Since legislatures and administrators often copy their counterparts in neighboring or other similar states, there often is a relationship between the tendency to innovate and the social and political characteristics of the states. As discussed in chapter 2, early legislative innovators tend to be states that are heavily urban, industrial, with high median incomes and education, and with substantial political

competition, all environmental characteristics that are likely to produce novel political ideas and new public issues (Walker 1969).

But the contrast between courts and legislatures should not be
carried too far, for there is theory that leads in the opposite direction. States with complex and diverse societies and economies and
political competition are more likely to generate new demands for
courts as well as legislatures than states with traditional and homogeneous environments (Atkins and Glick 1976; Baum and Canon
1982; Caldeira 1985). Therefore, certain states are likely to rank
high repeatedly as *early* policy innovators. In addition, national political events external to individual states stimulate similar litigation
throughout the country (Nelson 1984; Jacob 1988), and it is likely
that these events will motivate litigants and groups in states with
complex and heterogenous political and social environments earlier
than in traditional and uniform settings. Therefore, patterns of innovation in the right to die may be more similar to patterns of innovation in other fields of policy than we might predict from previous judicial innovation research.

Timing of Innovation

The first task in studying innovation is to examine the adoption of
policies over time. Here, I examine the chronology of diffusion for
three purposes: to reveal how quickly new judicial policy has spread
among the state courts; to suggest the impact of national political
events on litigation, which provides the courts with policy-making
opportunities; and to relate innovation in this field of law to other
measures of judicial leadership.

Figure 5.1 tracks the expanding flow of right to die cases into
state appellate courts with three graphs. The solid line represents
the cumulative frequency over time, i.e., all cases decided by a certain year; the dashed line indicates the number of cases decided each
year; and the dotted line reveals the frequency of initial decisions
annually in each of the states. The purpose of the third frequency is
to distinguish between the annual production of cases and the entry
of new courts into this policy field. Subsequent decisions by the
same court are excluded from this third frequency. New Jersey and
Massachusetts led the nation with the first right to die decisions in

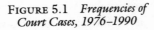

FIGURE 5.1 *Frequencies of Court Cases, 1976–1990*

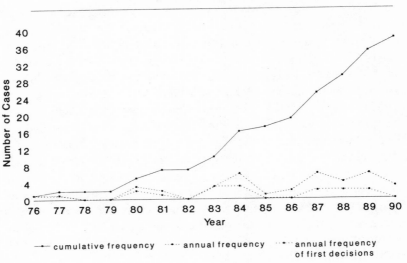

1976 and 1977. No additional appellate cases were decided until 1980 and the pace of litigation declined until 1983. In that year cases surged, followed by a substantial increase in 1984 and beyond. From 1984 to 1990, as indicated by the larger separation between the annual and first decision frequencies, several state courts made additional decisions beyond their preliminary entry into this policy field and the number of court decisions remained high to the end of the decade. Following my criteria of case selection, from 1976 to 1990 courts in seventeen states had made thirty-eight right to die decisions. (Additional intermediate appellate court decisions have been made in several of these states.)

The cumulative frequency of court cases resembles the beginnings of an S-shaped curve in which there is a lull following the earliest innovations, a second but modest increase in activity, followed later by a surge in policy adoptions (Rogers 1962; 1983; Gray 1973; Mahajan and Peterson 1985). Rogers has identified the surge or take-off point as coming after 20 to 30 percent of the adopters have sanctioned an innovation. However, after most adopters have joined the earlier innovators, adoptions typically slow and some potential users never get on the bandwagon. In the case of the right to die several states joined New Jersey and Massachusetts between 1980 and 1982, but a greater number of adoptions came in 1983 and beyond. By 1983 state appellate courts had decided over one-quarter of all cases decided to the end of 1990. The diffusion curve has not flattened off, however, since the states are in the midst of diffusion, and it is unclear how the curve will develop. However, given the complexity and controversy of treatment withdrawal decisions and the U.S. Supreme Court's acceptance of Missouri's strict evidence requirement regarding patients' wishes—but the Court's apparent willingness to accept a variety of other state policies on this issue—it is very likely that additional litigation will reach the state courts, and the current surge in cases will continue.

Spurs to innovation. The spurts in judicial policy-making activity beginning in 1983 and again in the late 1980s undoubtedly are linked broadly to the accumulation of information, news, and political events surrounding the right to die which has been on state public agendas since the late 1960s. But, as discussed in chapter 2, prominent events external to the politics of the individual states also may stimulate litigation in various states at approximately the same time. There are two closely linked early events that sharply increased awareness among potential litigants but, equally important, provided lawyers with new ammunition to seek remedies to medical treatment problems in the courts. In turn, success in court, especially in highly publicized cases, reinforces public interest in using the courts to solve medical treatment problems. Therefore, certain highly publicized cases also become significant events that spur further litigation.

The early events reflect the impact of prestigious medical and governmental organizations that gave their support to withholding or discontinuing life support for the terminally ill. In 1982 the American Medical Association announced for the first time that it was ethical for physicians to withhold or withdraw life-support systems from hopelessly ill patients. The following year, the President's Commission on ethical, medical, and legal issues related to treatment decisions *(Deciding to Forego Life-Sustaining Treatment* 1983) concluded that life-support systems may ethically be withheld or withdrawn from terminally ill and permanently comatose patients. While not explicitly endorsing any particular legislation or judicial policy, the commission largely followed the position of the New Jersey Supreme Court in the Quinlan case and encouraged new legislation to cover a wide range of medical circumstances. As discussed in chapter 3, these and other events also stimulated increased public discussion of the right to die.

The likelihood that these events stimulated litigation and the policies of the courts is supported by their frequent appearance in written court opinions. Beginning with the first appellate decision following the President's Commission Report through the end of 1988, the report was cited in 70 percent and the AMA announcement was cited in 55 percent of subsequent cases. No other noncase citation received such prominent attention. These pronouncements became shopworn in time, however, and courts deciding cases in 1989 and 1990 referred exclusively to the mounting volume of other state supreme court opinions as precedents for their decisions.

Another indicator of the importance of these events, especially of the Commission report, is the amount of space given the report in written opinions.[1] As will be discussed further below, the Quinlan decision is cited more often and receives more space in the written opinions of all subsequent courts than any other decision. However, to the end of 1988, courts discussed the Commission report more heavily than Quinlan in eight cases (40 percent) and in four others (20 percent), it is second only to Quinlan. In this combined total of 60 percent of cases, state courts gave less space to all other citations, including the opinions of other courts, than they gave either to the Quinlan decision or to the Commission report.

A second surge of litigation occurred in 1987, and there are two additional prominent events that stimulated this new wave of cases. Late in 1985 the New Jersey Supreme Court decided that the artificial administration of food and water was part of medical treatment and could be removed from terminally ill and permanently comatose patients, allowing them to die from the underlying cause of their illness (*In re Conroy*). A few months later, in early 1986, the AMA endorsed this policy. As discussed more fully below, 85 percent of all cases decided after 1985 concerned this same issue and it is very likely that the Conroy decision and the new position of the

AMA stimulated this most recent wave of litigation. The artificial administration of food and water continues to be the most controversial right to die issue.

Judicial Leadership

It is not surprising that New Jersey and Massachusetts were among the earliest innovators in the right to die since these two states also place among the top five in general measures judicial reputation (Caldeira 1983). But other early courts that produced judicial policy in the right to die also tend to be among the leaders in other fields of policy. Six of the leading right to die courts are among the top eleven innovators in tort policy (Canon and Baum 1981), and seven of them are among the top fifteen in overall judicial reputation (Caldeira 1983). These seven courts also account for two-thirds of the right to die decisions that were produced by the earliest innovators. Consequently, early right to die innovation is concentrated in the courts that normally lead in judicial policy innovation.[2]

We generally can expect appellate courts in New Jersey, New York, California, Massachusetts, and a few other states to produce the first of new judicial policies. Of course, the relationship is not a perfect one, and some state courts diverge from this pattern. It is difficult to account for the early right to die decisions in Georgia, Arizona, and Maine—all states that do not figure high in general judicial reputation or innovation. Nevertheless, while novel litigation can develop anywhere, I suspect that it is most likely to arise in states that usually are among the policy leaders.

These results have implications for political theories concerning judicial innovation. I speculate that a small subset of states with large and diverse populations and complex economies and governmental structures are much more likely to generate model litigation than simpler, homogeneous states. In the early years of a diffusion process, a dozen or fifteen familiar states generally will be among the policy leaders. In time, however, as a new issue receives widespread news attention and becomes more visible and salient everywhere, the early innovations and other external political events motivate other potential litigants in states that tend to be late policy adopters. Litigation will increase in many states, making later diffusion less predictable than early innovation. If we were to look only at the diffusion of innovations in all fifty states innovation would appear to be idiosyncratic and chaotic, but if we were to look at the earliest innovators the same group of early leaders are likely to be on the list.

Innovation and Reinvention

One of the themes emphasized in chapter 2 is that innovation is not only a matter of being first with a novel solution to a problem. Innovation also involves creating additional solutions as new and unanticipated problems emerge. In social science terms, policies may be reinvented during the process in which they are being adopted.

Models of Policy

Despite their similar prestige and reputations for innovation, the early leading courts in the right to die produced different models of policy that had unequal impacts on other courts. A summary of the major elements of appellate judicial right to die decisions is presented in table 5.1. The table lists the cases chronologically, the basic substantive issue involved in the disputes, the direction of the decision (for or against withdrawal or withholding treatment), the key precedents relied upon, whether the decision is innovative or largely follows the lead of other courts (I or F), and a brief summary of the court's policy. Most court opinions cover a number of issues but only the major policies can be mentioned in this summary table.

The extent to which subsequent courts relied on a prior case as a precedent or as guidance for its own decision is indicated in the table by "Percentage Cited" and "Percentage Cited (1% +)." There is an important distinction between these two categories. The first indicates the percentage of later cases in which the listed case was cited. The second indicates the percentage of later cases in which the listed case received 1 percent or more of the space, measured in percentage of lines, of the citing court's majority opinions. One percent of a majority opinion was the natural breaking point in the

TABLE 5.1 *Elements of Right to Die Judicial Policy, 1976–1990*

Case[a]	Substantive Issue[b]	Decision[c]	Key Precedents	Percentage Cited	Percentage Cited (1%+)	Major Policy Content[d]
Quinlan, N.J. 1976	Withdraw respirator	+	*Griswold v. Conn., Roe v. Wade*; new	66.7	50.0	I. Extends constitutional right to privacy; no judicial intervention required; guardian may act with medical consultation.
Saikewicz, Mass. 1977	Withhold treatment	+	*Quinlan*; new	62.9	34.3	I. Accepts right to privacy, but judicial supervision required.
Perlmutter, Fla. 1/80	Withdraw respirator	+	*Saikewicz*; partly	38.2	20.6	F. Accepts constitutional right to privacy for competent patients; extensive call for legislation.
Spring, Mass. 5/80	Withdraw treatment	+	*Saikewicz*, modified	39.4	6.1	F. Interprets *Saikewicz*; court approval not required in some cases, but policy unclear.
Severns, Del. 9/80	Withdraw respirator	+	*Quinlan*	28.1	3.1	F. Grants authority to trial court; no general policy; extensive call for legislation.
Storar, N.Y. 3/81	Withhold treatment	–	none	54.8	16.1	F. Limits decision to a case by case approach; patient's wishes unknown; court approval required.
Eichner, N.Y. 3/81	Withdraw respirator	+	none	30.0	20.0	I. Facts in each case will determine outcome; requires unequivocal evidence of patient's wishes.
Colyer, Wash. 3/83	Withdraw respirator	+	*Quinlan*	55.2	24.1	F. Endorses *Quinlan*; guardian required; Natural Death Act does not apply.
Barber, Calif.[e] 10/83	Withdraw respirator and food/hydration	+	none	28.6	14.3	I. Extends basis beyond State Natural Death Act for terminating life-support systems.
Leach, Ohio[e] 5/2/84	Withdraw respirator	+	*Saikewicz*	51.9	0.0	F. Endorses *Saikewicz*.
Bludworth, Fla. 5/24/84	Withdraw respirator	+	*Colyer; Quinlan*	50.0	15.4	I. Endorses *Quinlan* and *Colyer*, but allows family decision making; validates living wills.
LHR, Ga. 10/84	Withdraw respirator	+	*Quinlan*	28.0	4.0	F. Endorses *Quinlan*, but allows family decision making.
Hamlin, Wash. 11/1/84	Withdraw respirator	+	*Colyer* modified	29.2	8.3	F. Interprets *Colyer*; no guardian required.
Torres, Minn. 11/2/84	Withdraw respirator	+	*Quinlan*	39.1	8.7	F. Endorses *Quinlan*; guardian may order withdrawal.

TABLE 5.1 Contd.

Case[a]	Substantive Issue[b]	Decision[c]	Key Precedents	Percentage Cited	Percentage Cited (1%+)	Major Policy Content[d]
Bartling, Calif.[e] 12/84	Withdraw respirator	+	*Barber; Quinlan*	41.0	18.2	F. Endorses *Barber* and *Quinlan*; right to refuse treatment.
Conroy, N.J. 11/85	Withdraw food/hydration	+	*Quinlan*; new	61.9	38.1	I. No distinction between "ordinary" and "extraordinary" procedures; provides rules; extensive call for legislation; recognizes living wills, durable power of attorney, and oral instructions.
Bouvia, Calif.[e] 6/86	Withdraw food/hydration	+	*Bartling*	45.0	25.0	F. Endorses *Bartling*; right to refuse treatment.
Brophy, Mass. 9/86	Withdraw food/hydration	+	*Conroy*	63.2	31.6	F. Endorses *Conroy*; guardian may order withdrawal; court approval not required; patient transfer.
Farrell, N.J. 6/24/87	Withdraw respirator	+	*Conroy; Quinlan*	58.8	11.8	F. Endorses *Quinlan* and *Conroy*; right to refuse treatment.
Jobes, N.J. 6/24/87	Withdraw food/hydration	+	*Conroy; Quinlan*; new	41.2	23.5	F. Endorses *Quinlan* and *Conroy*; guardian may order withdrawal.
Peter, N.J. 6/24/87	Withdraw food/hydration	+	*Quinlan; Conroy*	29.4	5.9	F. Endorses *Quinlan* and *Conroy*; guardian may act in every case.
Rasmussen, Ariz. 7/87	Withdraw food/hydration	+	*Hamlin; Quinlan; Torres*	40.0	20.0	F. Endorses *Hamlin, Torres,* and *Quinlan*; guardian may order withdrawal.
Gardner, Maine 12/3/87	Withdraw food/hydration	+	*Storar*	50.0	14.3	F. Limits decision to case by case; living will does not apply; patient's wishes are clear.
Grant, Wash. 12/10/87	Withdraw respirator and food/hydration	+	*Colyer*	38.5	0.0	F. Endorses *Colyer*; guardian may order withdrawal and withholding of future treatment.
Drabick, Calif.[e] 4/88	Withdraw food/hydration	+	*Barber*	50.0	16.7	F. Endorses numerous other decisions; guardian may order withdrawal; no judicial intervention required.
O'Conner, N.Y. 10/88	Withdraw food/hydration	–	*Storar*	27.3	9.1	F. Endorses *Storar*; clear and convincing evidence of patient's wishes required.

Case	Action[b]	[c]	Precedent			Decision[d]
Cruzan, Mo. 11/16/88	Withdraw food/hydration	–	none	30.0	0.0	I. Rejects other states' decisions; clear and convincing evidence of patients wishes required; guardian may not act; living will provides legislative intent.
Childs, Calif.[e] 11/30/88	Withdraw food/hydration	+	*Drabick*	11.1	11.1	F. Transfer patient to another facility for withdrawal; guardian may order withdrawal.
McConnell, Conn. 1/89	Withdraw food/hydration	+	none	0.0	0.0	I. Interprets living will law to permit withdrawal despite restrictive language; guardian may order withdrawal.
Couture, Ohio[e] 8/21/89	Withdraw food/hydration	–	none	0.0	0.0	I. Interprets durable power of attorney for health care to prohibit withdrawal, although patient had not designated proxy.
Westhart, Calif.[e] 8/24/89	Withdraw food/hydration	–	*Childs*	0.0	0.0	I. Denies damages for insertion of feeding tube.
Riddlemoser, Md. 10/89	Withhold treatment	+	none	0.0	0.0	F. Permits "DNR" under estates and trust statutes.
Longway, Ill. 11/13/89	Withdraw food/hydration	+	none	25.0	25.0	F. Court approval required for withdrawal from incompetent patient; cites many precedents and statutes.
McAfee, Ga. 11/21/89	Withdraw treatment	+	*LHR*	33.0	0.0	F. Patient has right to disconnect ventilator.
Swan, Maine 1/90	Withdraw food/hydration	+	*Gardner*	0.0	0.0	F. Mature minor may refuse treatment.
Greenspan, Ill. 7/90	Withdraw food/hydration	+	*Longway*	0.0	0.0	F. Orally expressed wishes are binding; guardian may order withdrawal.
Browning, Fla. 9/90	Withdraw food/hydration	+	*Bludworth*	–	–	I. Guardian of incompetent but not vegetative patient may seek withdrawal according to patient's living will; no distinction between right of incompetent and vegetative patients; oral instructions permitted.

[a] Unpublished New Mexico case excluded.
[b] Withdraw or withhold respirator, other treatment, or food and hydration.
[c] + = In favor of request to withdraw or withhold. – = Against request to withdraw or withhold.
[d] I. = Innovative. F. = Follows own or other state's precedent.
[e] Intermediate court of appeals decision.

amount of an opinion devoted to a particular precedent. These figures distinguish between the mere listing of a case, often among a long list of citations, in which courts cite many or even all other cases in the policy area, and in-depth consideration of a policy by other courts.

Quinlan.   In its 1976 Quinlan decision the New Jersey Supreme Court relied on the principle of the constitutional right to privacy and established the power of families as guardians, in consultation with doctors, to make decisions on behalf of incompetent patients. It permitted the withdrawal of a respirator without requiring prior judicial approval. The Quinlan policy is especially significant because it has been cited more frequently by other courts (in two-thirds of subsequent cases) than any other state court decision, and it has been explicitly embraced by most other courts as basic guidance for right to die policy. Courts frequently make legal distinctions between guardians exercising "substituted judgment," in which they choose what the patient would have decided, and acting in the patient's "best interest," in which a patient's desires are not clear. Other courts permit either form of guardian decision making. Regardless of legal terminology, however, nearly all courts permit the withdrawal or withholding of treatment from very seriously ill patients who are unable to express their own desires at the time.

Frequent citation of a case by a following innovator is a partial indicator that an early policy has had a long-lasting effect. Citation is a necessary but not a sufficient condition for a prior case to become a policy model. Courts may heavily cite a prior case but also distinguish or even reject it as a precedent. Also, as more cases are decided in the same policy field, later courts have many more opportunities to selectively use earlier cases. Therefore, for a case to be a model for policy-making, judges need to recognize it explicitly in their written opinions as the basis for their decisions.

This underscores the importance of Quinlan in right to die policy-making since, with the passage of time and increases in litigation in other states, later courts had many more cases to select from as precedents. But they still relied on Quinlan most heavily and explicitly referred to it as the leading precedent. Overall, two-thirds of appellate opinions cited Quinlan and half gave it substantial space in written opinions, but even precedents as prominent as Quinlan lose value over time. To the end of 1988 Quinlan had been cited in 80 percent of subsequent cases and it received substantial space in two-thirds of later written opinions. Nevertheless, while Quinlan has depreciated in recent years, it still leads all other cases as the model for the right to die. Several recent cases, particularly Georgia's McAfee and LHR decisions and Florida's Browning and Bludworth opinions, can be traced directly to Quinlan.

Citation without impact. Courts have cited and discussed other early cases heavily also, but they have not had the persuasive policy impact of Quinlan. The treatment given other cases underscores the need to distinguish between mere judicial citation and the explicit endorsement of previous policy. In Saikewicz, the Massachusetts Supreme Judicial Court adopted New Jersey's right to privacy view; however, unlike New Jersey, the court reinvented the policy by requiring prior judicial approval before medical treatment could be withheld. Although the Massachusetts court devoted nearly 13 percent of the space in its majority opinion to discussion of Quinlan, which is the heaviest attention given by any court to the Quinlan decision, it produced a substantially different policy with different potential effects on future litigants.

As discussed earlier, this decision was greeted with great confusion and concern among lawyers and doctors who worried that the court intended that prior judicial approval be required in *all* cases involving the removal or withholding of life-sustaining treatment. Numerous articles in legal and medical journals focused on the anticipated financial and emotional burdens that the decision would impose on patients, families, and medical institutions and personnel (Doudera and Peters 1982). The Massachusetts court later modified, but never explicitly abandoned, this policy. Significantly, it has been rejected by all but an Ohio appellate court. Nevertheless, the case has been cited in nearly 63 percent of other opinions and it has received substantial space in approximately one-third of other opinions—second only to the Quinlan decision and New Jersey's Conroy decision discussed below.

Other states also produced distinctive policies within the broad context of earlier rulings, but with little impact on other courts. The

New York Court of Appeals contributed two of the few court cases decided against patients' interests, and in 1981 it produced a policy requiring extensive proof of a patient's prior wishes before life-sustaining treatment could be withdrawn or withheld. This policy has been explicitly followed only by the Maine Supreme Court, although that court ruled there was sufficient evidence of the patient's wishes to withdraw treatment. The Florida Supreme Court in 1984 was the first to recognize the validity of living wills and it permitted the withdrawal of treatment. While it has been cited often, other courts have not discussed the case extensively. The California decisions all were produced by intermediate courts of appeals and relied solely upon prior California precedent.

Finally, in 1988 the Missouri Supreme Court deviated from all others by flatly refusing to grant permission for the withdrawal of artificially administered food and hydration from Nancy Cruzan. It also rejected other policies found in most other state court decisions. In that case, the court ruled there is no constitutional right to privacy that guarantees the right to refuse treatment in all circumstances; it is doubtful that individuals can make informed decisions about future medical treatment situations; Nancy Cruzan had not clearly indicated her wishes; and there is no basis in law for allowing guardians to exercise substituted judgment.

Overall, approximately 70 percent of the states that have produced appellate judicial policy concerning the right to die have followed the Quinlan model of permitting the withdrawal or withholding of various forms of medical treatment without requirements for prior judicial approval or extensive and clear proof of patient's wishes.

Policy Expansion

From 1976 to 1985 the substantive issue presented to most state supreme courts concerned the withdrawal or withholding of respirators and other medical treatment from terminally ill, incompetent patients.[3] Only 10 percent of the cases involved competent patients and all courts upheld the right to refuse medical treatment in these instances. As indicated earlier, judicial policy has varied on several dimensions, particularly whether prior judicial approval was required before medical treatment could be withheld or withdrawn and the amount of proof required to determine that a patient had expressed prior wishes concerning medical treatment.

However, besides creating distinctive policies to deal with traditional treatment decisions, the courts also created new policies as right to die issues evolved. As discussed in the previous chapters, many comatose patients are maintained only by artificial feeding. The withdrawal or withholding of traditional forms of medical treatment does not result in their deaths. Therefore, the early court decisions do not explicitly govern their situations. Recently, litigants have argued that artificial food and hydration should be considered part of medical treatment and the same principles enunciated in previous decisions should apply.

This issue first appeared before the New Jersey Supreme Court in 1985, and the court ruled that artificial food and hydration was part of medical treatment and also could be withdrawn, allowing a terminally ill or permanently comatose patient to die (*In re Conroy*). The New Jersey court relied on and expanded its prior Quinlan policy to apply to artificial food and hydration and established general rules that were to apply to similar conditions. The court also issued an extensive call for comprehensive state legislation. Except for three cases—one in New Jersey that concerned the removal of a respirator; one in Washington state that concerned all forms of medical treatment, including food and hydration; and a recent case in Maryland concerning a "do not resuscitate order"—*every* case that followed Conroy raised essentially identical issues regarding food and hydration.

Since the content of litigation changed abruptly after Conroy, it is very likely that the Conroy decision stimulated additional litigation concerning food and hydration and, with few exceptions, courts reached similar conclusions.[4] The Conroy decision has been cited nearly as heavily as Quinlan, but it has received more space in subsequent written opinions than any other later case. Many courts did not rely explicitly on Conroy as the key precedent but mentioned several cases instead of or in addition to Conroy as binding, which probably reflects the greater number of available precedents as more litigation was produced. Significantly the Massachusetts Supreme Judicial Court, which produced the early Saikewicz policy of requiring court approval before treatment could be withheld or withdrawn, also endorsed the New Jersey decision in its own food and hydration case (*Brophy v. New England Sinai Hospital, Inc.*). Like New Jersey, it did not distinguish between food and hydration and other forms of medical treatment, but also did not require prior judicial approval for its removal.

New Jersey's Conroy decision illustrates the enormous impact that courts and novel litigation can have in rapidly altering state governmental agendas. Following Conroy, the artificial administration of food and hydration became one of the most controversial right to die issues in years. This single case quickly stimulated others to initiate similar litigation; along with later cases it put the food and hydration issue on legislative agendas; and most state courts and some legislatures adopted comparable policies that permitted the withdrawal of all forms of treatment. Cases such as Conroy underscore the need to examine the power of courts to place new issues on governmental agendas and the interaction of different political institutions in policy-making.

The difference between citation and policy leadership is clearest in Missouri's Cruzan decision. Its refusal to permit the withdrawal of artificially administered food and hydration from a permanently comatose patient is diametrically opposite of the clear trend established by every other court. Nevertheless, the Missouri Supreme Court cited *every* right to die precedent and devoted a substantial 8 percent of its majority opinion to the Quinlan decision. But, it also rejected all precedents and produced an innovative policy of its own.

Reactions to the U.S. Supreme Court

Overall, the state appellate courts have been permissive concerning the withdrawal or withholding of medical treatment, including the artificial administration of food and hydration both for competent and incompetent patients. Competent patients may refuse medical treatment and incompetent patients may indicate their wishes in advance or have family or court-appointed guardians act on their behalf to obtain the end of medical treatment. Missouri's *Cruzan* decision is the clearest exception, although a few other courts have imposed stringent requirements on evidence of a comatose patient's wishes regarding medical treatment.

Although the overall direction of state judicial policy permits the withdrawal of treatment, there is no national consensus on the details of implementing the right to die, and the states probably will continue to travel in more than one policy direction for years to come. In particular, cases involving people who have not indicated their wishes in writing and disputes over food and hydration will continue to reach the state courts.

This has become even more apparent since the U.S. Supreme Court's review of the Cruzan case. The Supreme Court has not provided definitive guidance to the states. Although the Court accepted Missouri's stringent requirements, the Supreme Court has not required state courts or legislatures to change their previous policies, or to require written evidence of patients' wishes. The Court said that written evidence is more convincing and preferable, but it did not mandate new state policy on this issue. The Court also recognized that there is no distinction between traditional medical care and artificially administered food and hydration, but even on this issue, the Court did not explicitly declare such distinctions null and void.

State courts. The Supreme Court's decision already has been interpreted and used in a number of ways in the states. In 1990, soon after the decision, the Illinois Supreme Court permitted a guardian to request the withdrawal of treatment based on the patient's previous oral statements that, in the event of a terminal illness or vegetative state, he would not want to be maintained by life-support equipment (*In re Estate of Sidney Greenspan*). The court did not cite the Supreme Court's Cruzan decision nor adopt a similar policy calling for unequivocal, clear, written instructions. Instead, the Illinois decision follows the well-worn path of other state courts.

A few months later the Florida Supreme Court permitted a guardian to seek the withdrawal of a feeding tube from an incompetent patient in accord with the patient's previously expressed wishes, in this case through a living will (*In re Guardianship of Browning*). Unlike Illinois, the Florida court cited the U.S. Supreme

Court in Cruzan, but not in ways that affected Florida's prior judicial policy. First, the Florida Supreme Court cited the U.S. Supreme Court's statement that there is no distinction between extraordinary and ordinary care. This is not new policy. This policy has been adopted by most state supreme courts since New Jersey's Conroy decision in 1985. Second, the court cited Justice Sandra Day O'Connor's concurring opinion in which she recommended written instructions.

But the Florida court produced its own distinctive and complex reinvented policy on this issue. It accepted as satisfactory either oral statements concerning a patient's wishes, or written instructions in living wills and other advance directives, including the designation of a health care proxy decision maker. However, it required the written designation of a proxy if the patient left no other instructions regarding future medical treatment. Oral communications already had legal status in Florida since the supreme court had previously allowed to stand without review an intermediate appellate court decision permitting the withdrawal of a feeding tube based on the patient's earlier oral communications (*Corbett v. D'Alessandro*).

An additional indication that the Supreme Court's Cruzan decision will have varied impact is the response of the Massachusetts legislature and interest groups to the decision. As discussed in the previous chapter, the Catholic church interpreted the Cruzan decision as requiring or at least encouraging new state policy that permits individuals to specify their wishes in advance in a written document. Given the continued support for living will laws, the Church preferred a proxy law to the alternative. However, the Massachusetts legislation deviates from the U.S. Supreme Court's policy by prohibiting the withdrawal of comfort care, which has been widely interpreted in other states to include artificially administered food and hydration. As suggested previously, since the Massachusetts Supreme Judicial Court permitted the withdrawal of food and hydration in the Brophy case, it is likely that a future court case will test the new legislative prohibition on the withdrawal of comfort care. Litigants can be expected to rely on the Supreme Court's Cruzan and the Brophy case to justify a different interpretation of comfort care than the one given by the legislature. Similar disputes in other states are bound to arise as well, and conflicts between courts and legislatures on having the last word on right to die policy will go on.

New agenda. While it has not provided definitive guidance on the right to die, the U.S. Supreme Court has stimulated additional agenda setting, particularly concerning acceptable standards of evidence of patients' wishes to terminate treatment. This is the central issue emphasized by the Court and the one that has received the greatest comment in the news. Clearly, the Court prefers written documents. However, few people have signed living wills or health care proxies and most states with court decisions accept oral communications or guardians acting on behalf of patients who are unable to communicate their desires.

But most states have not had appellate cases, which leaves the majority of Americans potentially uncovered on the right to die. This applies to most adults, but it is even more applicable to young children, teenagers, and young adults who frequently have not discussed life and death issues with others and have not indicated their wishes in any manner. Moreover, only two states recognize living wills for individuals under age twenty-one. If a court or other authority interprets the Supreme Court's Cruzan decision as requiring, not simply preferring, written evidence of a patient's intentions regarding terminal medical care, most people are vulnerable and are potentially dependent upon unknown medical and/or judicial decisions in their case.

Litigation involving young people has occasionally reached the appellate state courts, which have permitted the withdrawal of treatment from a severely brain-damaged infant, and accepted the earlier statements of a mature but now comatose teenager not to be maintained by life-support systems (*In re L.H.R.* and *In re Chad Eric Swan*). But others are caught in interminable legal limbo. For example, a case involving a teenager in Missouri who had not expressed her wishes in any form, and where parents or guardians may not obtain the removal of life-support systems without clear evidence of a person's prior wishes, would seem to be a candidate for appeal to the U.S. Supreme Court. The father's attempt to move her to another more permissive state has been blocked by the Missouri courts and there are new disagreements among medical staff and the child's father over whether his daughter actually is permanently comatose (*New York Times,* 2 January 1991:A8; 5 February 1991:A16; 6 March 1991:A10). Nevertheless, this case illustrates the additional, seemingly insoluble problems involved when there is no evidence whatever concerning the patient's wishes, but states require clear evidence before permitting the withdrawal of treatment. The case also illustrates the special plight of minors who are not legally permitted to execute binding living wills. New policy regarding the withdrawal of treatment for patients who have not left written instructions and those, including young people, who have provided no inkling of their desires are bound to be new agenda items.

Interest Groups in Court

Interest groups and public policy almost always evoke images of lobbying in the legislature, but interest groups also are important in litigation. Going to court sometimes is an alternative to the legislature, in which losers hope to win in a different branch of government by securing new judicial policies, favorable interpretations of statutes, or possibly having laws declared unconstitutional. In contrast, other groups sometimes enter court cases in order to protect the victories they have won elsewhere. Either way, interest groups go to court in order to influence the content of judicial policy.

The most widely used method for measuring interest group activity in the courts is the frequency of filing amicus curiae briefs (O'Connor and Epstein 1981–1982; 1983). These are written arguments submitted by groups in addition to the briefs filed by the litigants themselves. Through their briefs, groups emphasize policies and legal justifications supporting their view of the issues in a case, which they hope will influence judges' decisions. Interest groups may not offer verbal arguments. A large number of briefs submitted on behalf of both sides in a court case reveals intense interest group conflict in the courts, albeit a silent and largely invisible one.

Various interest groups have filed briefs in right to die cases and their involvement in litigation has increased over the years. In the 1970s and early 1980s it was uncommon for interest groups to submit briefs and only three cases prior to 1984 attracted outside groups. But since 1984, when litigation and legislation sharply increased and the right to die had become well established on the public and governmental agendas, as many as ten organizations submitted arguments for both sides in a single case and all but a few cases have involved interest groups. In all, interest groups have submitted ninety-six briefs in 57 percent of the appellate cases studied between 1976 and 1990. However, 90 percent of all amici briefs were submitted in 1984 and beyond. Clearly, by the mid–1980s, the right to die had become extremely salient to a variety of interest groups and many believed that state appellate courts were having an important impact on the content of the law.

Types of Groups

The distribution of amici briefs submitted by various types of interest groups is presented in table 5.2. Highest on the list are medical organizations (32.3 percent), including state medical societies, hospital and nursing home associations, individual hospitals, hospices, medical schools, and others. These are followed by national right to die advocacy groups (25 percent), principally the Society for the Right to Die and Concern for Dying; right to life organizations (16.7 percent), particularly state Catholic Conferences and right to life groups; and advocacy groups or associations of the disabled and retarded (16.7 percent). The nine briefs included in the "Other" category (9.4 percent) generally include various levels of government, legal groups, and civil liberties organizations.

The large majority of groups participating in the cases have favored policies enlarging the right to demand the withdrawal of treatment. In addition to the right to die advocacy groups, most medical associations and institutions have supported expansive policies and most of those in the "Other" category also have favored them. Opponents are found among right to life and organizations representing the disabled and retarded who, in their view, fear a march toward active euthanasia.

The elderly are very heavily affected by right to die judicial policies, and half of the cases have involved elderly patients, but groups representing the elderly have been nearly absent from right to die

TABLE 5.2   *Interest Groups in Right to Die Cases, 1976–1990*

Group	Percentage of Briefs (N = 96)
Medical	32.3
Right to Die	25.0
Prolife	16.7
Disabled	16.7
Other	9.4
Total	100.1[a]

[a]Rounded.

litigation. Only one brief was filed by an advocacy organization for the elderly in all of these cases. Although this is not a policy area that has attracted the elderly, there are some signs recently that seniors groups are becoming more concerned with it. Nevertheless, their level of political activity has been dwarfed by others. This seems perplexing, given the importance of these cases to them. Their role in right to die politics will be discussed more completely in the following chapter on legislation.

There is little evidence that interest groups have influenced the content of judicial opinions since judges rarely cite or quote from amici briefs. Nevertheless, interest groups believe it is valuable to present their point of view both in the hope that their arguments may have some effect on the judges' reasoning, but also to register their group's concern with the issue. Additionally, groups file briefs when the issues are very important but they fear that the attorneys representing the litigants whom the groups favor may not adequately represent their side of the case. Then, an amicus can supplement the main presentation. However, sponsoring litigation and preparing amici briefs is expensive and time consuming, and it strains the financial resources of various organizations. Therefore, groups carefully choose their battles and weigh the odds of influencing the courts.

Research on lobbying before the U.S. Supreme Court strongly indicates that groups that have no or limited access to legislatures, but that believe they can win before the Court are more likely to lobby than groups that perceive judicial policy as clearly going against them. In the 1960s and 1970s liberal civil rights and civil liberties groups, which generally have very poor access to conservative state legislatures, had good access to the U.S. Supreme Court and they appeared there often. However, as conservative Republican appointees of the Nixon and Reagan administrations gradually became the majority, liberal groups decreased their lobbying and conservatives increasingly took their place (O'Connor and Epstein 1983).

This discovery parallels the prominent role of right to die supporters in the state courts. The right to die advocates have had some success in state legislatures, but many state living will laws are restrictive and do not cover many patients. However, most state courts have been very supportive of patients' rights and have expanded the right to die beyond the bounds set by state legislatures. Right to life organizations, on the other hand, do not lobby as often in the courts. They either have been able to block living will laws entirely or to limit their breadth. They have used legislatures as a way of limiting liberal courts.

Courts and Legislatures

As the case studies and the discussion in this chapter make clear, state courts and legislatures interact on the right to die. Several state courts early in the innovation period called for legislation and have produced their own policies despite the failure of state legislatures to act. But the accumulation of court decisions has stimulated the adoption of living will laws in additional states as interest groups and legislatures have responded to the overall permissive thrust of judicial rulings. In turn, as legislation has been enacted, courts have new opportunities to interpret legislation.

Rising Volume of Policy

Except for the early adoption of living will laws in 1976 and 1977, courts generally have outstripped state legislatures in adopting right to die policy. The relationship between the frequency of court decisions and the adoption of legislation is portrayed by the graph in figure 5.2. It charts the number of appellate court cases and living will laws enacted from 1976 to 1990. The contours of the lines suggest that an increase in the number of cases precedes an increase

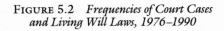

FIGURE 5.2   *Frequencies of Court Cases and Living Will Laws, 1976–1990*

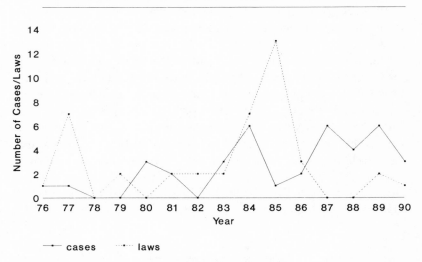

in the number of laws enacted in the 1980–1981, 1983–1984 and 1989–1990 periods. To test the hypothesis that litigation generally has preceded legislation, I have correlated the dates of appellate court cases lagged for one year with the dates of adoption of living will laws. This means that litigation in one year stimulates legislation the following year. The results are as expected, and the correlation is highly statistically significant ($r = .48$; $p < .01$).

Additional support for this hypothesis is provided by the lack of strong correlations for alternative relationships. No support exists for the hypothesis that rates of litigation and enactment of living will laws occur simultaneously or the hypothesis that the lagged adoption of living will laws precedes increases in litigation.[5] While other social forces and events stimulate state legislatures to act (these are discussed in the following chapter), support exists for the view that legislatures have responded to litigation.

As discussed regarding the right to die in Florida, an important catalyst for the courts' impact on the adoption of living will laws in many states appears to be a decision by many Catholic lobbyists to change their political position and strategy regarding legislation. Late in 1981 certain Catholic scholars recommended that the Catholic church reverse its opposition to living will laws (Paris and McCormick 1981). In their view, state courts increasingly were producing policies that promoted the right to die at a level well beyond that which state legislatures probably would approve if state Catholic conferences participated in bill drafting and lobbied for restrictive provisions. The National Conference of Catholic Bishops officially endorsed this view in 1984, and certain, but not all, state Catholic conferences took this position.

In states in which the Catholic population is large and the Church is especially powerful, such as Massachusetts, New Jersey, and New York, living will laws generally have not been enacted. These states generally rank high in policy innovation, but in this particular policy, it strongly appears that the Catholic church has successfully blocked legislation. However, the appellate courts in these states have served as important alternative sources of policy. While it might successfully oppose or limit legislation, the Catholic church and other groups cannot prevent individual citizens from putting an issue on the judicial agenda.

The courts also are much less likely to be influenced by interest groups, which can affect court cases only indirectly by submitting amicus curiae briefs. Since right to die cases are not plentiful or as visible as some criminal cases, it also is unlikely that an interest group can have much other influence, such as motivating the public to vote for judges according to their position on the right to die. But even in this regard many judges, particularly in the northeast, are appointed to office for life or for very long terms and never face the pressures of reelection. Moreover, judges elected elsewhere rarely lose their posts, and then only as a result of personal scandal or unpopular decisions in a series of highly visible cases, such as death penalty appeals. Consequently, the courts are much more insulated from direct political influence than state legislatures and, as evidenced, they generally have responded favorably to claims of privacy and patient or family control over medical treatment in the right to die.

Judicial Interpretation of Legislation

Courts have interpreted and applied living will laws in slightly more than half of the state appellate cases, but the rate of judicial interpretation is rapidly rising. From 1976 to early 1986 approximately 40 percent of state court decisions included the interpretation of state law, but from 1987 to 1990, following the big surge in living will legislation in the mid–1980s, three-quarters of the cases have involved judicial examination of living will statutes. Several recent cases also have interpreted newly adopted durable power of attorney for health care laws which swept the nation in the late 1980s.

As in all areas of law, when cases and legislation abound, the growing body of law gives judges numerous choices about which law to use and how to apply it. In addition, while the facts in many right to die cases are similar, judges frequently emphasize certain ones more than others and fit the law differently to those facts. The increase in state legislation has not impeded the state courts from making policies that coincide with their earlier rulings.

The right to die cases support a policy-making model of judicial behavior. Like legislators, judges have political and social attitudes and lean toward a particular policy or result. They find precedents or interpret law and facts in support of their views and the conclusion they wish to reach (Shubert 1974; Spaeth 1979; Glick 1988). One person interviewed for the three case studies summarized this view well when he said that state supreme courts and legislatures are political competitors and go their own way in making policy. The U.S. Supreme Court in particular is motivated by the attitudes and values of the justices. In the Cruzan case the Court split along its usual liberal-conservative ideological lines with Justices Rehnquist, White, O'Connor, Scalia, and Kennedy forming the conservative majority that approved Missouri's restrictive policy regarding evidence of patients' wishes, while Justices Brennan, Marshall, Blackmun, and Stevens dissented in favor of a broader interpretation of patients' rights and the power of guardians to act on a patient's behalf.

Constitutional rights.   Courts have revealed their policy-making power concerning state legislation in several ways. First, state courts have viewed living will laws as only one avenue for determining the right to die. Patients with or without living wills do not give up other rights. The first appellate case involving a substantive interpretation of a state living will law is a 1983 California intermediate appellate court decision (*Barber v. Superior Court*). The court concluded that the withdrawal of all medical treatment from terminally ill and comatose patients, including food and hydration, was within the normal practice of medicine and could be done per the wishes of the patient or surrogate decision maker, and that such decisions were not limited by the state's living will law (the Natural Death Act) or the brain death statute. Citizens have rights to refuse treatment which cannot be limited by statutes. It added that few people have executed living wills and it criticized as inhibiting the California statute which requires a fourteen-day waiting period after a patient has been declared terminally ill before a valid living will can be executed. By that time, many patients are too ill or comatose and cannot sign a document or indicate their wishes in any other way.

The Maine Supreme Court and a Florida intermediate court of appeals produced similar interpretations of legislation in 1986 and 1987 (*Corbett v. D'Alessandro* and *In re Gardner*). They condoned the withdrawal of artificial feeding and hydration from permanently comatose patients despite state living will statutory language that could be interpreted as requiring the administration of artificial food and hydration for "comfort care and to alleviate pain." Both courts added that state statutes were but one of several ways that patients' rights in these circumstances could be defined and that statutes could not limit the constitutional right to refuse medical treatment. Thus these decisions vastly extended the right to die beyond the states' living will laws and created an independent role for appellate courts in states with legislation.

Elastic legislation. Courts also can interpret restrictive legislative language to substantially expand patients' rights. A Connecticut case is an illustration. Connecticut's living will law explicitly excludes the *mechanical* administration of food and hydration from medical treatment which may be withdrawn. The statute also calls for comfort care and alleviation of pain *in all cases* and the provision of nutrition and hydration for *all patients* who are not terminally ill.

Therefore, removing food and hydration from patients in a permanent vegetative state seems to be prohibited.

But in keeping with the overall trend toward expanding patients' rights, the Connecticut Supreme Court interpreted the language of the law to achieve the opposite result (*McConnell v. Beverly Enterprises-Conn, Inc*). The court reasoned that individual provisions of the law had to be considered within the context of the purpose and meaning of the entire statute—giving the judges considerable latitude to interpret and apply other words and phrases. An additional sentence of the statute refers to the provision of "beneficial medical treatment," which, the court decided, did not include artificial technology to assist in nutrition and hydration. Normal eating and drinking by mouth are required, but artificial feeding and hydration are not. Therefore, the seemingly clear food and hydration provision of the state's living will law did not require the artificial administration of food and hydration.

The relevance of statutes.   Courts also view legislation as applicable to their cases or reject it as not binding. As discussed earlier, in denying the withdrawal of all forms of life-sustaining medical treatment, the Missouri Supreme Court relied on the state's living will law in the Cruzan case. The court concluded that the prolife preamble revealed the intent of the Missouri legislature concerning the right to die, and that the legislation applied to Nancy Cruzan even though she was not terminal and had not signed a living will, both of which seemingly are required by the legislation.

The Missouri Supreme Court had available an extensive set of judicial precedents, which it rejected in favor of its own distinctive application of statutory law. By doing so, it also rejected a constitutional or common law basis used in other courts for permitting the end of treatment.

Decisions of Ohio and Illinois appellate courts also illustrate judicial options for using state statutes. In an unusual case involving family disagreement over the withdrawal of treatment from a 29-year-old comatose patient, an Ohio intermediate appellate court ruled against the withdrawal of feeding tubes, relying on the state's restrictive durable power of attorney for health care law as an indication of legislative intent—even though the patient had not selected a proxy decision maker or executed a durable power of attorney document (*Couture v. Couture*).

According to the court the durable power of attorney law defines patients' best interests and prohibits the withdrawal of food and hydration unless death is imminent or such withdrawal would shorten life. The court cited only two right to die precedents, but it did not discuss either of them in detail. Although the court agreed the patient was terminal, death was not imminent, making the removal of the food and hydration tubes unlawful.

In contrast to Ohio, the Illinois Supreme Court ruled a few months later that artificially administered food and hydration could be withdrawn from an elderly incompetent patient who had expressed her wishes orally before becoming ill (*In re Estate of Longway*). The court cited the Illinois living will and durable power of attorney laws which defined artificially administered food and hydration as death-delaying treatments that may be withdrawn. But, opposite the Missouri and Ohio decisions, the court stated that since the patient had not signed documents indicating her wishes regarding medical treatment, these laws were *not* applicable. Instead, the court said the right to refuse treatment can be found in the Illinois Probate Act and the extensive body of right to die precedents, which the court cited extensively. However, the court required that judicial approval be obtained before artificially administered food and hydration could be withdrawn at the request of a patient's guardian. Guardians should seek to learn the intent of patients, but if it is not available guardians may exercise substituted judgment.

Many state laws have various food and hydration and other restrictive clauses in them, and based on these recent cases, state courts will interpret and use them in various ways. Possibly, as new cases arise, supreme courts in the generally liberal northeast and far west will follow the Connecticut model while those in the conservative South and Midwest may opt for the Missouri or Ohio routes. It certainly is unlikely that a single judicial policy will emerge in the states, or that the U.S. Supreme Court can or will rule on most of these issues in a single future decision.

Conclusion

Following the early lead of the New Jersey and Massachusetts supreme courts, prominent national events stirred additional litigation and judicial policy-making in the right to die. Many of the early leading courts rank high in general measures of judicial innovation and reputation, suggesting that judicial leadership in the right to die parallels early innovation in other fields of policy. However, while several familiar leading courts were among the early innovators, they and other courts have not produced a single uniform innovation, but have continuously reinvented the right to die. And the decisions of the early leaders have not had equal impact on subsequent judicial policy. New Jersey's Quinlan decision has become the model selected by most of the states, while the early Massachusetts and New York decisions have had little impact. Later, New Jersey also provided the major stimulus to new litigation and policy regarding artificially administered food and hydration. Nearly all litigation that followed this ground-breaking decision has concerned food and hydration, which remains a very controversial right to die issue.

Although the New Jersey decisions have become the general models for most states, neither the state courts nor the U.S. Supreme Court have provided a uniform body of law that solves right to die disputes or establishes clear standards concerning how individual decisions ought to be made. Most state courts permit the withdrawal of all forms of treatment, allow guardians to act on behalf of patients, and do not require prior judicial approval for withdrawal. Most also accept either written or oral evidence of patients' wishes, but they also allow guardians to act if a patient's wishes are unclear. However, a few courts differ concerning the appointment of guardians, particular circumstances under which courts must approve the withdrawal of food and hydration, and standards of evidence concerning patients' wishes.

Growth in the amount of legislation also gives state courts new opportunities to add the interpretation of statutes to the body of law regulating the right to die. Several courts have interpreted restrictive living will or durable power of attorney laws to permit the withdrawal of treatment, including the artificial administration of food and hydration, either by declaring that these laws do not apply because patients had not signed documents, or through inventive interpretation of legislative language. Clearly, judges who support the right to die are not substantially hampered by state legislation. But a few courts have gone in the opposite direction, and limit the right to die according to the conservative legislative intent found in state statutes, even though patients have not signed living wills or designated proxy decision makers. Probably these judges also are motivated by their own attitudes.

Despite the large majority of permissive judicial policies on the right to die, litigation continues to develop in the states on similar treatment issues. It might appear that since the Quinlan and Conroy models have been followed by most of the states, they would guide potential litigants concerning resolving disagreements or doubts on the withdrawal of treatment. But this has not occurred. An important reason is that no state's judicial decisions and laws are binding on another state, and most states have not had cases. Since the political environment and culture of the states differs it is likely that judges and legislators will resolve these issues in various ways. As long as doctors, families, and state officials, and hospitals and nursing homes (many of which are affiliated with religious organizations) disagree on the withdrawal of treatment or worry about their legal liability, doubts sometimes will be resolved in court. Many more cases and varied outcomes are likely to appear in the states.

The U.S. Supreme Court also is not a source of definitive right to die policy. The Court has approved one state's rigid evidence requirements regarding patients' wishes, but early evidence from state decisions following its Cruzan decision indicates that the Supreme Court's decision will not have one single impact. The lessons from much prior research on the effect of U.S. Supreme Court decisions are that high court decisions are open to various interpretations by lower court judges and other officials since the Court's opinions usually are drafted as general policy statements designed to apply to a range of circumstances. But, since they are general statements, they cannot cover each set of facts or conditions perfectly, and new issues constantly arise. Consequently, U.S. Supreme

Court decisions are implemented by lower courts and others in a variety of ways (Johnson and Canon 1984).

The attitudes and values of state judges and other public officials are crucial for determining exactly how supreme court decisions are translated into practice. State officials also have a large and growing body of state law on the right to die as well. Therefore, continuous change or reinvention of policy is bound to occur.

6 Lawmaking
and the
Right to Die

Although state courts took the early lead in creating the right to die and stimulated the adoption of living will laws in many of the states, the sources of right to die policy have not been entirely judicial ones. Early proposals were placed before the Florida, California, and other state legislatures years before court cases developed, and many individual medical tragedies served as sources of agenda setting in various states. As discussed earlier, the close proximity of New Jersey's Quinlan case and California's first law in 1976 has led some commentators to assume that the New Jersey decision put the issue on California's legislative agenda, but California considered a living will bill in 1974, a year before the Quinlan case entered the trial court.

Today many more states have legislative policy than judicial doctrines on the right to die. In states that have both legislative and judicial policy, courts and legislatures frequently compete for having the last word on policy for governing treatment in hopeless cases, but since most states have no judicial rulings, state legislatures are the only sources of governmental policy.

This chapter focuses mainly on the adoption of living will laws, since these were the first right to die legislative policies and they required a long time to diffuse among the states. Recently, however, in a very short period of time, most of the states also have enacted health care proxy decision maker laws, expanded their durable power of attorney statutes to apply to health care decision making, or included proxy provisions within their living will laws. Some of the states without living will laws have adopted one of these more recent innovations while continuing to reject the living will. Therefore I also will discuss these laws as the most recent form of innovation in the right to die.

As in judicial innovations, there are two basic parts to the politics of adopting living will laws. The first concerns the chronology of enactment—the ordering of the states over time according to when each passed a living will law. Unlike the courts, which are dependent on litigants to bring cases, legislatures are not passive institutions that must rely on constituents, interest groups, or others to generate their business. Individual legislators can introduce any bill they wish, and research on the adoption of legislative innovations anticipates much less idiosyncrasy in the adoption of legislative policy. Major national events as well as individual state characteristics account for when states enacted living will laws.

The second focus is on policy reinvention, or changes in the content of legislative policy that occur during the period of diffusion. Although much writing about living will laws tends to lump similar legislation together as one, each state has a distinctive law. Some of them provide great latitude to patients and families to obtain the end of treatment while others place many obstacles in the way. An important political question is how these laws differ and to discover if there are common changes that have occurred over time. Since most of the state laws have similar types of provisions—although their specific content varies—it is possible to assign each provision of each law a numerical score in order to compare the laws and to analyze the effects of the passage of time on their changing policy content.

This chapter has four main sections. The first examines the diffusion of living will laws over time and the impact of national events and trends and state characteristics on the timing of adoptions. The following section analyzes the content of these laws, particularly the reinvention of policy during the diffusion process. The third section discusses recent innovations, particularly the adoption of durable power of attorney for health care laws (DPAHC) and health care proxy (HCP) laws. Since most of the states adopted these laws over just a few years, there are few major differences in the politics of policy adoption. However, as in living will laws, some have restrictive provisions.

Finally, I examine the role of interest groups in the adoption of living will laws, with the main emphasis on the role of groups representing the elderly. My discussion of interest groups thus far has concentrated on the opposition of the Catholic church and right to life organizations to living will laws, but right to die policy directly affects the elderly more heavily than any other group of citizens. They would seem to be a natural constituency for this policy and we might expect them to lobby for living will laws.

The Diffusion of Living Will Laws

Between 1976 and 1990 forty-one states and the District of Columbia enacted living will laws.[1] The distribution of the states over this period is found in table 6.1. California was first in 1976 and was followed by five other western states and Arkansas and North Carolina the following year. It is not surprising that many of California's western neighbors enacted living will laws soon after California, since communications among state officials on new policies is common and geographic neighbors often follow their regional leader (Walker 1969; McVoy 1950; Foster 1978). Three of the five western states that followed California enacted nearly identical laws. The bill sponsor of Nevada's legislation, which varies from California's on only one provision, stated, for example, that the purpose of his bill was "to bring our law into conformity with California" (Hearings, Senate Judiciary Committee, March 24, 1977).

Regional fidelity, however, may have the opposite effect for states outside the orbit of a leading innovator. In response to one witness' testimony before a legislative committee that the California law should become a model for a midwestern state, a legislator responded sarcastically that it made no difference in his state what California did. Overall, regional emulation is much less clear after 1977, since few states enacted laws until 1984 and 1985 and many states from different regions had joined in by then.

Like the diffusion of judicial policy, the distribution of living will adoptions reveals the typical S-shaped diffusion curve in the cumu-

TABLE 6.1 Dates of Adoption of Living Will Laws, 1976–1990

1976	1977	1978	1979	1980	1981	1982	1983	1984	1985	1986	1987	1988	1989	1990
CA	AR	—	KS	—	AL	DE	IL	FL	AZ	AK	—	—	MN	KY
	ID		WA		DC	VT	VA	GA	CO	HI			ND	
	NV							LA	CN	SC				
	NC							MS	IN					
	NM							WV	IA					
	OR							WI	ME					
	TX							WY	MD					
									MO					
									MT					
									NH					
									OK					
									TN					
									UT					

lative adoption of laws (figure 6.1). The curve shows that a few states enacted laws early, followed by a lull in which there was only a scattering of adoptions in the next few years. But following 1983 when 30 percent of the states had adopted laws—falling within Rogers' estimated 20 to 30 percent threshold for a take-off in adoptions (Rogers 1983)—there is a huge surge in adoptions. That is followed once again by a period in which few additional states embraced the innovation.

But unlike diffusion among the state courts, where litigation still is active, the diffusion curve for living will laws has flattened. Adoptions dropped off in 1986, no additional states enacted laws in 1987 and 1988, and only three others adopted living will laws to the end of 1990. The remaining states may never adopt this innovation, although some of them have leap-frogged living wills and enacted more recent health proxy innovations.

Since legislatures may act on their own to create policy, there is a compelling reason to uncover explanations for patterns of living will diffusion. Why do certain states lead and others follow, and what accounts for the wholesale adoptions by many states in a one- or two-year period? As discussed in chapter 2, there are two likely explanations based on previous innovation research. The first is multiple state tipping, which occurs when many of the states respond at about the same time to similar national events. The second explanation is interstate communications in which information flows among decision makers in different states. Both of these need to be explored in order to account for the adoption of living will laws.

National Events

Accounting for the big surge in living will adoptions in 1984 and 1985, when twenty states enacted laws, is the most straightforward part of the living will story. There are two closely related events that probably tipped many of the states toward living will laws in these two years. First, in 1984 the National Conference of Catholic Bishops, in reaction to the national surge in liberal state court decisions, changed its approach to legislation and certain state Catholic conferences soon joined in drafting legislation rather than continuing to oppose it. With opposition from the Catholic church removed or

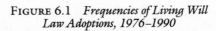

FIGURE 6.1   *Frequencies of Living Will*
Law Adoptions, 1976–1990

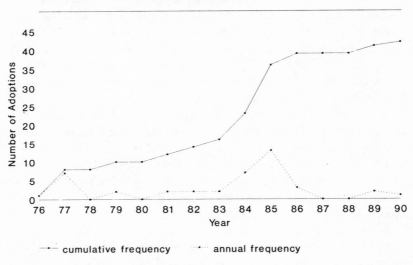

moderated in various states, state legislatures were much more likely to move toward innovation. The power of the Catholic church to largely determine the fate of living will laws in many states is reinforced by the case studies but also from previous research on legislative lobbying, which reveals that *any* interest group opposition is likely to kill a bill, and that the large majority of bills that are passed have no opposition (Wiggins and Brown 1982).

The second major event was the announcement of a model uniform living will law by the National Conference Commission on Uniform State Laws (NCCUSL). The NCCUSL began drafting a uniform living will law in 1984, and it announced the model officially in 1985. NCCUSL representatives from all states meet annually to examine laws already adopted by a number of states and that, in their view, require uniform models to ensure all states have similar legislation. The chairman of the NCCUSL conference on living will laws stated that it was appropriate for the organization to draft a uniform law since nearly half the states already had them, but the content and quality of state laws varied tremendously (Proceedings, August 1, 1984).

It is common in many states that have not yet enacted a law for one or more legislators to put a uniform law on the legislative agenda, and as occurred in California some earlier adopters considered the uniform law as a basis for amending their own legislation. A close examination of the hearings before legislative committees in states that enacted living will laws in 1984 and 1985 revealed that half of the bill sponsors were stimulated by the NCCUSL and based their bills on the uniform law. However, the states did not pass laws identical to the NCCUSL model or to each other (see also Jacob 1988), since interest groups and legislators negotiated specific changes in each of the states. But the presence of a uniform model adds legitimacy to a new policy and often stimulates states to enact new legislation.

Although actions by the NCCUSL and the Catholic church are most closely linked with the 1984 and 1985 living will law adoptions, these two important national events were preceded by the President's Commission report on life-sustaining treatment in 1983, which recommended comprehensive state legislation on the right to die. It seems clear that by 1984 living will innovation was "in the air" nationally, opposition had softened, and many states adopted new laws by 1985.

Varied State Responses

Even though many states enacted laws at about the same time, national events do not fully account for the diffusion of living will laws. Many states had enacted living will laws prior to 1984, some waited until the end of the 1980s or have not enacted laws, and those that enacted during the 1984–1985 surge waited until they were prompted by major national events. What held them back until then? Accounting for living will adoptions over the entire span of diffusion is a more complex task.

The search for other explanations requires identifying and examining two additional sources of influence on state decisions to enact living will laws. The first is state responses to changes occurring gradually over time on the national right to die agenda. The second is the effect of characteristics of the individual states that enhance or impede the odds they will innovate early, late, or not at all.

The changing agenda.   Evidence of the effect of the right to die agenda can be obtained through the number of articles published each year in the professional and mass media and the annual incidence of appellate court cases. My previous discussion indicates that the issue was on the professional and mass public agendas long before state legislatures began to act in numbers, and it is likely that rising public awareness stimulated legislative responsiveness. In addition, it appears that litigation generally preceded legislation and it is likely that the rising wave of court cases is partly responsible for legislative action. Since I hypothesize that publications and litigation influence later legislative enactments, I have lagged publications and court decisions by one year so that the adoption of living will laws in every year is correlated with the previous year's publications and court cases. Public opinion polls are not considered here because there is convincing evidence that polling did not become plentiful until the right to die already had taken off as a political issue.

State characteristics.   In addition to national trends, many differences in state political and social characteristics may affect the decisions of state legislatures to enact living will laws. One possibility is the influence of regionalism. As suggested earlier, much previous research suggests that states within particular regions are likely to identify with each other and to follow regional leaders. When regional leaders adopt a policy it becomes more legitimate for others in the same region to do so, and following the leader may become a political resource for overcoming other state political obstacles to policy adoption (Berry and Berry 1990). Early adoption of living will laws was partially related to states being in the western region, which suggests that the regional identity of the states may be a basis for their diffusion.

   In addition to regional membership, the states possess different internal characteristics. Certain state socioeconomic and political contexts are likely to foster innovation while others impede it. Generally, I hypothesize that innovation is most likely to be found in states that rank high in social and political diversity and political competition. Diversity and competition produce conflict and thus heightened awareness and responsiveness to new social issues.

Measures of social diversity include urbanism, total state population, education, and wealth. High scores on these factors indicate that populations vary between cities, suburbs, and rural areas and high and low levels of education and wealth.

Political characteristics that are likely to promote innovation include previous tendencies to innovate and governmental capability, which includes the professional quality of state legislatures, gubernatorial power, and financial support for governmental agencies and services. States that have modern and effective state legislatures and governors are more likely than others to become aware of innovations and to adopt them earlier. In addition, overall state policy liberalism is likely to affect decisions to enact living will laws. The right to die can be viewed as a liberal policy since it confers a constitutional and/or common law right on individuals to control their own bodies, and freedom from medical and governmental interference.

Finally, political competition and the policy relevance of political parties are expected to relate positively to innovation. States with active two-party electoral competition—where Democrats and Republicans alternate in controlling the governorship and a majority of seats in the legislature—are more likely to generate new policy proposals and be attuned and responsive to demands for change than governments in one-party states. More important are differences in the policy relevance of political parties. Policy relevance distinguishes among states according to whether the two major parties take distinctive positions on important social issues. In some states the two parties oppose each other in the legislature on major social issues such as welfare spending, but in others legislative divisions are based on personal or factional coalitions having little to do with political parties. States having policy-based parties probably are more likely to innovate early as each party responds to different constituencies and policies which affect them.

I expect these characteristics to be related to innovation, and I have obtained measures for all of them in order to test their relationship to the dates of adoption of living will laws.[2] However, while many of these variables have been shown in previous research to be related to a *general* tendency of states to innovate, few of them are proximate to the politics of creating *particular policies,* such as living will laws. While urbanism and high levels of education, for example, generally correspond with state tendencies to innovate, it is uncertain that they will distinguish among the states on the living will. Massachusetts, New Jersey, New York, and Pennsylvania all rank high in urbanism, state population, wealth, and various measures of governmental capability and competition, and generally they are among the states most likely to adopt innovations early. Yet they all lack living will laws, probably because the Catholic church in each of these states has been able to block their adoption.

Therefore state characteristics that are much more closely linked to the politics of the right to die also need to be included in order to develop a complete explanation of living will innovation. The politics of the right to die strongly indicate that a measure of the influence of relevant interest groups, particularly the Catholic church, must be included. Previous research on the adoption of morals policies, including birth control, divorce, gambling, and liquor laws, also has shown that innovation was much more heavily affected by the size of Catholic and fundamentalist Protestant populations than by other state social, economic, and political characteristics (Fairbanks 1980). These policies tap sensitive and deeply held personal values and generate intense political conflict. Political party leaders often do not take a stand on these policies, leaving individual legislators to vote according to their conscience or what they perceive to be the views of constituents (Smith 1975:90). Since living will laws raise similar concerns, it is likely that the diffusion of living will laws will be more heavily affected by the strength of Catholic and fundamentalist religious groups than by other variables.

I have obtained the percentage of each state's population that is Catholic as an indirect measure of the power of the Catholic church, and the percentage of the state population that adheres to fundamentalist Protestant religions as an additional indirect indicator of prolife sentiment and interest group power. Despite spotty evidence that the elderly have been active in right to die politics, I have included the percentage of each state's population over age 65 as an indirect indicator of senior power since right to die treatment decisions affect the elderly more heavily than any other population group.[3]

Results. I analyzed the relationships between these variables and the dates that states enacted living will laws through event history analysis, which is used to examine the likelihood of an event occurring at a particular time, in this case, annual adoptions of living will laws.[4] The variables that retained their significance throughout the analysis were *the size of the state's Catholic population, publications in mass periodicals, and the number of court decisions.* The direction of these relationships also was as expected. The larger a state's Catholic population the less likely states are to adopt living will laws. In contrast, the rising number of mass media publications and court decisions tended to enhance the tendency of the states to innovate. The three variables are moderately powerful predictors of state adoptions of living will laws.[5] The impact of court decisions reinforces the earlier observation that the rising tide of court decisions led to a change in the political posture of the Catholic church toward living will laws.

The other variables had no appreciable impact. The annual rate of publication in professional media is not related to innovation, probably because this literature is not visible to most government officials, lobbyists, and the public. Regionalism has no general effect on the tendency of states to enact living will laws, despite cohesion among some of the western states in the early years. All of the other state social, economic, and political characteristics also fail to influence the pattern of adoptions. These variables probably are too remote from the specific politics of the right to die.[6]

Finally, the size of the state's elderly and Protestant fundamentalist populations also failed to affect the tendency of states to innovate. Although the elderly might be expected to have a special interest in this issue, their presence is not felt in the statistical analysis and it generally has failed to appear in the case studies as well. Protestant fundamentalists have participated in living will battles as part of right to life organizations, but fundamentalists are not plentiful in the northeast and the role of the Catholic church generally overshadows their importance there and in other states.

These results closely fit the findings of the case studies and the connections between court decisions and legislation, which I discussed earlier. However, the event history analysis has shown in addition that publications in the mass media contribute to legislative decisions to enact living will laws. Publications in the professional literature do not correlate with enactments, however, which reinforces the two-stage process in media effects on state legislation (Nelson 1984:56). The professional literature emerges first, and in the early stages of agenda setting only certain professionals are keenly aware of the issue. In time, however, the professional literature provides information and ideas to writers for the mass literature, and the volume of articles in popular journals and newspapers increases. This popular or mass literature arouses general public awareness—including legislators and other political activists—and increases the propensity of states to innovate.

The Reinvention of Living Will Laws

Like judicial policy, living will laws have been reinvented over time, and recent legislation generally is more responsive to patients' rights and freedom than the earlier laws. Another parallel between judicial policy and legislation is that, like the states that have had several court cases in which judges have expanded the scope of the right to die in later decisions, legislatures in many states have amended their living will laws, also generally in the direction of providing greater freedom for patients and families.

State living will laws, however, are not as consistent or uniform as most state judicial policies. With few exceptions state courts have broadly interpreted the right to refuse and terminate treatment and they place few hurdles before patients, but living will laws vary much more. Some provide wide latitude to patients and families while others hem them in, and certain provisions are very restrictive. I shall discuss original legislation and laws after amendment separately in order to demonstrate how legislation has changed since 1976.

In order to analyze the reinvention of living will laws, I have coded each original law and all amendments through 1990 along a common dimension or scale termed *living will facility,* which reflects the ease of producing and carrying out the provisions of advance medical directives. The scale is based on eighteen similar legal provisions covering four main areas of living will laws: drafting; executing (signature and witnessing requirements); coverage of various medical contingencies; and enforcing a living will. A higher total score indicates that a state has a living will law that makes it easier for patients and their families to control medical decision making and treatment. The scoring technique is similar to that used in much policy research in which provisions of state law are content analyzed and coded in order to tap the particular requirements or coverage of various state policies (Bingham 1976; Fairbanks 1980; Glick 1981).

Original Legislation

The scores for each state's original legislation are presented in Table 6.2. If a state were to score in the highest category on all provisions of living will laws, the score would be 28. However, no state reaches that level since all have some restrictive provisions. Substantial variation exists among state scores, ranging from a high facility score of 20 to a very restrictive score of 6. Significantly, many of the states that were among the early adopters—the chronological innovators—have produced legislation that is much more restrictive than that of many recent adopters. Of the eight earliest adopters (table 6.1), seven have scale scores below the mean of 12.2, and several have the lowest scores in table 2: California scores 8; Idaho 6; and Texas 7.

An illustration of the important difference between state scores is found in the contrast of California (1976) and Montana (1985) legislation. In California, which has a low overall facility score of 8, a valid living will can be executed by a patient no sooner than two weeks after he or she has been diagnosed as terminally ill, and a living will cannot be created on behalf of a patient who is unable to sign for him- or herself. In Montana, with a high score of 20, a valid living will can be created any time and there is a provision for creating a living will for an incompetent or incapacitated individual. These provisions have enormous consequences for the usefulness of a living will law to residents of different states. As reported previously, a survey of California doctors found that as many as 50 percent or more patients are not diagnosed as terminally ill until after

179

TABLE 6.2   *State Living Will Facility Scores*

State	Score	State	Score	State	Score
Alaska	20	Alabama	13	Illinois	10
Maine	20	Arizona	13	Mississippi	10
Montana	20	Hawaii	13	North Carolina	10
		Indiana	13	Wisconsin	10
		Iowa	13		
Louisiana	18	North Dakota	13	Kentucky	9
Virginia	18	Tennessee	13	Nevada	9
		West Virginia	13	New Hampshire	9
				South Carolina	9
Washington, D.C.	16	Missouri	12		
Maryland	16	New Mexico	12	California	8
Minnesota	16	Vermont	12	Oklahoma	8
		Washington	12		
Florida	15	Wyoming	12	Georgia	7
Utah	15			Texas	7
		Arkansas	11		
Kansas	14	Colorado	11	Connecticut	6
		Delaware	11	Idaho	6
		Oregon	11		

Mean = 12.2; Median = 12; Std. Dev. = 3.7

they have become permanently comatose, making it impossible for these patients ever to execute a valid living will (*The California Natural Death Act* 1979). Since no other person may act on their behalf, the law puts a living will out of reach of most people.

In addition, in California living wills are valid for no longer than five years whereas Montana has no time limit. California imposes complicated and restrictive witnessing requirements, while Montana does not. In California a living will is invalid if the patient is pregnant, while in Montana the document is invalid only if it is clear the fetus will develop if life-sustaining treatment is given to the patient. In California a doctor who refuses to comply with a living will faces no penalties, while in Montana a doctor who refuses to carry out a patient's wishes to withdraw or withhold life-sustaining treatment is subject to criminal prosecution. Overall, Montana's recent law makes it much easier for patients or their families to control final medical treatment and enforcement provisions are likely to compel doctors to comply with their wishes.

Arkansas provides another contrast with California and most early adopting states. Arkansas enacted a restrictive living will law in 1977 with a facility score of 11, higher than California's but still well below the scores of later adopters. However, in 1987 Arkansas substantially amended its law, which has become the ideal model for the Society for the Right to Die. Arkansas' total score increased to 25, the highest in the nation. It differs from the Montana law in four important ways. First, unlike most other state laws that limit living wills to patients declared to be in a terminal condition, the Arkansas legislation applies also to patients who are in a permanent comatose state. Arkansas also allows for creating living wills on behalf of minors and permits the designation of a proxy decision maker in a living will. It also includes a procedure for terminating life-support systems for patients who lack a living will. This latter provision exceeds the coverage of many other laws and it applies to circumstances usually found only in state court policies.

Chronology and policy content. The position of the states on tables 6.1 and 6.2 suggests that the states that recently have enacted living will laws have produced more facilitative legislation. By correlating the date of adoption with the facility score, it is possible to assess more precisely the strength of the relationship between chronological innovation and policy reinvention. I do not argue that date of adoption explains or causes reinvention in a theoretic sense. The roots of reinvention likely include accumulating social experience from the application of medical technology, changes in the policy positions and priorities of interest groups, and patterns of emulation among the states—all of which occur over time—as well as differences in individual state political and social characteristics. However, the correlation between the dates of enactment and the facility scores can demonstrate the general tendency of later adopters to create more facilitative law.

I have correlated state scores with the date of adoption.[7] A plot of the state scores by year is presented in figure 6.2. The rising horizontal line of central tendency and the array of the states shows that living will legislation becomes more facilitative over time, although the relationship is a modest one. The relationship between these variables is most clear in the comparison between the earliest and middle adopters. The earliest innovators have very restrictive laws while those adopting in 1980 and 1981 have higher scores. By

FIGURE 6.2   *Plot of Facility Scores with*
Date of Adoption

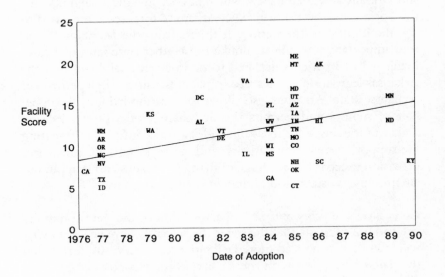

r = .316   R² = .10   Sig. = .04   Slope = .315

1984 and 1985 the scores begin to span a broader spectrum, although more states have higher than lower scores. Therefore, while the overall direction of the relationship reveals increasingly facilitative laws over time, there are other dimensions to reinvention.

Variations on reinvention.   Intense political conflict has developed over certain elements of living will laws, and some recent legislation contains restrictive provisions that contribute to lower overall states scores. As discussed earlier, an exceptionally controversial provision concerns the artificial administration of food and hydration. Political activists in the three case study states volunteered that this was the most controversial issue on the right to die agenda. Right to die advocacy and other groups maintain that food and hydration should be viewed as a form of medical treatment that may be refused, withheld, or withdrawn, but the Catholic church and right to life groups are opposed and have lobbied for provisions in living will laws that would prevent the withdrawal or withholding of artificial food and hydration from any patient.

The entry of new and controversial issues, such as food and hydration, is likely to lower overall state facility scores if legislatures respond to groups that want to limit the scope of living will laws. Additional analysis confirms that several provisions, especially those concerning food and hydration, have evolved opposite the overall trend of increasingly facilitative laws. Recent adopting states either have created new restrictive provisions or they have modified earlier ones in a more restrictive manner.

In order to identify all restrictive provisions in recent laws, I performed another set of correlations. First, I obtained correlations for each provision of each law with the date of adoption and noted those which became more restrictive over time, i.e., had negative signs. Five of the eighteen provisions produced negative results: regulation of the artificial administration of food and hydration; validity of living wills in the case of pregnancy; creation of living wills for minors; provisions permitting interested parties to block the implementation of living wills through court order; and penalties for failing to transfer patients to another medical facility if the original institution and/or staff refused to comply with a living will. I then analyzed these five provisions together to determine which of them had the greatest negative impact on the overall positive correlation between date of adoption and facility scores.

As anticipated from the current political conflict that dominates the right to die, the food and hydration provision was the only one that produced a large and statistically significant negative relationship with date of adoption.[8] The other four provisions had little impact. Removing the scores on the food and hydration provisions from the overall state facility score increases the relationship between date of adoption and facility score from .316 to .436 (sig. < .002).[9] In other terms, if none of the states had food and hydration provisions in their living will laws the overall facility scores would increase over time more than they do.

In addition to demonstrating the powerful impact of the food and hydration provisions on state living will laws and amplifying the intense political conflict over this issue, these findings have implications for the study of state public policy. They suggest that while states are likely to reinvent policy during diffusion and late adopters often have higher innovation scores (here, more facilitative living will laws), specific provisions of state law contribute to contrary hidden currents in policy-making, which partially mask the overall tendency of recent states to reinvent policy along a dominant dimension or theme. Policy researchers need to be sensitive to how particular provisions are treated by state institutions, for there may be several directions to innovation—those which facilitate and those which limit the options of groups affected by the law.

Amendment

Early enactment and reinvention by later adopters does not exhaust the reinvention process. Eighteen states amended their living will laws. Seven produced only technical changes that did not affect their facility scores, but eleven others made various substantive changes. *Most important, all eleven made their laws more facilitative,* in keeping with the trend established during the take-off period of original adoptions. Amending states changed their scores from 1 to 14 points, but the median change in score was a modest 2.5. In six states, legislatures adopted both more facilitative and restrictive amendments, but nevertheless increased their overall scores. *All but one restrictive amendment concerned food and hydration and pregnancy,* and reveal that these states adopted limitations favored by state Catholic conferences and right to life organizations.

Amendment can be expected to occur when early adopters change their laws to conform to the most recent reinventions. However, seven of the eleven states with substantive amendments changed their laws prior to or during the take-off period of original adoptions (1983 and 1985). Thus many of the early innovators often renovated their laws before others had gotten on the bandwagon. The early innovators remain in the communications network and are affected by the same national events and trends that affect later adopters during their initial decision to enact living will laws.

The process of amending legislation complicates the diffusion of policy innovation and the leadership position of individual states in the adoption process. It also indicates that policy analysts need to reconsider the diffusion of innovations as a simple straight line from early to late adoptions. The earliest adopters—particularly the first pioneering state—are due substantial credit as chronological innovators and for elevating an issue on the agenda, but their original facility scores tend to be lower than the later adopters. However, the status of some early adopters is reinforced since they amend before many initial adopters create *any* legislation. But, of seven 1977 adopters, only three substantially increased their scores through amendment and only one (Arkansas) exceeded the scores that later adopters achieved through their original legislation (table 6.2).

Consequently, it is difficult to evaluate the innovative role of early adopters that amend but do not exceed the original scores of late adopters. From the perspective of the chronology of innovation they are the leaders, but in terms of facilitative legislation they are among the pack and their laws have no greater benefits for citizens than original adoptions made later by other states. Finally, early restrictive laws that are not amended, such as the first living will law in California, continue to be much less useful to citizens than recent innovations in many other states including those that rarely are visible leaders in policy innovation—Maryland, Louisiana, West Virginia, Alabama, Vermont, and others.

A remaining question is how amendments have affected the original legislation and the relationship between date of adoption and state facility scores. First, amendment contributed to a slight increase in the overall range of facility scores. The range in the original legislation was from 6 to 20 with a mean score of 12.2. With the amendments, the range in scores changed from 6 to 25 with a mean of 13.3. *However, the effect of amendment on the relationship between date of adoption and final facility scores is to reduce the correlation to zero.* Figure 6.3 shows that the line of central tendency is nearly level, which indicates that the state scores are distributed nearly equally above and below the line over time. As indicated above, except for Arkansas, all of the amending states produced final scores that fell well within the range for all adopters. This does not mean that

FIGURE 6.3   *Plot of Amended Facility
Scores with Date of Adoption*

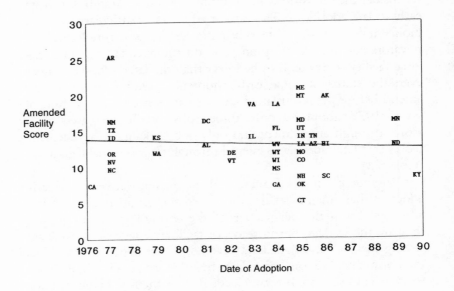

r = -.051   R² = .003   Sig. = n.s.   Slope = -.053

amendment resulted in nearly uniform legislation, but that through amendment most early adopters increased their scores to fall within the spread of scores of the later adopters.

Previous research on policy innovation has examined original legislation or initial court cases in particular fields of policy. Amendments and later judicial revisions rarely are considered (Eyestone 1977). My findings indicate, however, that it is important to distinguish between original and amended policy, and that amendment should be considered part of the ongoing cycle of innovation that affects the final content of policy and the relative position of the states as innovators.

In the case of living will laws, if someone were to examine only the content of the current set of laws, he or she would find that the laws vary substantially, but that the differences seem unrelated to political conditions at the time the laws were enacted. There would be no clues for understanding the impact on social and political events and trends on the evolving content of state law.

Continuous Innovation
Limits of Living Wills

Shortly after the living will became legal in California's Natural Death Act in 1976, doctors, patients, lawyers, and legislators became aware of its limited usefulness. Feedback from doctors and patients convinced Senator Barry Keene that the living will was not doing the job he intended, and he began to look for other ways to regulate medical treatment decision making in hopeless cases. Later adopting states generally have enlarged the coverage of living wills and avoided some of the crippling restrictions contained in the California law, particularly the requirement that a patient formally be diagnosed as terminally ill before a living will can be executed and the five-year time limitation on the validity of a living will.

But certain provisions and amendments that would enlarge the coverage of living wills, especially to permit the withdrawal of feeding tubes, have been resisted by right to life organizations and state legislatures (see also Coleman 1989). In 1990 nine states considered amendments to their living will laws. Seven of them would have permitted individuals to refuse food and hydration, but only three of them passed. An additional amendment that passed requires the administration of food and hydration in certain circumstances. Legislatures in nine other states without living will laws also considered bills. Only one living will law was enacted, and it requires the administration of food and hydration under certain circumstances. Five of the failed living will bills included provisions permitting the withdrawal of feeding tubes (Society for the Right to Die, 26 November 1990).

Commentators have noted many problems with living wills, particularly their limited applicability to various illnesses and the interpretation of living will language (Eisendrath and Jonsen 1983; Martyn and Jacobs 1984; Peters 1987; Weir 1989; Uniform Rights of the Terminally Ill Act, Amended 1989). First, most living will laws recognize only terminal illnesses as the basis for withdrawing treatment, which disqualifies other conditions from coverage. Patients in a permanent vegetative state and the very elderly, who linger with many chronic problems and injuries, including Alzheimer's disease—none of which are classified as terminal illnesses—and who drift between vague awareness and unconsciousness, can end up in living will limbo. With feeding tubes and other routine medical and nursing care, many such patients live for months or years even though they might have signed living wills and previously have stated to others that they wanted no life-sustaining treatment.

Even living will laws that apply to a permanent vegetative state or have provisions for terminating treatment for people without living wills pose problems of interpretation. Generally, disputes over the interpretation of statutes is a routine part of politics, and courts, administrators, and legislators deal with them as a regular part of government business. But when doctors, hospital administrators, and families are faced with life-and-death decision making, the problems of interpretation become acute and intense and carry enormous stakes.

There are numerous problems of interpretation, including what is meant by *terminal illness, no reasonable expectation of recovery, extraordinary treatment, when death is imminent, no hope, when the patient is no longer able to make decisions,* and other phrases. Although many serious illnesses from cancer to pneumonia cause death if they are untreated, patients' lives can be extended through aggressive treatment, and otherwise deadly conditions may not be classified as terminal illnesses so long as death can be postponed.

It is unclear when illnesses transform or should be reclassified from treatable conditions to terminal ones and when treatment should be ended. It also is difficult to get agreement on when death is expected to occur, so that *when death is imminent* can mean months from one point of view, but days or hours from another. Other phrases such as *no hope* or *no reasonable expectation of recovery* also are loaded with various meanings. For example, although there may be no hope or reasonable expectation that a patient can be fully restored to a previous condition of health following a stroke, heart attack, or onset of cancer, or brain damage caused by a serious accident, a patient may improve somewhat with treatment. What level

188

of improvement qualifies as recovery, and how should we measure hope or expectations?

In addition to the presence of many vague terms and phrases, living wills do not anticipate all future medical conditions and treatment options. Unless living wills were to include a list of many specific diseases or conditions and specify the kinds of treatment patients wish or reject for each of them—an impossible scenario—there are bound to be circumstances not explicitly covered by living wills and that leave room for physician and family discretion.

When a specific illness occurs doctors predisposed to treat are likely to deal with the symptom or problem and avoid considering the patient's earlier expressed wishes, which are contained in a document that cannot communicate about the immediate problem. Examples are various infections that patients may suffer in the course of dying from an otherwise deadly disease such as AIDS or cancer. Patients cannot anticipate and name every type of infection they might contract and treatments they might receive, but if doctors believe that an infection can be cured, even though the underlying illness cannot, many are apt to prescribe treatment. This occurs despite patients' living wills and even though a now unconscious patient probably would have objected. (*New York Times,* 17 January 1991:B7).

Limitations in the coverage and interpretation of living wills and political resistance to change has contributed to the search by right to die advocates for new solutions to the same treatment dilemmas. This new wave of agenda setting and innovation began in the 1980s at the same the time that many states were in the process of adopting living will laws. This recent innovation illustrates that innovation is a continuous process as many new ideas and policies surface as solutions or ways of coping with recurring problems. Durable power of attorney for health care and health care proxy laws are the current trend.

Powers of Attorney and Proxies

The durable power of attorney for health care (DPAHC) and health care proxy laws (HCP) permit individuals to designate another to make health care decisions on their behalf in the event patients are unable to make treatment decisions themselves. These laws presume that the decision maker has talked with the patient and understands his or her wishes concerning medical treatment. An advantage of this procedure over a living will is that the designated spokesperson has explicit legal authority to act on a patient's behalf and can interact with doctors concerning specific treatment decisions. A person takes the place of a formal document and communications can continue throughout treatment. It also removes concerns about internal family conflicts since the power of attorney or proxy specifies the person who has the power to act on a patient's behalf. Proxies also typically do not limit decisions to terminal illnesses, which allows discretion and latitude in dealing with specific but perhaps unexpected circumstances. However, some states have imposed particular limitations and others permit an individual to impose restrictions on their proxy if they wish. In all, thirty-eight states and Washington, D.C. have a form of proxy law that permits a spokesperson to refuse treatment on another's behalf.[10]

Political appeal.   DPAHC and HCP laws are attractive to many of the main political actors who have been involved in right to die policy-making. They appeal to doctors and medical institutions because they shift responsibility from them to a person with legal standing named by the patient. Doctors no longer need to worry about the meaning of a living will or sanctions for failure to comply, but can rely on another person who has the authority to speak for the patient. Doctors make recommendations about treatment, but proxies have the final power to decide. The Catholic church objects less to these documents than to living wills because they keep medical decision making between doctors and family members or another trusted person close to the patient, and avoid government involvement in defining life and death and penalties concerning the implementation of a living will. While bar associations have not been especially active in right to die politics, attorneys accept these new laws because they fit well within standard estate planning procedures.

These documents are attractive to political figures also because they are simple and generally avoid or postpone political conflicts that have occurred over living will laws. Since a person merely designates another to act on his or her behalf at a later unknown time, decisions concerning the meaning of *terminal illness, when death is imminent, no reasonable hope of recovery,* and other matters are put off until the patient actually falls ill and decisions have to be made. If conflicts are to occur, they occur at another time and another place, not in legislatures when laws are enacted.

Finally, these new laws have been enacted more easily than living will laws in many of the states because the innovations appear to grow naturally out of existing law. Instead of a brand new policy, which appears as a striking and controversial departure from the past, the DPAHC and HCP appear as an incremental change in existing ways of allowing people to handle their personal affairs. All of the states have had durable power of attorney laws that permit individuals to designate another person to make decisions concerning the disposition of property or other matters if they are unable to act for themselves. Compared with totally new legislation, it was relatively easy to convince legislators that applying the same principle to health care was not revolutionary, but a natural extension of previous policy. And, as indicated, the NCCUSL legitimized proxy laws before many of the states enacted them.

Limitations. There are caveats to the widespread support that seems to exist on this newest right to die innovation. Although new proxy laws or living will laws and amendments that permit proxies have been enacted recently in most of the states, their enactment has involved political compromises bound to stimulate additional litigation and legislation in the right to die. In several states the Catholic church has secured compromises prohibiting the withdrawal of food and hydration from terminal patients and/or those in a permanent vegetative state. As discussed earlier concerning Massachusetts, including a food and hydration prohibition was part of a settlement that made it possible to get any right to die legislation in the state. Similar curbs have been imposed in Ohio, New York, Connecticut, and Kentucky. In these states, proxies either cannot request the withdrawal of food and hydration or they need additional documentation showing that the patient did not wish to receive this form of treatment.

In states in which proxy provisions have been included as part of living will laws, proxies are affected by the same language problems that plague others in interpreting living wills. If living wills are applicable only to terminal illnesses, for example, proxies cannot obtain the withdrawal of treatment unless a patient has been diagnosed as terminally ill, and disagreements may flare over that decision. Doctors and proxies may confront each other also if doctors refuse to withdraw food and hydration, while proxies are certain that the patient would not have wanted that treatment. New court cases are likely.

Renewed political conflicts between courts and legislatures also are likely to occur in states where restrictive proxy laws appear to contradict earlier state court decisions that have decreed a constitutional or common law right to refuse treatment, including artificially administered food and hydration. Courts also have permitted the withdrawal of treatment from a wider set of seriously ill patients, including the terminally ill and those in a permanent vegetative state or other hopeless condition, than are covered by most living will laws. Since most courts already have decided that patients have the right to refuse treatment directly or through proxies or guardians, they probably will continue to do so. Restrictive legislative language may not restrict the courts that rely on their own sources of right to die policy.

Assisted Suicide

No state has enacted laws permitting a person to assist another in committing suicide, but this issue too is on the professional and mass agendas, and it is attracting additional media exposure and public interest, particularly concerning the proper role of doctors in treating terminally ill patients. Assisted suicide is not the same as mercy killing, since assisting a suicide contributes indirectly to another's death. However, the two sometimes are linked and discussed together in the news media since doctors or others take various active roles in ending the life of a terminally ill or suffering patient. The mercy killer directly administers the lethal dose or uses a weapon, sometimes involving a patient who is unable to express his or her own desires. In assisted suicide the patient intentionally commits the act after having obtained information or drugs or other means from a doctor or other person. To some, assisted suicide is less objectionable than mercy killing because it is the patient, not another person, who makes the decision and takes the action to end life. Of course right to life groups and others oppose suicide, assisted or otherwise, as a violation of moral and religious beliefs and law.

Medically assisted suicide has become visible recently through the "suicide machines" built by Dr. Jack Kevorkian and used in Michigan on two different occasions by three women, including one woman who traveled from Washington state to obtain Dr. Kevorkian's help. The suicide machines permitted the patients to self-administer a lethal dose of drugs. Following their deaths, which took place in a van and a remote vacation cabin, Dr. Kevorkian notified local police and sought publicity in order to stimulate public discussion of assisted suicide. His conduct and procedures aroused enormous controversy and he was indicted for first degree murder in the first case, but the judge ruled in a preliminary hearing that Dr. Kevorkian had not caused the woman's death, and since there was no law in Michigan against assisted suicide, no other charges could be brought against him. The judge called for new legislation (*New York Times* 14 December 1990:1; 25 October 1991:1).

A few months after the first incident involving Kevorkian, doctor-assisted suicide again was in the news when Dr. Timothy E. Quill of Rochester, New York, assisted a leukemia victim to commit suicide by advising her to seek information from the Hemlock Society, and then providing her with a prescription for barbiturates that he knew she would use to kill herself (*New York Times* 12 March 1991:B6).

Dr. Kevorkian's approach to assisted suicide gained few sympathetic supporters due to his personal notoriety and longstanding history as an outsider in the medical profession. Other doctors quoted in the mass media were careful to distinguish between Dr. Kevorkian's methods and the serious problems faced by terminally ill patients.[11] In contrast, Dr. Quill received a more careful and sympathetic reaction since he was well-established in medical practice and, although assisted suicide is not an accepted medical treatment, he reacted to his patient's desire and plans for suicide within the context of standard medical procedures.[12] Unlike Dr. Kevorkian, he had been treating his patient for a long period of time. She was not a stranger who came to town to use a specially designed and publicized device to take her life. The patient, her family, and the doctor had carefully discussed treatment options for her leukemia and her desire to die without further medical treatment before the disease caused her further suffering. The patient also was seen by a psychiatrist who determined that her desire to commit suicide did not stem from serious depression. In addition, Dr. Quill sought visibility in a more polished and professional forum by publishing an article in the prestigious *New England Journal of Medicine* describing the circumstances of the case and his actions.

Although assisted suicide is illegal in New York, Dr. Quill was not prosecuted. The county district attorney presented a case to the grand jury, but it refused to indict him (*New York Times* 27 July 1991:1). Like Dr. Kevorkian, Dr. Quill hoped that his article would stimulate professional discussion of doctors' roles in helping terminally ill and suffering patients to die, if that was their wish. His refined and professional approach to telling his story is vastly different from Dr. Kevorkian's treatment and exposure, and will contribute to keeping assisted suicide on the public agenda and probably will make it more legitimate.

In addition to these two highly visible incidents, assisted suicide has been an issue for public policy consideration since popular initiatives legalizing assisted suicide have been started in California and Washington state. The number of signatures was inadequate for getting the issue before the California voters, but in Washington the issue was on the November 1991 ballot. It was defeated by a margin of 54 to 46 percent. If passed, the law would have allowed doctors to aid in the suicide of a patient who had requested assistance in writing and been certified by two doctors as terminally ill and with no more than six months to live. Supporters, particularly the Hemlock Society, reportedly had raised over $1.5 million for the campaign while opponents, including the National Conference of Catholic Bishops, had contributed approximately $1 million to defeat the plan (*New York Times,* 4 November 1991:A9; 7 November 1991:A10).

Although these measures have not passed, recent polls indicate that approximately 50 percent of the public favors assisted suicide. If similar measures were put on the ballot in these or other states, it is possible they might be approved, although the Catholic church and right to life organizations would wage a mighty battle to prevent it. Judging by the history of living will laws, these groups probably will be able to keep assisted suicide out of state legislatures for the foreseeable future.

But assisted suicide will not disappear. Public interest is high, and it will possibly replace the artificial administration of food and hydration as the most controversial right to die proposal. Another indication of the salience of assisted suicide is the new book on how to commit suicide titled *Final Exit,* by Derek Humphry of the Hemlock Society, which became a controversial best-seller in the summer of 1991 (*New York Times,* 9 August 1991:A1).

With intense public interest and half the public in favor of it, assisted suicide may become a more widespread unofficial practice, as in the Netherlands. But given the heavy presence of government policy-making in the right to die, it will remain as part of the professional and mass agendas for years to come. Additional efforts surely will be made to legalize aid in dying.

Interest Groups and Legislation: The Elderly

As indicated throughout this book, state Catholic conferences universally are the most prominent interest groups affecting living will laws. The case studies and the analysis of the politics of innovation clearly establish their preeminent role in delaying or limiting the coverage of these laws as well as recent proxy legislation. As mentioned earlier, there has been little organized support for these laws. Although the elderly are disproportionately involved in and affected by the court cases as well as legislation, there is no evidence that advocates for the elderly or associations of retired individuals have been active in right to die politics. This cannot be due to their general lack of political participation since the elderly or groups that speak for them are very active in other policies, notably Social Security legislation and social services for the elderly. Their absence in the right to die requires explanation.

Of the three case study states, the elderly have been most active in California, although they have not been prominent there. Associations of the elderly and others indicated their support of the 1976 Natural Death Act, usually through letters written to the bill sponsor and legislative committees, but they were not active in drafting the bill, rounding up support in the legislature, or providing an alternative perspective to the CMA or CCC. The first indication of active senior involvement appeared in 1985 when the Gray Panthers urged Senator Keene to introduce the NCCUSL uniform living will law in the California legislature. This organization planned to coordinate support among other seniors' groups, including the American Association of Retired Persons (AARP), Older Women's League, and others. However, no amendments to California's law were introduced until 1987, and since then the Gray Panthers appear to have moved on to other issues.

Among the elderly, the AARP reportedly has shown the greatest recent interest in obtaining amendments to the law. Although seniors have been more active in California than in other states, and their recent activity may indicate more interest in the future, there has been no evidence of a sustained effort supporting living will laws, lobbying on behalf of changes in California's law, or in arousing large numbers of seniors to contact public officials.

The level of involvement of the elderly in living will laws has been even lower in Florida and Massachusetts. In Florida the Silver Haired Legislature once placed the right to die on its agenda, but it never considered policy alternatives and it has not endorsed legislation. The state chapter of the AARP has only recently indicated interest in living will laws, but there is no evidence that it has been active on this issue in the legislature. Another organization, the American Association of Retired Citizens, lobbied against a living will bill during one year but otherwise has not been active.

In Massachusetts the dominance of the Catholic church has shaped the political conflict and overshadowed the power of all other groups. As in Florida, in one particular year, the Silver Haired Legislature and the state secretary of elder affairs each endorsed a living will bill but they have not engaged in active lobbying. Political activists maintain that living will proposals have so sharply divided the state along religious lines that it is difficult for any other group to influence legislation or even to provide perspectives on living will legislation that differ from the themes established by opposing religious organizations. Overall, the elderly are not perceived as important politically in this area of policy.

Why Inactivity?

The elderly have not been active in right to die politics probably for several reasons. First, the elderly generally have not been prominent in state politics and policy. Advocates and organizations of the elderly have directed most of their attention to national policy-making since the federal government has established the major programs benefiting the elderly, and state and local governments participate through matching funds and parallel government programs and bureaucracies. Many state and local officials and advocates for the elderly have perceived the federal government, not the states, as having responsibility for the elderly (Dobson and Karnes 1979; Dobson and St. Angelo 1979; Browne 1985). There are signs, however, that senior lobbying is increasing in the states. The AARP, for example, has established state committees to monitor and influence legislation, and states with active senior organizations include Michigan, Minnesota, New York, and California.[13] Nevertheless, with few exceptions, senior interest in the right to die is low in comparison with other state issues, such as tax relief, health care, housing, transportation, and others (Browne 1985; Browne and Ringquist 1985). However, in 1987, the Minnesota Board of Aging—a state agency established to advise the governor on aging—sponsored a living will bill, but a living will law was not enacted until 1989.

Lack of interest probably is linked to the specific content of this issue. First, it may reflect the tendency of many citizens—young and old alike—to avoid issues of death and dying. The right to die, in particular, deals with medical treatment and hospitalization associated possibly with a prolonged and painful death in which the individual is intruded upon beyond his or her control. Contemplating this issue in personal terms and promoting public policy regarding the right to die is troublesome and unpleasant for many. The right to die also competes with other health care and financial issues that have more immediate and compelling importance to the elderly. Similarly, organizations of the elderly often have stressed tangible economic benefits such as discounts on insurance, travel, and pharmaceuticals. In addition, living wills may be executed by any person over age twenty-one, making the right to die technically unrelated to age, although the elderly are more heavily affected than other age groups.

Finally, the elderly divide along political, socioeconomic, and other lines, and age is not a good predictor of political attitudes or loyalties (Hendricks and Hendricks 1977; Dobson and St. Angelo 1979; Hudson 1980; Binstock 1984). Moreover, the well-educated and economically well-off elderly—those most likely to actively participate in political organizations—are *least likely* to identify with the elderly as a group. They tend to link themselves to various other social and economic groups, such as particular occupations, coreligionists, or the middle class, or they do not identify with any segment of society.

When policies benefit certain groups of elderly differently, political divisions occur and the elderly send mixed and competing messages to public officials. The right to die probably cleaves the elderly along similar religious and political lines found in the general population. Elderly Catholics may be equally or even more inclined than younger Catholics to follow church leaders, and elderly conservative Protestants may share a right to life orientation with their younger coreligionists. Consequently, associations of the elderly may be reluctant to take a position on this issue if it might divide the membership. The few organizations of the elderly that have testified for the enactment of living will legislation find it difficult to convince legislators that they widely represent the elderly since opposing groups sometimes make identical claims.

Professional associations that advocate the interests of the elderly might appear to have greater opportunities to influence state legislatures, but since they are advocates *for* the elderly and not *of* the elderly they probably would not be convincing as genuine representatives of the elderly on this sensitive issue (Hudson 1980). Politically-appointed government officials who serve as advocates of the elderly also must balance their political security with the interests of the elderly, and strong advocacy on controversial issues sometimes is sacrificed to political survival. Advocacy groups also have organizational interests that do not necessarily coincide with the interests of their clientele or customers. In living will laws, for example, medical, hospital, and nursing home associations frequently state that they are deeply concerned with the interests of patients, but the provisions of law that they have addressed most often concern liability for terminating life-support systems and dampening efforts to impose civil or criminal penalties for not complying with patients' wishes. In other instances, these groups have opposed all legislation as an interference with traditional doctor/hospital-patient relationships.

Political Potential

Many commentators and researchers perceive enormous political potential for the elderly in state politics, but almost all agree that the potential has not been realized. The size of the elderly population is growing rapidly and the social and political contours of the United States are changing. The proportion of the elderly population in Florida probably will become the model for the rest of the nation in the next century (Lammers 1983). Many issues concerning the elderly, including the right to die, are bound to become more relevant and salient to the elderly and to policymakers alike.

Group size offers significant potential for influencing state politics. State legislatures may perceive the elderly as a growing and deserving group in need of additional services and support as well as an increasingly important voting bloc. Research both on the American states and among nations indicates that the proportion of the elderly population is an important factor explaining government support for pension and other legislation for the elderly (Browne 1985; Pampel and Williamson 1985; 1988; 1989). This could carry over to other policies if the elderly become interested and concerned with them.

The growing size of the elderly population also creates potential for group cohesion and identification, not just as a demographic category, but as a distinctive entity with particular life-styles, needs, problems, and aspirations. The elderly may congregate more in separate living arrangements and meet increasingly in senior centers—convenient locations for social and political organization (Hendricks and Hendricks 1977; Dobson and St. Angelo 1979). The elderly also remain active in many forms of politics. They continue to vote at levels equal to or higher than other age groups and they participate in other ways, such as paying close attention to political news and information and making campaign contributions. However, as they age, people become less involved in the most active forms of participation, notably talking to and persuading others about politics (Jennings and Markus 1988). Since many groups representing the elderly rely on volunteer amateur lobbyists (discussed below), the decline of active political participation among the elderly is a limitation on their power in state politics.

The elderly also generally enjoy a favorable public image and empathy from most other age groups, which might enhance their status and access in politics (Hudson 1980; Pampel and Williamson 1989). The middle-aged are most likely to be supportive since they foresee becoming elderly themselves. In contrast, it is more difficult to empathize with the young, an age to which no one can return, or with other racial, religious, gender, or sexual groups since people cannot or do not change these characteristics and may be less able to imagine themselves in the position of these others.

Limitations.   But size and empathy are not enough. Active lobbying is necessary for the elderly to obtain particular legislative victories, especially where their proportion of the population is small and others oppose bills they might favor, such as in the right to die. Obtaining gubernatorial support also is crucial, for governors have vetoed legislation favorable to the elderly when expenditures exceed governors' budgets (Browne 1985). Conservative governors in California and Florida and other states also have vetoed living will laws and amendments, so supporters of this legislation must obtain and maintain access to all branches of government if they want to increase their chances at political success. Finally, it also is necessary for the elderly to coordinate activities among mass membership organizations and for many groups to devote more of their energies to lobbying. In some states, associations of the elderly are interested mainly in social functions, and lobbyists for the elderly report that it is difficult to mobilize the membership for political action or other demonstrations of political support (Browne 1985).

The elderly have other political disadvantages. Most state legislators do not perceive the elderly as active in state politics nor do many legislators self-identify as advocates for the elderly or specialists in aging legislation. Nongovernmental advocates for the elderly rarely report that they participate in bill drafting or lobbying or serve as lobbyists for the elderly. Many see themselves as guardians and managers of existing federal programs and do not encourage further state or local government involvement (Dobson and Karnes 1979; Dobson and St. Angelo 1979; Browne 1985). Also, most senior citizens' groups do not employ professional lobbyists (Browne 1985). Although some amateur lobbyists have several years of lobbying experience, they often work part-time and lack the breadth and penetration enjoyed by business or other occupational and professional groups which sometimes employ the same professional lobbyists and large staffs for many years.

These limitations are compounded since the elderly usually seek to change the political status quo, such as in living will laws, which requires enormous energy and constancy to get new items on crowded legislative agendas, shift the attitudes of legislators, and shepherd bills into laws. In sharp contrast, a Catholic lobbyist volunteered that he did not find it difficult to defeat living will bills since it always is much easier to kill a bill than to enact a law. The many stages of the legislative process provide many locations and opportunities to shelve or vote down legislation, whereas obtaining passage means a bill has to get over every parliamentary hurdle.

Despite political disadvantages, the elderly usually are cohesive on certain issues, notably health care and income support, and the potential for political solidarity and growing impact remains. In addition, each generation undergoes distinctive life experiences during different historical periods which influence their political socialization and perceptions and attitudes throughout life. It is likely that future generations of elderly will see social issues differently from those of today. Regarding the right to die, as more public attention and public policy focuses on this issue—most of which supports the right to die—the current young-old and middle-aged populations

201

are likely to develop more knowledge and sophistication and perhaps will develop similar attitudes toward final health care decision making. The polls indicate wide support for the withdrawal of treatment, and these attitudes are likely to stay with people as they age. If there is growing interest in this issue and opinion solidarity among the future elderly, lobbyists will be motivated to concentrate on this policy and develop greater legitimacy as representatives of the elderly.

Conclusion

The tendency of most of the states to enact living will and other right to die laws is shaped by the rising tide of litigation and publications in the mass media, but they are affected too by the power of the Catholic church in state politics. No other interest group has been as concerned with these laws as the Catholic church, nor have they had nearly the impact. It appears that the Catholic church was able to prevent the enactment of living will laws in most of the states for many years. However, as litigation and publications in the mass media increased, the Church recognized that the right to die was being put into place by the courts and that legislation also was increasingly likely. Therefore Catholic strategies changed toward producing limited laws, which also are counterweights and alternatives to liberal court decisions.

Although most of the states have living will and proxy decision maker laws, individual state political processes have produced important variations among them that affect their application to various illnesses and how effective they are in permitting individuals to control medical treatment at the end of life. Differences in state laws are due to the impact of changing national trends and events over time and, generally, recently enacted or amended laws are more useful or facilitative than the earliest legislation. However, many laws contain crucial restrictions, particularly limitations on the withdrawal of artificially administered food and hydration, which is most important for patients in a permanent vegetative state or other slowly debilitating disease. In these cases, despite living wills calling for the end to treatment, individuals may linger for a very long time.

Dissatisfaction with living will laws has led to recent innovation and the enactment of simpler durable power of attorney for health care or proxy decision maker laws. These laws have been more easily enacted because they contain fewer provisions and are less controversial and seem to be routine expansions of existing law. However, enacting these laws has not been entirely routine in some states, for right to life groups have been able to attach restrictions on withdrawing food and hydration identical to those found in many living will laws.

At first glance it seems that these new simpler laws, which transfer decision making to another person sometime in the future, solve the problem of implementing the right to refuse treatment. But proxies in many states will find legal restrictions on food and hydration limit their ability to have their decisions put into effect. Where proxies derive their powers from living wills, they will have the added problem of coping with conflicts interpreting the meaning of these documents. Conflicts over these issues among doctors, medical institutions, and proxy decision makers and between courts and legislatures are bound to continue.

Research on the diffusion and reinvention of living will laws has general implications for state policy research. It has demonstrated that the date of enactment is not the only important information about the adoption of policy innovations by the states. Similar state laws vary while recent adopters pick up the innovation. Generally, recently enacted or amended laws are more useful or facilitative of the right to die than the earliest innovations. While the earliest adopters deserve credit for being pioneers and for stimulating other states to follow, their laws probably are not very useful to their citizens. Unless they are amended or augmented by additional legislation, they never will be very effective for dealing with the problems that motivated their enactment. The restrictions found in the first laws and problems with implementing living wills motivated the innovators to seek entirely new solutions to the old problems, but even these laws will produce mixed results due to political efforts to limit them in the same ways.

7 A
National
Right to Die?

Although by 1990 all but two of the states had either legislative or judicial policy regarding the withdrawal or withholding of medical treatment in hopeless cases, there is no uniform policy on the right to die. Living will, durable power of attorney for health care and proxy decision-maker laws, and court opinions all contribute to state policy, but they do not add up to a consistent, comprehensive, or uncomplicated set of rules. Moreover, we get a false or a fleeting impression of right to die policy if we assume that simply by having various laws or judicial rulings in place, individuals are assured they can avoid unwanted treatment if they make their wishes known. What is clear is that there is no agreement among the states on right to die policy and that citizens are affected differently depending upon where they live. Recent federal policy on the right to die also has not unified the law.

State Policy
Legislation

Many differences exist among state living will laws, and their content and application frequently limit their usefulness in ending medical treatment. Probably most important, most living will laws apply only to individuals who have been diagnosed as terminally ill. By the end of 1990, only a few states had amended their laws to include individuals in a permanent vegetative state.

However, there are some recent signs of change. The Supreme Court's Cruzan decision appears to have stimulated much additional state law making. Following its decision in June 1990, four additional states enacted living will laws, and eighteen others amended their living will statutes. Two of the new laws and ten of the amendments include provisions for withdrawing treatment in cases of permanent unconsciousness, such as Nancy Cruzan's. Five include proxy decision making as part of living wills, and seven allow proxies to refuse artificially administered feeding and hydration. None of the new laws require artificial feeding (Society for the Right to Die, November 26, 1990; Choice in Dying, November 25, 1991).

While recent law making probably indicates a shift toward recognizing the permanent vegetative state as qualifying for the withdrawal of treatment, including artificial feeding, the large majority of living will laws continue to apply only to terminal illnesses. Not only do these laws fail to cover many patients, they are crippling in another way. A diagnosis of terminal illness often comes during the last stages of a serious illness so that many patients undergo various life-saving treatments before doctors and/or families decide that further treatment is fruitless and the patient should be allowed to die. In addition, there are limitations on when and how documents can be executed, often weak sanctions on doctors and hospitals for failure to comply with a living will and limitations regarding the withdrawal of artificially administered food and hydration.

Durable power of attorney for health care and proxy decision maker laws appear to be more flexible and uniform than living will laws because they are simple documents that contain little additional language beyond the designation of a substitute decision maker. There are fewer qualifying clauses that need to be interpreted at a later time, and proxies can object to particular treatments. Although they probably are improvements over living will laws for obtaining the withdrawal of treatment, some of the new laws also limit withdrawal in various ways. Several states do not specifically give a proxy the power to refuse any treatment, and others have imposed specific restrictions on the withdrawal of comfort care or food and hydration. Proxies who are named as part of a living will also must deal with the same problems of interpretation and application of these documents that occur with living wills without designated proxies.

However, as in the most recent living will innovations, most proxy laws and amendments adopted following Cruzan provide for greater patient and surrogate control over treatment decisions. Ten states recently have enacted new DPAHC laws, and three others have amended their earlier statutes. Six of the new laws permit proxies to reject artificial feeding and hydration, and three others allow the withdrawal of treatment for patients in a permanent vegetative state. None of the most recent laws require the articifical administration of food and water, as in the 1990 Massachusetts law and other statutes.

Even though the Supreme Court upheld the Missouri Supreme Court's restrictive interpretation of the state's living will law, it appears that the Supreme Court's acceptance of the withdrawal of all forms of treatment for patients in Nancy Cruzan's condition has led some states to enact or renovate living will and proxy laws to provide greater patient or surrogate control over treatment decisions. But other earlier laws on the books in most of the states still restrict individual autonomy.

It is too soon to assess the value of proxy documents in obtaining the end of treatment, but in up to one-third of the states with various limitations, it is likely that proxies will encounter problems similar to those involved with living wills. In addition, where limited laws conflict with state judicial policy, or more generally, if a proxy's request for the withdrawal of treatment conflicts with the values of doctors or the policies of health care institutions, obtaining withdrawal still may require a court order.

Judicial Policy

State judicial policies generally cover more contingencies than legislation since they have dealt most frequently with patients who are in a permanent vegetative state, and who have not executed advance directives or have not expressed their wishes orally concerning final medical treatment. In contrast, only a half dozen living will laws include provisions for terminating treatment for individuals who have not drawn up formal documents. In sharp constrast to other recent facilitative innovations, only one new living will law enacted in 1991 includes a provision for withdrawing treatment from patients who have not executed advance directives.

In cases involving living wills or conscious patients, the courts have required that the patient's wishes be followed. In the other more plentiful cases, most courts have permitted family members or court-appointed guardians to act on behalf of an unconscious patient, through the rule of "substituted judgment" and/or "the best interests of the patient." The formal rules differ depending upon whether or not there is evidence of a patient's wishes, but the results are the same.

National Policy

As of 1990 federal policy exists on the right to die, but neither the U.S. Supreme Court nor Congress has developed rules that come close to the detail or scope of policies created in the states.

Cruzan

The U.S. Supreme Court, in approving the Missouri Supreme Court's decision in the Cruzan case, produced a very limited national right to die policy. First, it placed its decision within the narrow context of a patient's long-established right to refuse medical treatment, and it declined to endorse a broad constitutional right to die. The Court also limited itself to reviewing the central issues in the Missouri case.

The Court approved of the Missouri Supreme Court's requirement that a patient's wishes regarding medical treatment must be clear and convincing, and it ruled that the state court was not required to accept the principle of substituted judgment that is employed by other courts. The majority explicitly stated that state constitutions, statutes, and the opinions of other state courts were "not available" to the Court, and that the only issue was whether the Missouri Supreme Court had acted properly. The U.S. Supreme Court endorsed written evidence of patients' wishes through living wills or proxies, noting that oral communications either were prohibited as evidence in other types of cases or were highly suspect in legal transactions. The Court did not address the frequent conflicts between the limited applicability of state living will laws and more comprehensive state court decisions, nor did it imply that restrictive state laws might be unconstitutional. However, it did agree with most other state courts that there is no meaningful distinction between ordinary and extraordinary medical treatment, and that food and hydration may be withdrawn.

Living wills got a political boost by the decision, and those who favor liberal treatment withdrawal policies, including food and hydration and their application to the permanent vegetative state, can point to the Supreme Court for support. But, the Court has not explicitly imposed any of these policies on the states, which are free to go their own way in adhering to their previous rules or formulating new ones. Nevertheless, as was the case in Massachusetts, which has resisted legislation until recently, the Supreme Court's Cruzan decision has added to the sense that innovation is in the air. Not since the mid–1980s, when many states enacted living will laws or recently adopted DPAHC laws, have so many legislatures enacted new laws or amended earlier ones. However, since the Cruzan decision and all but a few state laws emphasize written advance medical directives, this flurry of new law making does not apply to the vast majority of Americans who have not signed living wills or health care proxies. Most people are still without coverage.

Congress

The U.S. Congress also has entered the right to die realm through its new Patient Self-Determination Act. Effective December 1, 1991, all medical facilities, including hospitals, nursing homes, home health organizations, and hospices receiving federal funds—which includes most of them since many patients are covered by Medicare or Medicaid—must inform patients upon their admission of the existence of state laws and the institution's policies regarding patients' rights. This includes the right to refuse treatment and the availability of advance medical directives. Patients' records also are to include information about whether the patient has executed a living will or other advance directive, and the institutions are required to follow state law. The law also requires education for medical staff on state laws concerning advance medical directives, and the federal government will distribute information to social security recipients about appropriate forms. Congress authorized $5 million for fiscal year 1991, and $12 and $13 million for fiscal years 1992 and 1993 to create educational programs and to implement the policy in the states.

This law does not create a national right to die, nor does it set out the conditions under which medical treatment may be withdrawn. Instead of producing a national version of a living will or proxy law, it actuates or mobilizes a process for making state right to die policies more visible and meaningful to medical institutions and patients.

The law was proposed by Senator John C. Danforth, Republican of Missouri. Senator Danforth, who is a Protestant minister, has reportedly been concerned with the impact of high-tech medicine on American citizens for several years and his interest was heightened by the Cruzan case in Missouri. His proposal was a response to the U.S. Supreme Court's decision that emphasized written instructions as the best way of protecting patients' rights. The hearings before the Senate Subcommittee on Medicare and Long-Term Care emphasized the Cruzan decision, the committee's estimate that only 10 percent of Americans have executed living wills, and the fact that perhaps one million people are being artificially sustained by medical machines—many more than the ten thousand mentioned in the U.S. Supreme Court's Cruzan opinion. The purpose of the bill was to educate Americans about their need to put their desires in writing to avoid unwanted life-sustaining technology (Hearings on Living Wills, U.S. Senate, Subcommittee on Medicare and Long-Term Care, Committee on Finance, July 20, 1990).

This new federal law has the potential for dealing with one of the fundamental and continuing limitations in the right to die—the failure of all but 10 or 15 percent of Americans to sign living wills or other advance medical directives. Following the Supreme Court's Cruzan decision, the Society for the Right to Die reported that several hundred thousand people had written to the society requesting living will or proxy forms (Concern for Dying and Society for the Right to Die, *Newsletter,* Fall 1990). While many thousands were motivated to act at the time of that decision, many millions more either are unaware of right to die policies and their options, or they fail to take the steps to obtain and sign the necessary documents. Certainly, it is an issue that most people would like to avoid thinking about, and it is easy to put it off.

The new federal law makes it much more likely that everyone who enters a hospital, nursing home, or other facility will receive information and available forms so that they can make a decision about potential medical treatment near or at the time they are admitted to the facility. There is no guarantee, of course, that people will sign these documents, but there is a better chance that they will learn about them and use them.

Concern for Dying and the Society for the Right to Die plan to coordinate a lobbying effort aimed at the Health Care Funding Administration, which is responsible for developing regulations for health care facilities covered under the act. They have organized a study committee that includes representatives from various national health care and medical organizations, including the American Medical Association, American Association for Homes for the Aging, American Hospital Association, and many others. The committee hopes to influence the way in which the new law is put into effect so that maximum exposure to advance directives occurs throughout the United States (Concern for Dying and Society for the Right to Die, *Newsletter,* Spring 1991).

Unsolved Problems

While the new federal law and the Supreme Court's Cruzan decision will make advance medical directives more visible and available to many people, neither addresses the circumstances of many accident victims or those who suffer massive heart attacks and strokes and who enter hospitals and nursing homes already unconscious and doomed to a permanent vegetative state. If they have not signed living wills or proxies in advance, the availability of these documents upon admission to the emergency room or nursing home will not benefit them. People under age twenty-one also are not covered since few state laws apply to minors.

More than 60 percent of the patients who have been the subject of state appellate right to die cases entered medical facilities already unconscious or incompetent and without advance medical directives. Since most living will laws do not provide for discontinuing treatment for individuals who have not signed documents, and proxies must be executed in advance, many patients will continue to be in the same legal/medical predicament as Karen Quinlan in 1976 and Nancy Cruzan in 1990. Recent action by the federal government cannot help them.

Public Information

Policies requiring written instructions inevitably affect social classes differently. The highly educated and well informed are much more likely than the poor and uneducated to become aware of right to die news events and to feel that they can and should plan ahead for medical contingencies. They are much more likely than most of the poor, who probably are only faintly aware of the right to die, to write for information about living wills and proxies, or to contact local organizations for help. But the poor, especially the young, are even more vulnerable to accidents, violence, and acute serious illness than the wealthy and the educated, and they, as much as anyone, need written evidence of their wishes regarding medical treatment. But so long as policies continue to emphasize written documents and advance planning, only a few among the better educated and well off are likely to have right to die coverage.

If written instructions are required in order for people to avoid unwanted treatment, more effective ways need to be found to make the public aware of its options. Many public institutions other than hospitals and nursing homes could distribute information. Perhaps simplified packets of instructions and documents could be dispersed by doctors, health maintenance organizations, and county health clinics. Information could be given to school children to take home to parents, and people registering to vote or applying for drivers' licenses could receive packets. Forms could be included in county property and state income tax notices.

Similar to the intent of the federal law, the broad dissemination of information would provide access to existing state law and necessary documents. No additional policy-making other than procedures and minimal costs for printing and distribution would be required. Opponents to living will and other right to die laws may object to heightening public awareness, which allows people to take advantage of state laws, but since this policy would be a natural outgrowth of existing policy, opposition should not be difficult to overcome.

In 1991, a few states enacted laws that require broader dissemination of information about advance medical directives or that increase the chances advance directives will be effective. Maine requires that living will forms be provided to applicants for driver's and hunting licenses, and Oregon requires health care facilities to provide advance directives to all adult patients. Illinois requires that an individual's execution of an advance directive be noted on the driver's license, which increases the chances that a person's wishes concerning medical treatment will be noted and honored by medical personnel.

Limitations.   Providing more information would probably increase the number of people protected by advance directives, but it would not address the needs of the many millions who are unfamiliar with or suspicious of legal documents and do not or cannot take action to protect themselves through written documents.

Judicial policies that cover people without written instructions also fall short. State judicial policy is fairly uniform on this issue, but most states do not have judicial policies, and one state's judicial decisions are not binding on another. Among states with court decisions some disagreement exists concerning procedures for discontinuing treatment and the specific therapies that may be withdrawn. While the Supreme Court's Cruzan decision probably will stimulate more state law making, it also probably will encourage some state courts in the future to require written evidence of patients' wishes instead of oral evidence, and to prohibit guardians from exercising substituted or best interests judgments.

Judicial policies are also limited because the facts in every court case always vary. This leads some potential litigants, such as doctors, hospitals, and others to resist withdrawing treatment in particular cases under their control, despite the general trend in judicial policy to the contrary. Even when state courts draft general policies intended to govern similar cases in the future, potential litigants always can claim that the facts in their case are unique and, therefore, they are not bound by prior judicial rulings. Equally important, most doctors and other medical staff are not intimately familiar with state judicial right to die policy and the differences and conflicts that often exist between courts and legislatures. It is tempting to assume that doctors and hospital and nursing home staff know the law since they deal with life and death regularly, but understanding and implementing right to die policy undoubtedly is not their highest priority. Their understanding of the right to die is likely influenced by their own values and the policies of their hospital or other health care institution.

More Facilitative Policy

Despite these limitations, there is growing support for more facilitative policy. First, public opinion strongly supports withdrawing treatment in hopeless cases, either upon a patient's direct request or by the family if the patient is unable to communicate. Therefore, one of the necessary conditions seems to be in place for moving toward policies permitting the withdrawal of treatment for patients in a permanent vegetative state whether or not they previously have recorded their wishes in writing or expressed them orally.

Organized groups also keep this issue on the public agenda. The Society for the Right to Die has called for national discussion and consideration of treatment policies for those in a permanent vegetative state. Citing the recent case in Minnesota in which hospital staff have sought to withdraw treatment from an elderly permanently comatose patient over the objections of her family, SRD suggests that perhaps there is a national consensus that treatment for those in a permanent vegetative state should be withdrawn unless there is evidence a patient would want treatment continued (*Newsletter*, Spring, 1991).

This suggests shifting from a policy that *permits* to one that *encourages* the withdrawal of treatment, and it implies that the permanent vegetative state should be viewed as similar to brain death. Others have suggested that severely ill Alzheimer's patients, whose disease has progressed to the point where they have lost all bodily functions and awareness, but who are not terminally ill or in a permanent vegetative state in the strictest sense of these terms, should not be maintained through artificial feeding and hydration. As the size of the elderly population increases in the next century, and many people live to age eighty-five and beyond, there will be many millions of such patients (*Time*, 15 April 1991:10–12).

In reaction to the Supreme Court's emphasis on written instructions, the National Center for State Courts, a federally funded corporation that encourages research devoted to the improvement of state court systems, has solicited research proposals for the formulation of proposed judicial rules governing the cessation of treatment for patients based upon oral rather than written communications of their wishes. But despite this continued interest in covering people without written instructions, judicial policy can always be avoided by medical professionals, institutions, and individuals who are not litigants in a case. Therefore, comprehensive legislation is more likely to be broadly effective.

Concerns with the quality of life and increased attention to the enormous cost of sustaining life in hopeless cases for more, not fewer, people are bound to lead to new definitions and proposed policies for getting the very aged and the Nancy Cruzans off respirators and artificial food and hydration, and for preventing others from being connected to such devices that prolong life.

Conclusion

The U.S. Supreme Court's ruling and the new federal law that requires notice of patients' rights can be viewed as incremental changes in the right to die. It is common for governments to move in small steps rather than in giant leaps, especially regarding controversial issues. The willingness of the U.S. Supreme Court to decide the Cruzan case and Congress's requirements concerning public notice of advance directives came years after the states and the NCCUSL already had developed right to die policies. Early restrictive living will laws and court decisions that permitted the withdrawal of respirators contrast with later more facilitative living will and proxy laws and court rulings that permit the withdrawal of artificially administered food and hydration from permanently unconscious patients.

Right to life organizations probably interpret new policy-making in the right to die as further evidence of the slide down the slippery slope toward active euthanasia, but while incrementalism often has implied small steps in a single direction, as in incremental increases in state and federal budgets, incrementalism can mean small steps in the opposite or other directions as well. In the right to die, there is nothing inevitable about the content or direction of state policies. Restrictive policies, particularly limitations on the withdrawal of food and hydration, often have been enacted at the same time that other facilitative procedures have been adopted.

State courts and legislatures also frequently move in conflicting directions. State legislatures have restricted the right to die to terminally ill patients and have limited the withdrawal of food and hydration at the same time that state courts have permitted the withdrawal of all forms of treatment for those in a permanent vegetative state. The nation's most restrictive state court decision in the right to die also has been endorsed by the U.S. Supreme Court. While new proxy laws have been enacted, they too often contain limitations that prevent or make it difficult for proxies in certain states to secure the withdrawal of treatment. Public opinion clearly supports the withdrawal of treatment, but it is much less in favor of voluntary active euthanasia and assisted suicide and it is all but unanimous in opposing active euthanasia under the control of doctors and courts. There is no reason to assume that policies that apply the right to die to patients who are in a permanent vegetative state or similar condition inevitably will lead to totalitarian policies that require or permit the killing of the aged, retarded, dependent, or the unpopular.

It is possible, but not inevitable, that new policies that call for the end of treatment for those in a permanent vegetative state will be developed and put into effect at the same time that the public agenda continues to add newer and more controversial issues, such as assisted suicide for those suffering from terminal illnesses or other debilitating conditions. But assisted suicide is unlikely to be approved soon, and political conflicts on the right to die will continue with competing interest groups and institutions seeking the last word on treatment decisions for the end of life.

Notes

1. Death, Technology, and Politics

1. Information on the Cruzan case is derived from *Cruzan v.Harmon; Cruzan v. Director; New York Times,* 25 July 1989:1; 27 November 1989:11; 7 December 1989:1; 26 June 1990:A7; and 27 June 1990:A10; *Kansas City (Missouri) Times,* 7 December 1989:n.p.; *Los Angeles Times,* 29 July 1990:1; *Time,* 19 March 1990:62.

2. For extensive discussion of these and related issues see Weir 1989; Meisel 1989; and Horan and Mall, eds., 1980.

3. The following discussion partly relies on *Deciding to Forego Life-sustaining Treatment* 1983; Humphrey and Wickett 1986; Callahan 1987, 1990; Miesel 1989; Weir 1989; and Society for the Right to Die. 1988. For much earlier writing on these subjects, see the extensive notes and bibliography in Weir 1989, especially chapter 6.

4. A more complete discussion of my research on the impact of literature as an indicator of social concern on the development of right to die policy is found in chapter 3.

3. The Rise of the Right to Die Issue

1. Although the number of "don't know" responses on right to die surveys has always been low, the polls may overstate public involvement with the right to die as a social issue. Issues concerning personal values and experiences permit most people to figure out a response other than "don't know," indicating surface evidence of public opinion, but there may be little deep understanding or few consistent underlying attitudes related to the issue. The possible lack of firm attitudes on the right to die is also suggested by the different levels of support obtained by questions with slightly different wording. On these points, see Converse 1970 and Converse and Traugott 1986.

2. The following subject headings included articles limited to the right to die: euthanasia; death with dignity; living wills; mercy killing; mercy death; Quinlan; and right to die. Except for articles on euthanasia for animals and duplicate listings, all articles under these headings were counted. Other headings that included some articles on the right to die were death,

death and dying, and medical ethics. Only articles in which the titles clearly indicated reference to the right to die were counted. The following terms placed articles in the right to die category: discussion of particular court cases and state statutes; living wills; withdrawal of treatment for the terminally ill or permanently comatose; extraordinary care; right to die; or death with dignity.

3. The various effects of professional and mass literature on the adoption of living will laws are analyzed further in chapter 6.

4. Most polls include questions on several social and political issues, not exclusively the right to die. I have identified and obtained all available polls including right to die questions from the 1940s to the present. The following sources were examined for this analysis: the files of American Public Opinion, Opinion Research Service, Boston, Mass; George H. Gallup, *The Gallup Poll, 1972–1977* (Wilmington, Del.: Scholarly Resources, 1978); Roper Center for Public Opinion Research, University of Connecticut, Storrs, Conn.; Harris Polls, University of North Carolina, Chapel Hill, N.C.; The General Social Survey, National Opinion Research Center, University of Chicago, Chicago, Ill.; *New York Times;* Inter-University Consortium for Political and Social Research, University of Michigan, Ann Arbor, Michigan; *Public Opinion Magazine;* Susan Waller, "Trends in Public Acceptance of Euthanasia Worldwide," *The Euthanasia Review,* 1(1986):33. It is likely that I have identified most of the polls since my sources produced many duplicate references to the surveys, but there may be others that I have not identified, especially local polls that have not been published in the media or identified by polling resource organizations, or perhaps some very early polls that have never been made public or have not been saved by polling organizations.

5. V. O. Key, a leading founder of modern research on public opinion and political behavior put it this way:

> Observers of public opinion have been perturbed by the gaps between public opinion and governmental action. On many issues interviewers obtain from heavy majorities of national samples concurrence with views that have not been transmuted into public policy and are not likely to be in the predictable future. . . . A 10 percent dissent may include small pockets of the most determined opposition whose members command controlling points in the governmental mechanism. The 90 percent concurrence may not include driving clusters of determined leadership, or it may consist largely of persons not strongly attached to their stated position. *Public Opinion and American Democracy* (New York: Knopf, 1963), p. 32.

5. The Right to Die in Court

1. The AMA policy is contained in a very short one-page announcement while the President's Commission report is a text of several hundred pages. Consequently, even if the AMA report were reprinted in its entirety in a written opinion, it would not consume much space.

2. Based on the fixed marginals, the difference between the observed and expected values on the distribution of states in right to die innovation and Caldeira's reputation rankings of state supreme courts is statistically significant at $< .02$.

3. An exception is *Barber v. Superior Court* in 1983. However, unlike all other cases, this was a California criminal case involving two doctors who, at the request of the family, had removed all life- support systems as well as feeding tubes from a terminal patient. It is also an intermediate appellate court decision, which is unlikely to be relied on by other courts.

4. The impact of Conroy on the shift in judicial policy is comparable to an interrupted time series in which Conroy changed the issues and the focus of policy from standard medical treatment to food and hydration. The relationship is statistically significant at the $< .001$ level.

5. These correlations are $r = .21$; not sig. and $r = .13$; not sig.

6. Lawmaking and the Right to Die

1. The results of my analysis in this section differ slightly from my other writing on living will innovation since my earlier work was based on enactments through 1988 and this treatment includes legislation through 1990.

2. The sources for these variables include:

regionalism: United States Census categories of region

urbanism: United States Census, percentage population living in urban areas

total state population: United States Census

education: United States Census, percentage population twenty-five years and older having completed at least four years of high school

wealth: United States Census, per capita income

state policy liberalism: David Klingman and William W. Lammers, "The 'General Policy Liberalism' Factor in State Politics," *American Journal of Political Science,* 28:598–610. Their measure is a composite of measures of innovation, civil rights policy adoptions, level of welfare support, support of the equal rights amendment, and consumer protection laws.

late twentieth-century innovation: Robert L. Savage,"Policy Innovativeness as a Trait of American States," *Journal of Politics,* 40 (1978):212–24. His measure is a score of the state on innovation in sixty-nine policy fields since 1930.

governmental capability: three separate measures of government capability are included. The first concerns legislative professionalism, from John Grumm, "The Effects of Legislative Structure on Legislative Performance," in Richard Hofferbert and Ira Sharkansky, eds., *State and Urban Politics* (Boston: Little Brown). The Grumm index has been updated several times, but the state scores are very similar. The second measure is Ann O'M. Bowman and Richard C. Kearney, "Dimensions of State Government Capability," *Western Political Quarterly,* 41 (1988):341–62. Their measure includes thirty-two measures of legislative professionalism and support and gubernatorial and executive power in the states. The third measure is the amount spent on legislative services for each year from 1976 to 1988. It is derived from *State Government Finances,* Annual, United States Bureau of the Census, and *Book of the States,* Biannual, Council of State Governments.

political party competition and the policy relevance of political parties: These variables were measured in three ways. The first is a general measure of political party electoral competition and the alternation of majority party control of the legislature and the governorship over time. It is an update of the Ranney index found in John F. Bibby et al., "Parties in State Politics," in Virginia Gray, Herbert Jacob, and Kenneth N. Vines, eds., *Politics in the American States,* 4th ed., pp. 59–96 (Boston: Little, Brown, 1983). The second is a measure of divided party control of both houses of the legislature and the governorship. It has been obtained for each year from 1976 to 1988 from the *Book of the States.* The final measure is an indicator of the policy relevance of state political parties. It is derived from Thomas R. Dye, "Party and Policy in the States," *Journal of Politics,* 46 (1984):1097–1116.

3. The data for these variables was obtained from the following sources:

percentage population Catholic: Official Catholic Directory, Annual (New York: P. J. Kennedy).

percentage Protestant fundamentalist: Douglas W. Johnson, Paul R. Picard, and Bernard Quinn, *Churches and Church Membership in the United States* (Washington, D.C.: Glenmary Research Center, 1971); Bernard Quinn, Martin Bradley, Paul Goetting, and Peggy Shriver, *Churches and Church Membership in the United States* (Atlanta: Glenmary Research Center, 1980).

percentage population over age sixty-five: United States Census

4. I have conducted this analysis through 1988, which is the last year for which a complete set of variables for the states was available. Event history analysis conducted through probit or logit regression is preferred over ordinary least squares analysis because it does not exclude (censor) states that have not adopted an innovation or force the coding for these

states into a single nonadopt category. It also permits including independent variables whose values are constants or change over the period studied. The dependent variable is a dichotomous adopt/nonadopt code for each state for each year covering the entire period under investigation. For detailed discussion of these techniques, see Allison 1984; Aldrich and Nelson 1984; Berry and Berry 1990; and Pavalko 1987.

5. Using ordinary least squares regression, I examined all the independent variables for multicollinearity and determined that all the relationships between the independent variables and date of adoption were linear. The statistics for the logit analysis of these relationships in the event history is as follows:

Variable	MLE	S.E.	MLE/S.E.
% Catholic	−.0599	.0175	−3.42*
Lagged Cases	.3644	.0895	4.07*
Lagged Mass Lit.	.0885	.0057	15.53*

*Sig. <.001

Pseudo R^2 = .55

Percent Adoptions correctly predicted = 90.8

6. General state policy liberalism came closer than the other variables to reaching a statistically significant relationship with the date of enactment of living will laws, but the direction of the relationship was contrary to what would have been expected. It was a negative relationship, meaning that the most liberal states were least likely to enact these laws. The liberal states also tend to be heavily Catholic, and on living will laws the size of the Catholic population is a much more important determinant of adoption than the general liberal tone of the states' policies.

7. The date of adoption is coded as 100 minus the last two digits of the date—giving early adopters higher scores. Since I am studying a single issue and only those states that have adopted legislation, I have not used the scoring techniques used in most previous innovation research. With an aggregation of many policies, adoption scores for each policy are measured by the time between the first and last adoption, and states are assigned a score for the percentage of time that has elapsed between the first adoption and their adoption of the policy. All scores are averaged and subtracted from 1.000 to give early adoptors higher scores (Walker 1969).

8. The standardized beta coefficients for the five provisions regressed on date of adoption are as follows: penalty for nontransfer −.148 (n.s.); blocking a living will −.132 (n.s.); living wills for minors .038 (n.s.); pregnancy provisions .112 (n.s.); food and hydration −.437 (sig. < .02).

9. With the four additional provisions removed, the correlation between date of adoption and facility score improves to .559 (sig. < .001). Removing the food and hydration provision alone accounts for nearly the same increase in the R_2 as removing the four additional variables.

10. California led the states in 1983 with the nation's first DPAHC law. Since then twenty-four other states and Washington, D.C., have enacted

proxy laws that explicitly permit the withdrawal of treatment. However, few states enacted these laws until 1989 (six states) and 1990 (thirteen states). These new laws probably became acceptable then because the NCCUSL acted quickly in 1989 to amend its earlier model living will law to include a provision for a proxy decision maker. Ten additional states have proxy provisions in their original living will laws or through amendment, also enacted since 1983. In three other states, courts or the state attorney general have interpreted existing durable power of attorney statutes to apply to health care decision making, including the withdrawal of treatment. In five other states, durable power of attorney laws apply to health care, but only explicitly to the power of a proxy to accept treatment, not to refuse or request the withdrawal of treatment. In these states, it is unclear if proxies have the power to demand the end of treatment. Finally, seven states have no provisions for health care proxies. Only Michigan and Nebraska have neither a living will law nor some form of proxy decision-maker law.

11. The editor of the *New England Journal of Medicine* stated "I think the whole episode, which certainly had its bizarre aspects, underscored a very real problem. . . . Whatever you thought of what Dr. Kevorkian did, it certainly wasn't murder. And we in medicine have got to come to better grips with the fact that increasing numbers of our patients will be seeking our assistance in ending their lives" (*New York Times,* 14 December 1990:B10).

12. Dr. Quill's story was analyzed sympathetically by various columnists. See, for example, the column by syndicated *Chicago Tribune* writer Joan Beck, "When the Only Mercy Left Is Death," seen in *Tallahassee Democrat,* 12 March 1991; and Lawrence K. Altman, M.D., "More Physicians Broach Forbidden Subject of Euthanasia," *New York Times,* 12 March 1991:B6.

13. Based on unpublished research by Douglas St. Angelo, Florida State University.

Case References

Barber v. Superior Court. 1983. 195 Cal. Rptr. 484 (California).
Bartling v. Superior Court. 1984. 228 Cal. Rptr. 847 (California).
Bouvia v. Superior Court. 1986. 225 Cal. Rptr. 297 (California).
Brophy v. New England Sinai Hospital, Inc. 1986. 497 N.E.2d 626 (Massachusetts).
Browning v. State of Florida. 1988. 530 A.2d 258 (Florida).
Browning (Florida v. Doris F. Hebert, etc.) 1990. 568 So.2d 4 (Florida).
Childs v. Abramovice (Conservatorship of Thelma Morrison). 1988. 253 Cal. Rptr. 530 (California).
Colyer. 1983. 660 P.2d 738 (Washington).
Conroy. 1985. 486 A.2d 1209 (New Jersey).
Couture v. Couture. 1989. 549 N.E.2d 571 (Ohio).
Corbett v. D'Alessandro. 1986. 487 So.2d 368 (Florida).
Cruzan v. Harmon. 1988. 760 S.W.2d 408 (Missouri).
Cruzan v. Director, Missouri Department of Health. 1990. 110 S.Ct 2841.
Dinnerstein. 1978. 380 N.E.2d 134 (Massachusetts).
Drabick. 1988. 245 Cal. Rptr. 840 (California).
Eichner. 1976. 420 N.E.2d 64 (New York).
Elbaum v. Grace Plaza of Great Neck. 1989. 140 A.D.2d 244. (New York).
Farrell. 1987. 529 A.2d 404 (New Jersey).
Gardner. 1987. 534 A.2d 947 (Maine).
Grant. 1987. 747 P.2d 445 (Washington).
Greenspan. 1990. 558 N.E.2d 1194 (Illinois).
Hamlin. 1984. 689 P.2d 1372 (Washington).
In re, or In the matter of . . . See name of party.
Jobes. 1987. 529 A.2d 434 (New Jersey).
John F. Kennedy Hospital v. Bludworth. 1984. 452 So.2d 921 (Florida).
L.H.R. 1984. 321 S.E.2d 716 (Georgia).
Leach et al. v. Shapiro. 1984. 469 N.E.2d 1047 (Ohio).
Longway (Keiner v. Community Convalescent Center. 1989. 549 N.E.2d 292 (Illinois).
McConnell et al. v. Beverly Enterprises-Conn, Inc. 1989. 553 A.2d 596 (Connecticut).
Peter. 1987. 529 A.2d 419 (New Jersey).
Quinlan. 1976. 355 A.2d 647 (New Jersey).

CASE REFERENCES

Rasmussen v. Fleming. 1987. 741 P.2d 674 (Arizona).

Riddlemoser. 1989. 564 A.2d 812 (Maryland).

Satz v. Perlmutter. 1980. 379 So.2d 359 (Florida).

Severns v. Wilmington Medical Center, Inc. 1980. 421 A.2d 1334 (Delaware).

Spring. 1980. 405 N.E.2d 115 (Massachusetts).

State v. McAfee. 1989. 385 S.E.2d 651 (Georgia).

Storar. 1981. 420 N.E.2d 64 (New York).

Superintendent of Belchertown State School et al. v. Joseph Saikewicz. 1977. 370 N.E.2d 417 (Massachusetts).

Swan. 1990. 569 A.2d 1202 (Maine).

Torres. 1984. 357 N.W.2d 332 (Minnesota).

Webster v. Reproductive Health Services. 1989. 109 S. Ct. 3040.

Westchester County Medical Center v. Helen Hall (O'Conner). 1988. 531 N.E.2d 607 (New York).

Westhart v. Mule, et al. 1989. 261 Cal. Rptr. 640 (California).

General References

Adams, Gerald R., Nancy Bueche, and Jay D. Schvaneveldt. 1978. "Contemporary Views of Euthanasia: A Regional Assessment." *Social Biology* 25:62–68.

Aldrich, John H. and Forrest D. Nelson. 1984. *Linear Probability, Logit and Probit Models.* Beverly Hills, Ca.: Sage Publications.

Allen, Russ and Jill Clark. 1981. "State Policy Adoption and Innovation: Lobbying and Education." *State and Local Government Review* 13:18–25.

Allison, Paul D. 1984. *Event History Analysis.* Beverly Hills, Ca.: Sage Publications.

Almgren, Gunnar. [1991]. "Bedside Decisions Pertaining to Artificial Nutrition and Hydration: Influences of Public Policy Versus Nursing Home Industry Structure." Unpublished paper, Ogburn-Stouffer Center for the Study of Population and Social Organization. Chicago: University of Chicago.

Atkins, Burton M. and Henry R. Glick. 1976. "Environmental and Structural Variables as Determinants of Issues on State Courts of Last Resort." *American Journal of Political Science* 20:97–114.

Bachrach, Peter and Morton S. Baratz. 1962. "Two Faces of Power." *American Political Science Review* 56:947–52.

——. 1963. "Decisions and Nondecisions: An Analytical Framework." *American Political Science Review* 57:632–42.

Baum, Lawrence and Bradley C. Canon. 1982. "State Supreme Courts as Activists: New Doctrines in the Law of Torts." In Mary Cornelia Porter and G. Alan Tarr, eds., *State Supreme Courts: Policymakers in the Federal System,* 83–108. Westport, Conn.: Greenwood Press.

Berry, Frances Stokes and William D. Berry. 1990. "State Lottery Adoptions as Policy Innovation: An Event History Analysis." *American Political Science Review* 84:395–415.

Bingham, Richard D. 1976. *The Adoption of Innovation by Local Governments.* Lexington, Mass.: Lexington Books.

Binstock, Robert H. 1984. *Reframing the Agenda of Policies on Aging.* In Meredith Minkler and Carroll C. Estes, eds. *Readings in the Political Economy of Aging.* Farmingdale, N.Y.: Baywood Publishing.

225

Blumberg, Melanie J. and Michele Wharton-Hagen. 1988. "How Dead Is Dead? Policy-making on Questions of Morality at the State Level." Presented at the annual meeting of the American Political Science Association, Chicago.

Bosso, Christopher J. 1987. *Pesticides and Politics*. Pittsburgh: University of Pittsburgh Press.

Browne, William P. 1985. "Variations in the Behavior and Style of State Lobbyists and Interest Groups." *Journal of Politics* 47:450–68.

Browne, William P. and Delbert J. Ringquist. 1985. "Sponsorship and Enactment: State Lawmakers and Aging Legislation, 1956–1978." *American Politics Quarterly* 13:447–66.

Burstein, Paul. 1985. *Discrimination, Jobs, and Politics: The Struggle for Equal Employment Opportunity in the United States*. Chicago: University of Chicago Press.

Caldeira, Gregory A. 1983. "On the Reputation of State Supreme Courts." *Political Behavior* 5: 83–108.

——. 1985. "The Transmission of Legal Precedent: A Study of State Supreme Courts." *American Political Science Review* 79:178–192.

——. 1988. "Legal Precedent: Structures of Communication Between State Supreme Courts." *Social Networks* 10:29–55.

"California Natural Death Act: An Empirical Study of Physicians' Practices." 1979. *Stanford Law Review* 31:913–45.

Callahan, Daniel. 1987. *Setting Limits*. New York: Simon and Schuster.

——. 1990. *What Kind of Life*. New York: Simon and Schuster.

Canon, Bradley C. and Lawrence Baum. 1981. "Patterns of Tort Law Innovations: An Application of Diffusion Theory to Judicial Doctrines." *American Political Science Review* 75:975–87.

Clark, Jill. 1985. "Policy Diffusion and Program Scope: Research Directions." *Publius* 15:61–70.

Clark, Jill and Lawrence French. 1984. "Innovation and Program Content in State Tax Policies." *State and Local Government Review* 16:11–16.

Clark, Terry N. 1968. "Community Structure, Decision-making, Budget Expenditures, and Urban Renewal in 51 American Communities." *American Sociological Review* 23:576–93.

Clines, Francis X. "Dutch Quietly in Lead in Euthanasia Requests." *New York Times*, December 31, 1986, p. 6.

Cobb, Roger W. and Charles D. Elder. 1972. *Participation in American Politics: The Dynamics of Agenda-building*. Boston: Allyn and Bacon.

Cobb, Roger W., Jennie-Keith Ross, and Marc Howard Ross. 1976. "Agenda Building as a Comparative Political Process." *American Political Science Review* 70:126–38.

Cohen, Michael, James March, and John Olsen. 1972. "A Garbage Can Model of Organizational Choice." *Administrative Science Quarterly* 17:1–25.

Coleman, Barbara. 1989. "New Issues Sidetrack Living Wills." *AARP News Bulletin* 30:1.

Converse, Philip E. 1970 "Attitudes and Non-attitudes: Continuation of a Dialogue." In Edward R. Tufte, ed., *The Quantitative Analysis of Social Problems*. Reading, Mass.: Addison-Wesley Publishing.

Converse, Philip E. and Michael W. Traugott. 1986. "Assessing the Accuracy of Polls and Surveys." *Science* 234:1094–98.

Crane, Diana. 1978. "Consensus and Controversy in Medical Practice: The Dilemma of the Critically Ill Patient." *Annals* 437:99–110.

Danis, M. et al. 1991. "A Prospective Study of Advance Directives for Life-sustaining Care." *New England Journal of Medicine* 324:828–88.

Deciding to Forego Life-sustaining Treatment: A Report on the Ethical, Medical, and Legal Issues in Treatment Decisions. 1983. Washington: President's Commission for the Study of Ethical Problems in Medicine and Biomedical and Behavioral Research.

Dister, John M. 1988. "The Supreme Court, Constitutional Agenda Setting, and Reapportionment." Presented at the annual meeting of the American Political Science Association, Chicago.

Dobson, Douglas and David A. Karns. 1979. *Public Policy and Senior Citizens: Policy Formation in the American States*. Final Report. U.S. Department of Health, Education and Welfare, Administration on Aging.

Dobson, Douglas and Douglas St. Angelo. 1979. *Politics and Senior Citizens: Advocacy and Policy Formation in a Local Context*. Final Report. U.S. Department of Health, Education and Welfare, Administration on Aging.

Doudera, Edward and J. Douglas Peters, eds. 1982. *Legal and Ethical Aspects of Treating Critically Ill Patients*. Ann Arbor: AUPHA Press.

Downs, George W. 1976. *Bureaucracy, Innovation, and Public Policy*. Lexington, Mass.: Lexington Books, D. C. Heath.

Downs, George W. and Lawrence B. Mohr. 1976. "Conceptual Issues in the Study of Innovation." *Administrative Science Quarterly* 21:700–14.

Drechsel, Robert E. 1983. *News Making in the Trial Courts*. New York: Longman.

Duff, Raymond and A. G. M. Campbell. 1980. "Moral and Ethical Dilemmas: Seven Years into the Debate about Human Ambiguity." *Annals* 447:19–28.

Eisendrath, Stuart J. and Albert R. Jonsen. 1983. "The Living Will: Help or Hindrance." *Journal of the American Medical Association*. 249:2054–58.

Erickson, Robert S., Norman R. Luttbeg, and Kent L. Tedin. 1980. *American Public Opinion*, 2d ed. New York: Wiley.

Eyestone, Robert. 1977. "Confusion, Diffusion, and Innovation." *American Political Science Review* 71:441–47.

Fairbanks, J. David. 1980. "Politics, Economics, and the Public Morality: Why Some States Are More Moral Than Others." In Thomas R. Dye and Virginia Gray, eds., *Determinants of Public Policy*, pp. 95–105. Lexington, Mass.: Lexington Books.

Fletcher, Joseph. 1954. *Morals and Medicine: The Moral Problems of the Patient's Right to Know the Truth—Contraception, Artificial Insemination, Sterilization, Euthanasia.* Princeton: Princeton University Press.

Fletcher, Joseph. 1973. *To Live and to Die: When, Why, and How.* New York: Springer-Verlag. Reprinted in part as "Ethics and Euthanasia,"in Horan and Mall, eds., pp. 293–304, *Death, Dying and Euthanasia.*

Foster, John L. 1978. "Regionalism and Innovation in American States." *Journal of Politics* 40:179–87.

Gibbs, Nancy. "Love and Let Die." *Newsweek,* March 19, 1990, pp. 62–71.

Glick, Henry R. 1981. "Innovation in State Judicial Administration: Effects on Court Management and Organization." *American Politics Quarterly* 9:49–69.

——. 1988. *Courts, Politics, and Justice,* 2d ed. New York: McGraw-Hill.

Gray, Virginia. 1973. "Innovation in the States: A Diffusion Study." *American Political Science Review* 67:1174–85.

Gray, Virginia and Bruce Williams. 1973. *The Organizational Politics of Criminal Justice.* Lexington, Mass.: Lexington Books.

Griliches, Zvi. 1957. "Hybrid Corn: An Exploration in the Economics of Technological Change." *Econometrica* 25:501.

Haug, Marie. 1978. "Aging and the Right to Terminate Medical Treatment." *Journal of Gerontology* 33:586–91.

Hendricks, Jon, and C. Davis Hendricks. 1977. *Aging in Mass Society.* Cambridge, Mass.: Winthrop.

Horan, Dennis J. and David Mall, eds. 1980. *Death, Dying and Euthanasia.* Frederick, Md.: University Publications of America.

Humphrey, Derek and Ann Wickett. 1986. *The Right to Die: Understanding Euthanasia.* New York: Harper & Row.

Hudson, Robert B. 1980. "Old Age Politics in a Period of Change." In Edgard F. Borgatta and Neil G. McCluskey, eds., *Aging and Society: Current Research and Policy Perspectives.* Beverly Hills, Ca.: Sage Publications.

Jacob, Herbert. 1988. *Silent Revolution: The Transformation of Divorce Law in the United States.* Chicago: University of Chicago Press.

Jennings, M. Kent and Gregory B. Markus. 1988. "Political Involvement in the Later Years: A Longitudinal Survey." *American Journal of Political Science* 32:302–16.

Johnson, Charles A. and Bradley C. Canon. 1984. *Judicial Policies: Implementation and Impact.* Washington: CQ Press.

Kamisar, Yale. 1958. "Some Non-Religious Views Against Proposed 'Mercy-Killing' Legislation." *Minnesota Law Review* 42:696–1042. Reprinted in Horan and Mall, eds., pp. 406–79, *Death, Dying and Euthanasia*.

Kelly, David F. 1979. *The Emergence of Roman Catholic Medical Ethics in North America*. New York: The Edwin Mellen Press.

Kingdon, John W. 1973. *Congressmen's Voting Decisions*. New York: Harper & Row.

———. 1984. *Agendas, Alternatives, and Public Policies*. Boston: Little, Brown.

Lammers, William W. 1983. *Public Policy and the Aging*. Boston: Little, Brown.

Mahajan, Vijay and Robert Peterson. 1985. *Models for Innovation Diffusion*. Beverly Hills, Ca.: Sage Publications.

Martin, Susan R. and Lynn Balshone Jacobs. 1984. "Legislating Advance Directives for the Terminally Ill: The Living Will and Durable Power of Attorney." *Nebraska Law Review* 63:779–803.

McVoy, E. C. 1950. "Patterns of Diffusion in the United States." *American Sociological Review* 5:219–27.

Meisel, Alan. 1989. *The Right to Die*. New York: John Wiley.

Melnick, Shep. 1983. *Regulation and the Courts: The Case of the Clean Air Act*. Washington, D.C.: The Brookings Institution.

Menzel, Donald E. and Irwin Feller. 1977. "Leadership and Interaction Patterns in the Diffusion of Innovations Among the American States." *Western Political Quarterly* 30:528–36.

Nelson, Barbara J. 1984. *Making an Issue of Child Abuse*. Chicago: University of Chicago Press.

O'Conner, Karen and Lee Epstein. 1981–1982. "Research Note: Amicus Curiae Participation in U.S. Supreme Court Litigation." *Law and Society Review* 16:311–20.

———. 1983. "The Rise of Conservative Interest Group Litigation." *Journal of Politics* 45:480–89.

Ostheimer, John M. and Clay L. Moore. 1981–82. "The Correlates of Attitudes Toward Euthanasia Revisited," *Social Biology,* 28:145–49.

Paige, Connie. 1983. *The Right to Lifers*. New York: Summit Books.

Pampel, Fred and John B. Williamson. 1985. "Age Structure, Politics and Cross-National Patterns of Public Pension Expenditures." *American Journal of Sociology* 50:782–99.

———. 1988. "Welfare Spending in Advanced Industrial Democracies, 1950–1980." *American Journal of Sociology* 93:1424–56.

———. 1989. *Age, Class, Politics and the Welfare State*. Cambridge: Cambridge University Press.

Paris, John J. and Richard A. McCormick. "Living-Will Legislation, Reconsidered," *America,* September 5, 1981, pp. 86–89.

Pavalko, Eliza Keith. 1987. "Labor Process and Welfare State Formation in the United States, 1900–1930." Unpublished doctoral dissertation, Florida State University.

Perlin, Terry M. "On the Physician's Role in Hastening Death." *The Aging Connection,* August-September, 1989.

Peters, David A. 1987. "Advance Medical Directives: The Case for the Durable Power of Attorney for Health Care." *Journal of Legal Medicine* 8:437–64.

Pius XII. 1957. "Allocution 'Le Dr. Bruno Haid.'" *Acta Apostolicaie Sedis,* November 24, 1957, pp. 1031–32.

———. 1957. "The Prolongation of Life: Address to an International Congress of Anesthesiologists." February 24, 1957.

Polsby, Nelson. 1984. *Political Innovation in America: The Politics of Policy Initiation.* New Haven: Yale University Press.

Price, David E. 1985. "Policy Making in Congressional Committees: The Impact of 'Environmental Factors.'" *American Political Science Review* 72:548–73.

Regens, James L. 1980. 'State Policy Responses to the Energy Issues: An Analysis of Innovation." *Social Science Quarterly* 61:44–57.

Rogers, Everett. 1962; 1983. *Diffusion of Innovations.* New York: Free Press.

Sackett, Walter F. 1971. "Death with Dignity." *Southern Medical Journal* 64:330–32.

Savage, Robert L. 1978. "Policy Innovativeness as a Trait of American States." *Journal of Politics* 40:212–24.

———. 1985. "Diffusion Research Traditions and the Spread of Policy Innovations in a Federal System." *Publius* 15:1–27.

———. 1985. "When a Policy's Time Has Come: Cases of Rapid Policy Diffusion in 1983–1984." *Publius* 15:113–25.

Schaeffer, Sherri. 1988. "Death with Dignity: Proposed Amendments to the California Natural Death Act." *San Diego Law Review* 25:783–828.

Shubert, Glendon. 1974. *Judicial Policy Making.* Glenview, Ill.: Scott, Foresman.

Serow, William J., David F. Sly, and J. Michael Wrigley. 1990. *Population Aging in the United States.* New York: Greenwood Press.

Singh, B. K. 1979. "Correlates of Attitudes Toward Euthanasia." *Social Biology* 26:247–54.

Smith, T. Alexander. 1975. *The Comparative Policy Process.* Santa Barbara, Ca.: ABC-Clio.

Society for the Right to Die. 1988. *The First Fifty Years: 1938–1988.* New York: Society for the Right to Die.

Spaeth, Harold J. 1979. *Supreme Court Policy Making.* San Francisco: W. H. Freeman.

Steinhoff, Patricia G. and Milton Diamond. 1977. *Abortion Politics: The Hawaii Experience.* Honolulu: The University Press of Hawaii.

Tatalovich, Raymond and Byron W. Daynes. 1981. *The Politics of Abortion.* New York: Praeger.

Tribe, Laurence H. 1990. *Abortion: The Clash of Absolutes*. New York: Norton.

Walker, Jack L. 1969. "The Diffusion of Innovations Among the American States." *American Political Science Review* 63:880–99.

Waller, Susan. 1986. "Trends in Public Acceptance of Euthanasia Worldwide." *The Euthanasia Review* 1:33–47.

Ward, Russel A. 1980. "Age and Acceptance of Euthanasia." *Journal of Gerontology* 35:421–31.

Weir, Robert F. 1989. *Abating Treatment with Critically Ill Patients*. New York: Oxford University Press.

Weissberg, Robert. 1976. *Public Opinion and Popular Government*. Englewood Cliffs, N.J.: Prentice-Hall.

Welch, Susan and Kay Thompson. 1980. "The Impact of Federal Incentives on State Policy Innovation." *American Journal of Political Science* 24:715–29.

Wiggins, Charles W. and William P. Browne. 1982. "Interest Groups and Public Policy Within a State Legislative Setting." *Polity* 15:548–58.

Index

AARP, 21, 196
ACLU, 2
Adkins, Janet, 11
Agenda and agenda setting, 29–52; *see also* Right to die, supporters of
  by the courts, 36–37
  decisional, 32, 35
  elitist model of, 33–34
  governmental, 31–42
  by interest groups, 32–33, 36–37
  for living will laws, 35–38
  mass, *see* Public
  media's role in, 37, 63–79; *see also* Media
  medical, 75–76
  pluralist model of, 32–33
  professional, *see* Public
  public, 31–41; *see also* Media
    mass, 31–34, 37, 70–75
    professional, 32–36, 39–40, 68–70
  research approaches, 49–52
  for the right to die, 53–77, 174
  and state politics, 29–30, 39–41
  theories of, 31–40
AMA, *see* American Medical Association
American Association of Retired Persons, 21, 196
American Civil Liberties Union, 2
American Euthanasia Society, 10, 54–58, 62, 66
American Medical Association, 21, 67, 74, 104, 108
Arkansas, 180–181
Artificial feeding, 16–19; *see also* Withholding treatment
  in California, 100–101

court rulings, 2–5, 15–19, 78, 140–141, 148–154,162–164
  effect on policy reinvention, 179, 182–187
  in Florida, 115–120
  in living will laws, 178–192
  in Massachusetts, 121–122, 128
  media coverage, 71–73
  in New Jersey, 14–15, 74–75
  nursing home policy on, 25–27
  public opinion on, 79–80
Artificial life support, 14–18; *see also* Artificial feeding
Assisted suicide, 11–12, 20, 192–195; *see also* Euthanasia, active; Public opinion, suicide

Barber v. Superior Ct., 100, 161
Bartling v. Superior Ct., 100
Bouvia v. Superior Ct., 100–101
Brain death, 23–24, 111
British Euthanasia Society, 54
Brophy v. New England Sinai Hospital Inc., 121–122, 149–152
Brown, Jerry, Governor, 98, 104
Bulger, William M., 125–127

California, 5, 15, 93–104
  comparison to other states, 35, 102, 128–132
  durable power of attorney, 101–102
  elderly, 103, 196
  judicial innovation, 5, 100–101
  living will law, 5, 15, 41–44, 53, 74, 93–104, 194
    amendment proposals, 101–104
    evaluation of, 179–181